International Journal on Advances in Networks and Services

2016 vol. 9 nr. 3&4

Printed from e-media with permission by:

Curran Associates, Inc.
57 Morehouse Lane
Red Hook, NY 12571

Some format issues inherent in the e-media version may also appear in this print version.

Printed by Curran Associates, Inc. (2018)

International Academy, Research, and Industry Association (IARIA)
412 Derby Way
Wilmington, DE 19810

Phone: (408) 893-6407
Fax: (408) 527-6351

petre@iaria.org

Additional copies of this publication are available from:

Curran Associates, Inc.
57 Morehouse Lane
Red Hook, NY 12571 USA
Phone: 845-758-0400
Fax: 845-758-2633
Email: curran@proceedings.com
Web: www.proceedings.com

The *International Journal on Advances in Networks and Services* is published by IARIA.
ISSN: 1942-2644
journals site: http://www.iariajournals.org
contact: petre@iaria.org

Sponsored by IARIA
www.iaria.org

International Journal on Advances in Networks and Services
Volume 9, Number 3 & 4, 2016

Diletta Romana Cacciagrano, University of Camerino, Italy
Maria-Dolores Cano, Universidad Politécnica de Cartagena, Spain
Juan-Vicente Capella-Hernández, Universitat Politècnica de València, Spain
Eduardo Cerqueira, Federal University of Para, Brazil
Bruno Chatras, Orange Labs, France
Marc Cheboldaeff, T-Systems International GmbH, Germany
Kong Cheng, Vencore Labs, USA
Dickson Chiu, Dickson Computer Systems, Hong Kong
Andrzej Chydzinski, Silesian University of Technology, Poland
Hugo Coll Ferri, Polytechnic University of Valencia, Spain
Noelia Correia, University of the Algarve, Portugal
Noël Crespi, Institut Telecom, Telecom SudParis, France
Paulo da Fonseca Pinto, Universidade Nova de Lisboa, Portugal
Orhan Dagdeviren, International Computer Institute/Ege University, Turkey
Philip Davies, Bournemouth and Poole College / Bournemouth University, UK
Carlton Davis, École Polytechnique de Montréal, Canada
Claudio de Castro Monteiro, Federal Institute of Education, Science and Technology of Tocantins, Brazil
João Henrique de Souza Pereira, University of São Paulo, Brazil
Javier Del Ser, Tecnalia Research & Innovation, Spain
Behnam Dezfouli, Universiti Teknologi Malaysia (UTM), Malaysia
Daniela Dragomirescu, LAAS-CNRS, University of Toulouse, France
Jean-Michel Dricot, Université Libre de Bruxelles, Belgium
Wan Du, Nanyang Technological University (NTU), Singapore
Matthias Ehmann, Universität Bayreuth, Germany
Wael M El-Medany, University Of Bahrain, Bahrain
Imad H. Elhajj, American University of Beirut, Lebanon
Gledson Elias, Federal University of Paraíba, Brazil
Joshua Ellul, University of Malta, Malta
Rainer Falk, Siemens AG - Corporate Technology, Germany
Károly Farkas, Budapest University of Technology and Economics, Hungary
Huei-Wen Ferng, National Taiwan University of Science and Technology - Taipei, Taiwan
Gianluigi Ferrari, University of Parma, Italy
Mário F. S. Ferreira, University of Aveiro, Portugal
Bruno Filipe Marques, Polytechnic Institute of Viseu, Portugal
Ulrich Flegel, HFT Stuttgart, Germany
Juan J. Flores, Universidad Michoacana, Mexico
Ingo Friese, Deutsche Telekom AG - Berlin, Germany
Sebastian Fudickar, University of Potsdam, Germany
Stefania Galizia, Innova S.p.A., Italy
Ivan Ganchev, University of Limerick, Ireland
Miguel Garcia, Universitat Politecnica de Valencia, Spain
Emiliano Garcia-Palacios, Queens University Belfast, UK
Marc Gilg, University of Haute-Alsace, France
Debasis Giri, Haldia Institute of Technology, India
Markus Goldstein, Kyushu University, Japan
Luis Gomes, Universidade Nova Lisboa, Portugal
Anahita Gouya, Solution Architect, France
Mohamed Graiet, Institut Supérieur d'Informatique et de Mathématique de Monastir, Tunisie
Christos Grecos, University of West of Scotland, UK
Vic Grout, Glyndwr University, UK
Yi Gu, Middle Tennessee State University, USA
Angela Guercio, Kent State University, USA
Xiang Gui, Massey University, New Zealand

Katsuhiro Naito, Mie University, Japan
Deok Hee Nam, Wilberforce University, USA
Sarmistha Neogy, Jadavpur University- Kolkata, India
Rui Neto Marinheiro, Instituto Universitário de Lisboa (ISCTE-IUL), Instituto de Telecomunicações, Portugal
David Newell, Bournemouth University - Bournemouth, UK
Armando Nolasco Pinto, Universidade de Aveiro / Instituto de Telecomunicações, Portugal
Jason R.C. Nurse, University of Oxford, UK
Kazuya Odagiri, Yamaguchi University, Japan
Máirtín O'Droma, University of Limerick, Ireland
Rainer Oechsle, University of Applied Science, Trier, Germany
Henning Olesen, Aalborg University Copenhagen, Denmark
Jose Oscar Fajardo, University of the Basque Country, Spain
Constantin Paleologu, University Politehnica of Bucharest, Romania
Eleni Patouni, National & Kapodistrian University of Athens, Greece
Harry Perros, NC State University, USA
Miodrag Potkonjak, University of California - Los Angeles, USA
Yusnita Rahayu, Universiti Malaysia Pahang (UMP), Malaysia
Yenumula B. Reddy, Grambling State University, USA
Oliviero Riganelli, University of Milano Bicocca, Italy
Teng Rui, National Institute of Information and Communication Technology, Japan
Antonio Ruiz Martinez, University of Murcia, Spain
George S. Oreku, TIRDO / North West University, Tanzania/ South Africa
Sattar B. Sadkhan, Chairman of IEEE IRAQ Section, Iraq
Husnain Saeed, National University of Sciences & Technology (NUST), Pakistan
Addisson Salazar, Universidad Politecnica de Valencia, Spain
Sébastien Salva, University of Auvergne, France
Ioakeim Samaras, Aristotle University of Thessaloniki, Greece
Luz A. Sánchez-Gálvez, Benemérita Universidad Autónoma de Puebla, México
Teerapat Sanguankotchakorn, Asian Institute of Technology, Thailand
José Santa, University Centre of Defence at the Spanish Air Force Academy, Spain
Rajarshi Sanyal, Belgacom International Carrier Services, Belgium
Mohamad Sayed Hassan, Orange Labs, France
Thomas C. Schmidt, HAW Hamburg, Germany
Hans Scholten, Pervasive Systems / University of Twente, The Netherlands
Véronique Sebastien, University of Reunion Island, France
Jean-Pierre Seifert, Technische Universität Berlin & Telekom Innovation Laboratories, Germany
Sandra Sendra Compte, Polytechnic University of Valencia, Spain
Dimitrios Serpanos, Univ. of Patras and ISI/RC ATHENA, Greece
Roman Y. Shtykh, Rakuten, Inc., Japan
Salman Ijaz Institute of Systems and Robotics, University of Algarve, Portugal
Adão Silva, University of Aveiro / Institute of Telecommunications, Portugal
Florian Skopik, AIT Austrian Institute of Technology, Austria
Karel Slavicek, Masaryk University, Czech Republic
Vahid Solouk, Urmia University of Technology, Iran
Peter Soreanu, ORT Braude College, Israel
Pedro Sousa, University of Minho, Portugal
Cristian Stanciu, University Politehnica of Bucharest, Romania
Vladimir Stantchev, SRH University Berlin, Germany
Radu Stoleru, Texas A&M University - College Station, USA
Lars Strand, Nofas, Norway
Stefan Strauβ, Austrian Academy of Sciences, Austria
Álvaro Suárez Sarmiento, University of Las Palmas de Gran Canaria, Spain
Masashi Sugano, School of Knowledge and Information Systems, Osaka Prefecture University, Japan

International Journal on Advances in Networks and Services
Volume 9, Numbers 3 & 4, 2016

CONTENTS

International Journal on Advances in Networks and Services, vol 9 no 3 & 4, year 2016, http://www.iariajournals.org/networks_and_services/

A System for Managing Transport-network Recovery Using Hybrid-backup Operation Planes according to Degree of Network Failure

Toshiaki Suzuki, Hiroyuki Kubo,
Hayato Hoshihara, and Kenichi Sakamoto
Research & Development Group
Hitachi, Ltd.
Kanagawa, Japan
E-mails: {toshiaki.suzuki.cs, hiroyuki.kubo.do,
hayato.hoshihara.dy, and
kenichi.sakamoto.xj}@hitachi.com

Hidenori Inouchi and Taro Ogawa
Information & Telecommunication Systems Company
Hitachi, Ltd.
Kanagawa, Japan
E-mails: {hidenori.inouchi.dw and
taro.ogawa.tg}@hitachi.com

Abstract*—A system for managing transport-network recovery using hybrid-backup operation planes according to the degree of a network failure is proposed. Under this management system, an entire network is separated into multiple areas. A network-management server prepares a three-step recovery procedure to cover the degree of network failure. In the first step of the recovery, an inside-area protection scheme is used to recover current data-transmission paths in each area. In the second step, an end-to-end protection scheme is applied to the current data-transmission paths. In the third step, the operation plane is changed. Each assumed operation plane is composed of recovery configurations for restoring failure paths for assumed area-based network failures. If a small network failure occurs, it is recovered by the inside-area protection and end-to-end protection schemes. If a catastrophic network failure (caused by a disaster) that cannot be recovered by those protection schemes occurs, it is recovered by changing the operation plane in accordance with the damaged areas. A prototype system composed of a network-management server and 96 emulated packet-transport nodes was developed and evaluated by configuring 1000 data-transmission paths. In case of a small network failure, 500 data-transmission paths were damaged, and they were reconfigured by the inside-area protection scheme and end-to-end protection scheme in about 5 seconds. If the network failure was not recovered by those protection schemes, 1000 data-transmission paths were reconfigured in about 1.2 seconds after the network-management server decided to change the operation plane. As a result, the proposed system could localize a network failure and recover a transport network according to the degree of network failures.

Keywords - network management; protection; disaster recovery; packet transport

I. INTRODUCTION

Lately, reflecting the rapid growth of the Internet and cloud systems, various services, for example, on-line shopping, net banking, and social-networking services (SNSs), are being provided via networks. Under these circumstances, networks have become an indispensable service supporting daily life. If a network is out of service due to failures of network nodes, people's lives and businesses would be considerably damaged. Therefore, if a network fails, it should be recovered promptly. Failures of a network can be envisioned as "small" failures (such as a failure of a node or a link) or "extensive" failures (due to natural disasters). It is therefore a crucial issue to develop a scalable network-recovery scheme that can cover recovery from either a small network failure or a catastrophic network failure.

In our previous work presented at INNOV 2015 [1], an entire system architecture was focused on a scalable network-recovery scheme by extending a prior system [2]. In this extended work, a prototype system for multiple tenant users was implemented, and its performance was evaluated in comparison with a conventional system.

As recovery procedures for network failures, two major schemes [3], namely, "protection" and "restoration," are utilized. As for protection, it is possible to recover from a network failure promptly because a backup path to a current path is prepared in advance. However, to recover from a network disaster, numerous backup paths must be prepared. Protection is therefore useful for small network failures. On the other hand, as for restoration, a recovery path is recalculated after a network failure is detected. It therefore takes much time to recover from a network failure if numerous current paths exist.

In light of the above-described issues, a robust network-management scheme is required. The overall aim of the present study is thus to develop a network-management scheme [1][2] for monitoring and controlling network resources so as to quickly restore network services after a network disaster.

The procedure for recovering from a network failure consists of three steps: the first step is to quickly detect a network failure; the second is to immediately determine how to recover from the failure; the third is to promptly configure recovery paths. The second step is focused on in the present study. In particular, a scalable network-recovery scheme—covering failures ranging from small ones to extensive ones—is proposed. The target network is a transport network, such as a Multi-Protocol Label

Switching - Transport Profile (MPLS-TP) network.

The rest of this paper is organized as follows. Section II describes related work. Section III overviews a previously proposed system and a requirement to apply it to not only catastrophic failures but also small network failures. Section IV proposes a new network-disaster recovery system. Sections V and VI respectively describe an architecture of a prototype system and present some results of evaluations of the system's performance. Section VII concludes the paper.

II. Related Work

Several standardization activities related to reliable networks have been ongoing. The International Telecommunication Union - Telecommunication Standardization Sector (ITU-T) [4] discussed specifications, such as Transport – Multi Protocol Label Switching (T-MPLS), in the first stage of standardization. In the next stage, the ITU-T jointly standardized MPLS-TP specifications with the Internet Engineering Task Force (IETF) [5]. Requests for comments (RFC) on requirements [6] and a framework [7] for MPLS-TP were then issued. In addition, RFCs on a framework for MPLS-TP-related operation, administration, and maintenance (OAM) [8] and survivability [9] were issued. Based on the OAM framework, the previously proposed system can detect network failures promptly.

Several schemes for failure recovery have been proposed. One major scheme, called "fast reroute" [10], prepares a back-up path. Another recovery scheme (for multiple failures) prepares multiple backup paths [11], and another one prepares a recovery procedure for multiple modes [12]. In the case of these protection schemes, to recover from a catastrophic network failure, a huge volume of physical resources for preparing a large number of standby paths is needed. These schemes are useful for limited network failures, namely failures of a few links or nodes.

In the case of restoration schemes, in contrast to protection schemes, recovery paths are calculated after a network failure is detected. Restoration schemes for handling multiple failures [13] and virtual networks [14] have been proposed. A scheme for reducing search ranges by using landmark nodes has also been proposed [15]. It is useful for recovering a seriously damaged network, since all reroutes are calculated after a failure is detected. However, if a large number of current paths exist, it might take much time to calculate all recovery paths.

III. Previous System and Requirements

The previously proposed network-recovery system is shown in Figure 1 [2]. The target network is composed of packet transport nodes (PTNs), such as those in an MPLS-TP network. The system only focuses on recovery from multiple area-based network failures on PTN networks. A critical issue in the case of a network disaster is the time consumed in recovering the numerous established paths (shown as solid blue arrows) in packet networks. (Note that "path" means a label-switched path (LSP) [16] and a pseudo wire (PW) [17].) A user is connected to one of the PTNs through a network such as an IP network. A server located in a data center (DC) is also connected to one of the PTNs through an IP network.

The previously proposed system could promptly recover from a catastrophic failure of a network by using prepared back-up paths (shown as dotted red arrows). However, it significantly changes network configurations, even if a network failure is small, since network conditions are managed on the basis of divided network areas. It must therefore be enhanced so that it can recover from a catastrophic network failure, as well as a small network failure, by using fewer configurational changes based on the degree of damage due to the network failure.

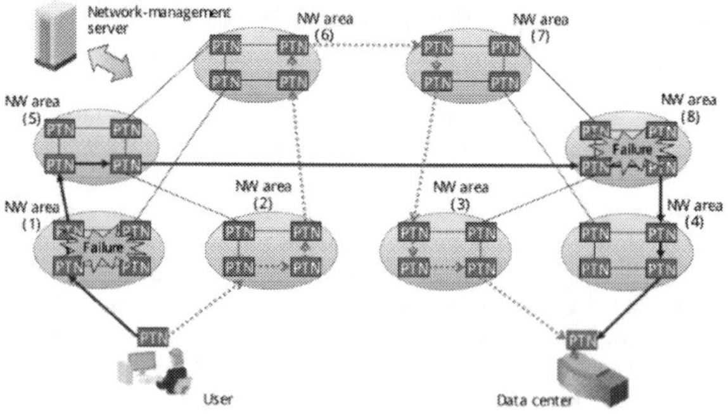

Figure 1. Previously proposed network-recovery system

IV. Proposed Transport Network-Recovery Scheme

To meet the above-described requirements, a three-step recovery procedure for covering the degree of network failures is proposed. The first step of the procedure is to execute "an inside-area protection scheme" to recover small failures, such as a node failure in each area formed by separating an entire network into small areas. The second step is to execute "an end-to-end protection scheme" to recover small failures, such as a failure of a link between areas not recovered by the inside-area protection scheme. The third step is to execute "an operation-plane change scheme" to recover extensive failures, such as network failures of multiple areas.

A. Path protection for small network failures in each area

The proposed system should promptly recover a network from a small failure, such as a link failure between PTNs or a PTN failure. A scheme called "inside-area protection"—for localizing and swiftly recovering from a small network failure—is overviewed in Figure 2. Using a conventional scheme (such as cluster analysis), the network-management server divides an entire PTN network into multiple (e.g., eight) areas, which it then manages. It configures a current path (shown as solid black arrows in the figure), composed of a LSP and a PW, for transmitting data from a sender to a receiver according to requests by end users. The network-management server configures a backup path for each current path, namely, an inside-area protection path (shown as dotted red arrows), between one edge PTN and another edge PTN in every area. Specifically, the network-management server finds an edge PTN pair that is related to the current path in every area. For example, PTN 14 and PTN 11 are the edge PTN pair in area (1), since packet data from PE1 are received by PTN 14 and then transmitted to area (5) by PTN 11, as shown in Figure 4. In addition, PTN 54 and PTN 53, PTN 84 and PTN 83, and PTN 42 and PTN 43 are the edge PTN pairs that are related to the current path. The network-management server calculates a detour path for each edge PTN pair by excluding network links that are parts of the current path. For example, a detour path between PTN 14 and PTN 11 through PTN 13 and PTN 12 is calculated as the backup path. All calculated detour paths in each area become the inside-area protection paths.

In each area, both edge PTNs exchange OAM packets to check if a disconnection exists between the PTNs. If a disconnection is detected, they send an alert to the network-management server, which keeps the received alert and monitors the degree of failures, namely, numbers of link and PTN failures, and damaged areas.

In the case shown in Figure 2, a link failure between PTN 14 and PTN 11 is assumed to occur in area (1). PTN 14 and PTN 11 detect the link failure, which is recovered by the inside-area protection. Specifically, a direct data-transmission path from PTN 14 to PTN 11 is changed to a backup transmission path through PTN 13 and PTN 12. On the other hand, the path between PTN 14 and PTN 11 is a part of an end-to-end path between provider-edge 1 (PE1) and PE2. The link failure between PTN 14 and PTN 11 is therefore temporarily detected by PE1 and PE2, since both PEs also exchange OAM packets. However, both PEs wait for 100 milliseconds to see whether the link failure is recovered by the inside-area protection. Therefore, when the link failure is recovered by the inside-area protection, neither PE executes further recovery action.

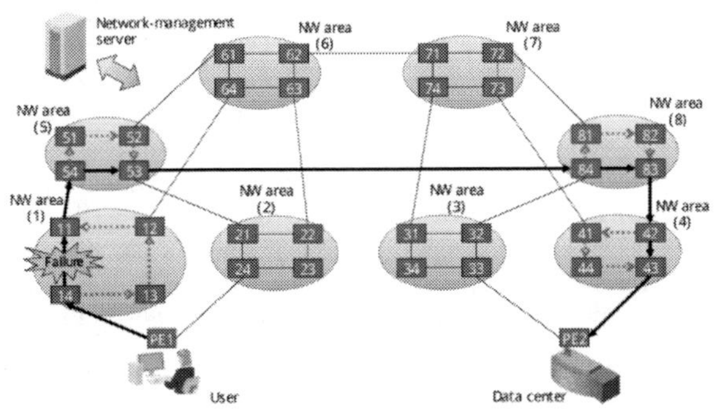

Figure 2. Configuration of path protection in each NW area

B. *End-to-end path protection for small network failures*

The proposed system should be able to immediately recover from a small failure that is not recovered by the above-described protection (such as a link failure between areas). A scheme called "end-to-end protection" to promptly recover from a failure that is not restored by the inside-area protection is overviewed as follows. The network-management server configures a backup path (called an "end-to-end protection path") for each current path between PE1 and PE2. PEs exchange OAM packets to check whether a disconnection exists between them.

Specifically, as shown in Figure 3, the network-management server configures a current path (shown as solid black arrows) between PE1 and PE2 [through areas (1), (5), (8), and (4)] for transmitting data packets between a user and a DC. In addition, the network-management server configures a backup path called an "end-to-end protection path (shown as dotted red arrows)" between PE1 and PE2. The end-to-end protection path is established so as not to travel through the same areas used by the current path as much as possible. In Figure 3, the backup path is configured to transmit data through areas (2), (6), (7), and (3).

During network operation, the end-to-end protection is executed when the data transmission between PEs is disconnected for a while (for example, 100 milliseconds). In the case of Figure 3, a link failure between areas (5) and (8) is assumed. This failure is not recovered by the inside-area protection; instead, it is recovered by the end-to-end protection because it occurs between areas. Specifically, a data-transmission path is changed from the current path (shown as solid black arrows) to a backup path (shown as dotted red arrows).

The end-to-end protection scheme is similar to a conventional protection scheme. In the case of a conventional scheme, the protection is immediately executed after one of the PEs detects a disconnection. However, in the case of the proposed end-to-end protection scheme, it is not executed for 100 milliseconds so that it can be checked whether a failure has been recovered by the inside-area protection or not.

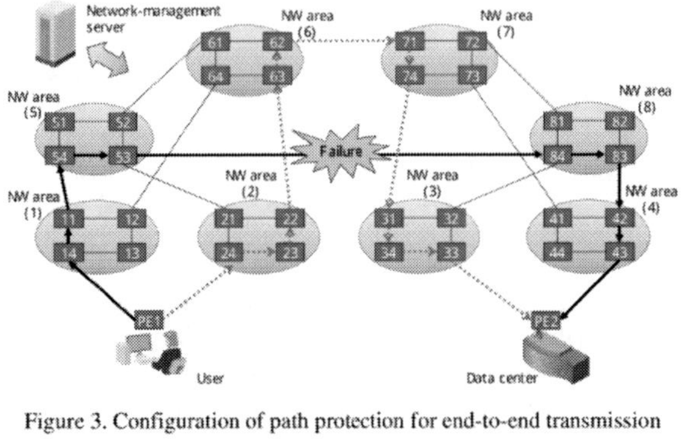

Figure 3. Configuration of path protection for end-to-end transmission

C. *Changing operation plane for network-disaster recovery*

The proposed system should be able to promptly recover not only failures inside a network area and between network areas but also catastrophic failures. A recovery scheme that changes the operation plane to recover from area-based network failures is overviewed in Figure 4. Before starting network operations, the network-management server prepares multiple backup operation planes for handling possible area-based network failures. Each backup operation plane is composed of recovery configurations for restoring failure paths due to assumed network failures. During network operation, if network failures are not recovered by both the inside-area protection and the end-to-end protection, the failures are recovered by changing an operation plane.

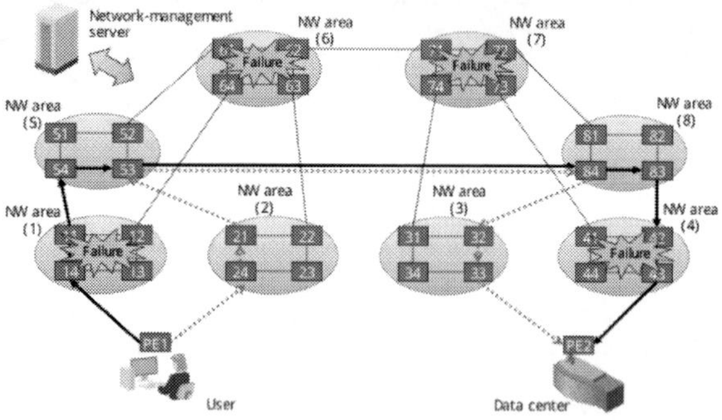

Figure 4. Configuration for changing an operation plane for network-disaster recovery

In Figure 4, as an example, the network-management server configures multiple currents paths [through areas (1), (5), (8), and (4)] for transmitting data packets between a user and a DC. It calculates all recovery paths preliminarily by assuming all possible area-based network failures. The number of possible combinations of areas is 256 (i.e., 2^8), and it includes a pattern by which no area-based network failure occurs. The network-management server therefore prepares 255 backup operation planes. It then assigns a unique recovery identifier (ID) for each backup operation plane, and sends all recovery IDs and recovery configurations to each PTN, which stores all received recovery IDs and configurations.

An example area-based network-failure recovery procedure is shown in Figure 4. In the figure, area-based network failures are assumed to occur in areas (1), (4), (6), and (7). In this case, PE1 (namely, an edge node of the current path) detects a disconnection between PE1 and PE2. PE1 waits 100 milliseconds to check whether the failures are recovered by the inside-area protection. It also checks the availability of the end-to-end protection path (which is not shown in Figure 4) by using OAM packets. If the failures are not recovered in 100 milliseconds and the end-to-end protection path is not available, PE1 sends an alert to the network-management server to inform it that the end-to-end protection is not available. The network-management server then checks which areas are not available. In this example, by receiving many alerts sent by multiple PTNs, the network-management server determines that area-based network failures occur in areas (1), (4), (6), and (7). By using the determined network-failure information, it then determines the most suitable backup operation plane to recover. To change an operation plane, the network-management server sends a recovery ID specifying the most-suitable backup operation plane to related PTNs, which change data transmissions according to the received recovery ID. By means of the above-described procedures, the operation plane is changed, and catastrophic network failures are swiftly recovered.

V. Architecture of Prototype System

In this section, the architecture of a prototype system is described. Specifically, the structure of the prototype system is shown first. Then, recovery procedures are overviewed. After that, calculation procedures for the inside-area protection paths and the end-to-end protection paths are described. (Note that calculation procedures for the backup operation planes are not described since they are explained in a previous work [2].) At the end of this section, an implemented viewer is depicted.

A. *Structure of prototype system*

A prototype system was implemented by using three servers. The structure of the prototype system—composed of an application server, a control server, and a node simulator server—is shown in Figure 5. Specifically, implemented software components are shown in the figure.

The application server is in charge of the entire network management. Specifically, it manages calculation and configuration of current paths and protection paths by sending commands. In addition, it calculates and configures back-up operation planes with multiple detour paths by assuming possible node failures or area-based network failures. Besides, it receives alerts and determines the degree of network failures. It then selects a recovery back-up operation plane and sends it an identifier specifying it to network nodes.

The control server is in charge of transmitting command messages from the application server to the simulator server. Specifically, it receives calculated route information of the current paths, protection paths, and back-up operation planes and distributes it to the simulated multiple network nodes. In addition, it monitors state of connections between not only current paths but also protection paths. When it detects a disconnection, it prompts the node simulator server to activate an alert. On the other side, it transmits alert information from the simulator server to the application server.

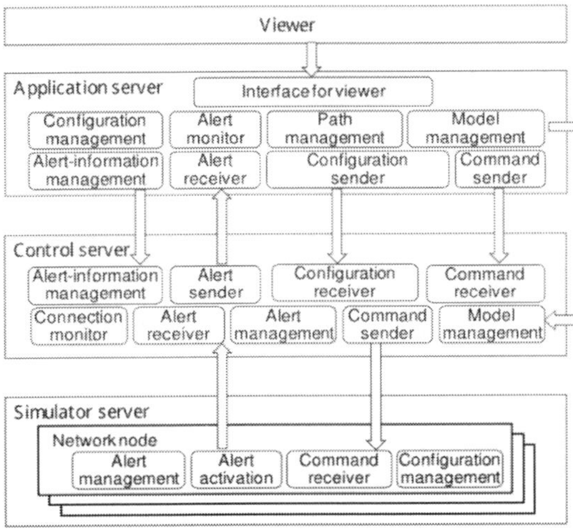

Figure 5. Structure of prototype system

The simulator server emulates certain parts of the functions of MPLS-TP network nodes. It receives configurations of LSP and PW paths and sets data-transmission paths on the basis of the received path information. When it is requested to activate alerts, it sends an SNMP trap to the control server.

B. *Overview of recovery procedures*

The structure of the proposed transport network-recovery scheme is similar to the previously proposed scheme (shown in Figure 1). Namely, it is composed of a network-management sever and multiple PTNs. The network-management server centrally manages the whole network. However, the recovery procedures differ from those of the previous system.

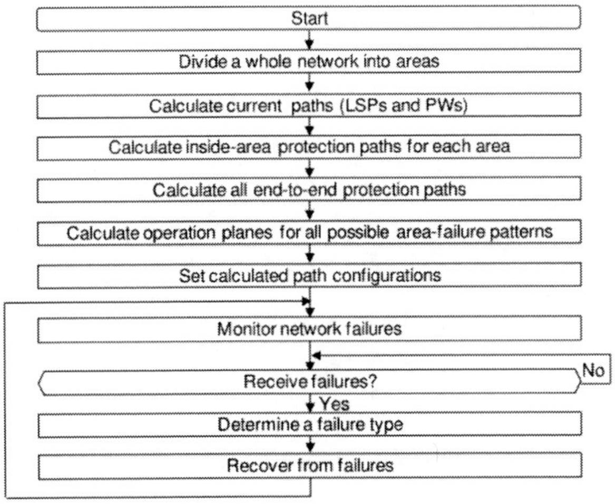

Figure 6. Overview of proposed recovery procedure

A flow chart of the new recovery procedure is shown in Figure 6. First, after starting a network-management function, the network-management server divides the whole network into multiple areas. It calculates current paths (composed of LSPs and PWs) for transmitting data from a sender node to a receiver node according to inputs by a network manager. The network-management server calculates "inside-area protection paths" for each area and "end-to-end protection paths" to recover current paths in case of network failures. In addition, it calculates virtual operation planes for all possible area-failure patterns. The protection paths and virtual operation planes are described in detail in later sections. The network-management server sets the entire configuration of the calculated paths to all network nodes and starts to monitor the network for failures. When it detects a network failure, it determines the type of failure, namely, an area-based or node-based failure. The network-management server then executes the appropriate failure-recovery procedures according to the determined failure degree.

C. *Calculation of inside-area protection paths*

An implemented flow chart of the calculation procedure of inside-area protection paths is shown in Figure 7.

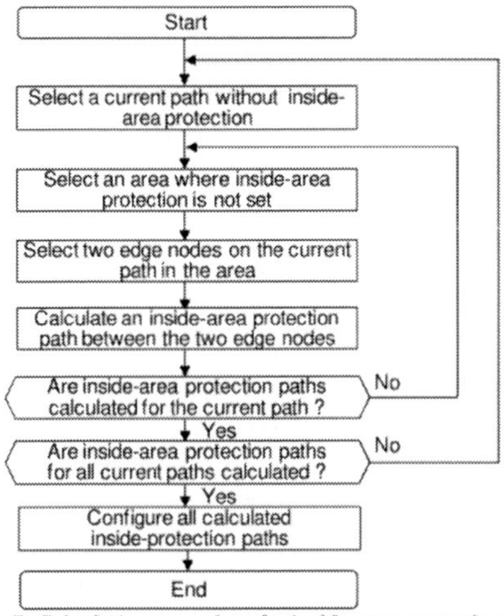

Figure 7. Calculation procedure for inside-area protection paths

The application server selects a current path that does not have an inside-area protection path. In addition, it selects an area where inside-area-protection for the selected current path is not set. Then, it selects two edge nodes on the selected current path in the selected area. One is the start point and the other is the end point for the selected path in the selected area. The application server calculates the inside-area protection path between the two selected edge nodes and stores it. After that, it checks whether the inside-area protection paths related to the selected current path are calculated or not. If they are calculated, it checks whether all inside-area protection paths for all current paths are calculated or not. If they are not calculated, it calculates other inside-area protection paths for the remaining current paths. If all inside-area protection paths are calculated and stored, it terminates the calculation procedures.

D. *Calculation of end-to-end protection paths*

An implemented flow chart of the calculation procedure for end-to-end protection paths is shown in Figure 8. The application server selects a current path that does not have an end-to-end protection path. In addition, it sets a high cost value for links in areas that the current path passes through. It then calculates an end-to-end protection path for the selected current path to minimize the cost of the summation of the links composing the protection path. After that, it checks whether all end-to-end protection paths for all current paths are calculated or not. If they are not calculated, it calculates other end-to-end protection paths for the remaining current paths. If they are calculated and stored, it terminates the calculation procedure.

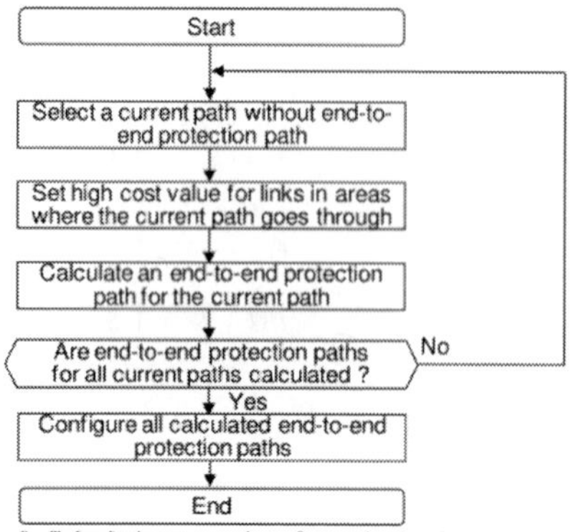

Figure 8. Calculation procedure for end-to-end protection paths

E. *Calculation of recovery paths for operation-plane change*

An implemented flow chart of the calculation procedure for recovery paths when changing the operation plane is shown in Figure 9. The detailed calculation procedure is described in our previous study [2]. The application server selects one of all possible patterns of area failures that does not have a backup operation plane. In addition, it excludes all nodes in the selected failure pattern of area failures. It then selects a current path that does not have a recovery path and calculates a recovery path for the selected current path. After that, it checks whether all recovery paths for the selected pattern of area failures are calculated or not. If they are not calculated, it calculates other recovery paths for the selected pattern of area failures. If they are calculated, it calculates recovery paths for other patterns of area failures. If all recovery paths for all possible patterns of area failures are calculated, it terminates the calculation procedure.

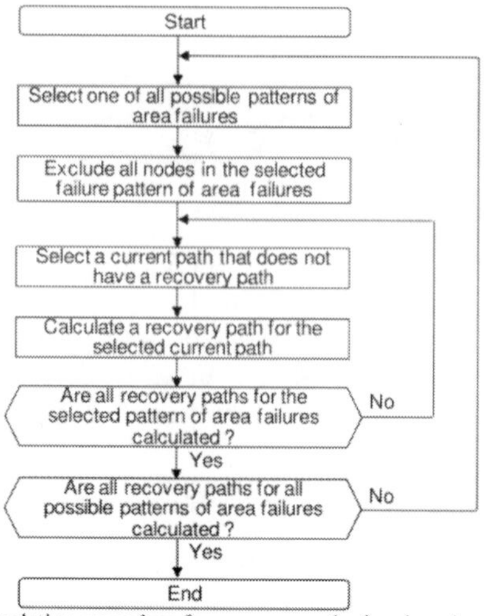

Figure 9. Calculation procedure for recovery paths for changing operation plane

F. *Implementation of viewer*

The primary-screen layout of the prototype system's viewer is shown in Figure 10. The function menu allows selection of a topology view or a system-configuration view. The operation ID means the number of a selected operation planes. If no failure occurs, the number zero is used. The recovery indicator shows conditions after execution of one of the recovery procedures, namely, inside-area protection, end-to-end protection, and a selection of a backup operation plane. The condition panel shows current operational status of the system. The topology tree shows a list and structure of connected nodes. The alert panel shows a list of failures, such as node failures. The "area object" tag indicates an existence of each area. The "user terminal" tag indicates each user terminal. The map location indicates the position of the displayed network.

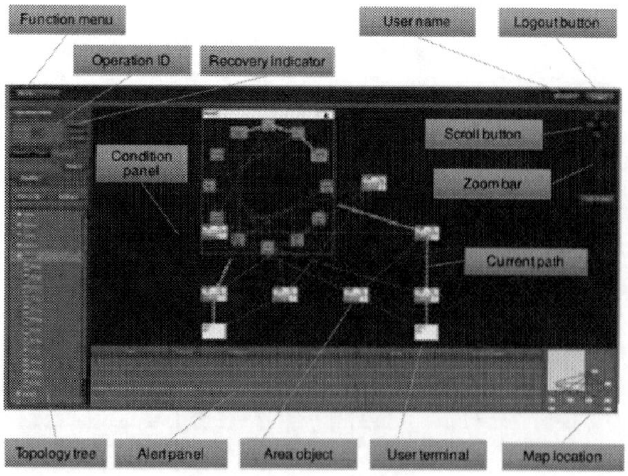

Figure 10. View of primary-screen layout

The "current path" tag highlights the currently used path. The "zoom bar" button provides a function to change the size of the displayed network. The "scroll" button provides a function to change the position of the displayed network. The "user name" tag shows the name of a current user. The "logout" button is used to terminate network management.

VI. PERFORMANCE EVALUATION AND RESULTS

The above-described recovery procedures were evaluated in the case of a small network failure and a catastrophic network failure by using the prototype system. In the evaluation, the times needed to calculate and to configure a table for current data-transmission paths (composed of PWs and LSPs) were evaluated. In addition, the times taken to configure recovery paths in the case of a failure of a PTN or an area-based failure were evaluated.

A. Evaluation system

The system used for evaluating the proposed recovery procedures is shown in Figure 11. It is composed of a network-management server and 96 PTNs. As shown in the figure, an entire PTN network is divided into eight areas. Each network area is composed of 12 PTNs, as shown in NW area (7). In each area, PTNs are connected in a reticular pattern. In addition, each user terminal is connected to PTN-network areas (1) and (2) through PE1 or PE3, and each application server in DC1 or DC2 is connected to PTN-network areas (3) and (4) through PE2 or PE4.

Note that the PTN networks (composed of 96 PTNs) are emulated by a physical server. The user terminal and application server are also emulated by the physical server, whose specification is listed in Table I. Another physical server, which executes the network-management function, has the same specifications as the former server.

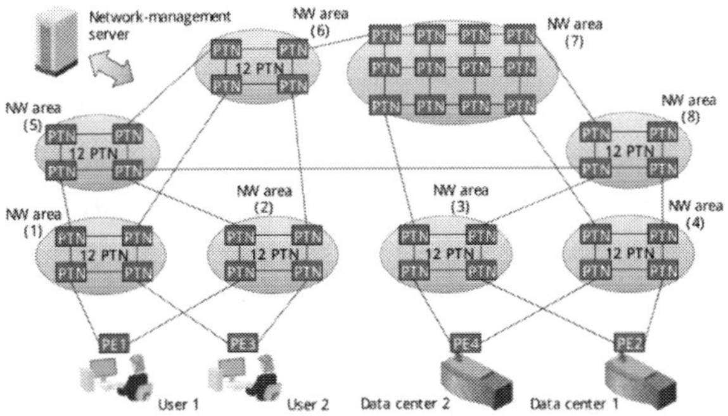

Figure 11. Evaluation system

TABLE I. SPECIFICATION OF SERVER

#	Item	Specification
1	CPU	1.8 GHz, 4 cores
2	Memory	16 Gbytes
3	Storage	600 Gbytes

TABLE II. EVALUATED ITEMS

#	Item	Evaluation specification
1	Current-path calculation time	Time to calculate 100 (=50+50), 500 (=250+250), and 1000 (=500+500) PWs
2	Current-path distribution time	Time to distribute all calculated current paths in case of 100 (=50+50), 500 (=250+250), and 1000 (=500+500) PWs
3	Protection-path calculation time for each area	Time to calculate all protection paths in each area for 100 (=50+50), 500 (=250+250), and 1000 (=500+500) PWs
4	Protection-path calculation time for end-to-end protection paths	Time to calculate all protection paths for all end-to-end current paths for 100 (=50+50), 500 (=250+250), and 1000 (=500+500) PWs
5	Recovery-path calculation time for changing operation plane	Time to calculate recovery 100 (=50+50), 500 (=250+250), and 1000 (=500+500) PWs for all possible area-failure patterns
6	Recovery-configuration time	Time to configure all protection paths after detecting path failures for 100 (=50+50), 500 (=250+250), and 1000 (=500+500) PWs
7	Recovery-ID distribution time	Time to distribute a recovery ID after detecting an area failure for 100 (=50+50), 500 (=250+250), and 1000 (=500+500) PWs

B. Evaluation conditions

The times taken to calculate multiple PWs between PE1 and PE2 and between PE3 and PE4 were evaluated. Each PW was included in a LSP. If a transmission path of a PW differed from the path of an already setup LSP, a new LSP was setup, and the PW was included in the new LSP. The evaluations were executed according to the patterns listed in Table II. Specifically, the times taken to calculate current paths, to distribute their configuration to all PTNs, and to calculate the inside-area protection paths and end-to-end protection paths were evaluated by changing the number of PWs (namely, 50+50, 250+250, and 500+500 for two users). In addition, the times taken to calculate recovery paths for changing the operation plane, to configure protection paths, and to distribute the recovery ID were evaluated.

C. Evaluation results

1) Current-path calculation time

The times taken to calculate current PWs requested by the two users are plotted in Figure 12. User 1 accesses a server in DC1 through PE1 and PE2. User 2 accesses a server in DC2 through PE3 and PE4. A scalability evaluation was executed by changing setup PWs for each user. As shown in the figure, the times taken to calculate 100 (=50+50) current PWs, 500 (=250+250) current PWs, and 1000 (=500+500) current PWs were respectively about 152, 570, and 1079 milliseconds.

2) Distribution time for configuring current paths

The times taken to distribute all configurations of the calculated current paths to all PTNs are plotted in Figure 13. As shown in the figure, the times taken to distribute all configurations of the 100 (=50+50) current PWs, 500 (=250+250) current PWs, and 1000 (=500+500) current PWs are respectively about 25, 330, and 923 milliseconds.

3) Protection-path calculation time for all current paths in each area

The times taken to calculate protection paths corresponding to all current PWs in each area are plotted in Figure 14. As shown in the figure, the times required for calculating all the inside-area protection paths for 100 (=50+50) current PWs, 500 (=250+250) current PWs, and 1000 (=500+500) current PWs are respectively about 600, 1392, and 2095 milliseconds.

4) Protection-path calculation time for all end-to-end current paths

The times taken to calculate end-to-end protection paths to all current PWs are plotted in Figure 15. As shown in the figure, the times taken to calculate all the end-to-end protection paths for 100 (=50+50) current PWs, 500 (=250+250) current PWs, and 1000 (=500+500) current PWs are respectively about 230, 952, and 1983 milliseconds.

5) Recovery-path calculation time for operation-plane change

The times taken to calculate all recovery PWs for 255 possible area-based network-failure patterns are plotted in Figure 16. As shown in the figure, the times taken to calculate all recovery PWs for 255 area-based network-failure patterns and 100 (=50+50) current PWs, 500 (=250+250) current PWs, and 1000 (=500+500) current PWs are respectively about 12.2, 44.8, and 85.5 seconds.

6) Recovery-configuration time required by both protection schemes for each area and end-to-end path

The times taken to set recovery configuration and to store a configured network topology by the inside-area protection and end-to-end protection schemes after detecting a path disconnection are plotted in Figure 17. Specifically, recovery configuration time was evaluated by intentionally invoking a node failure in area (5). In this case, half of the PWs were damaged and recovered. In the evaluation, if a disconnected path is not recovered for 100 milliseconds by the inside-area protection, it is automatically recovered by the end-to-end protection. Actually, disconnected paths were recovered by the end-to-end protection. As shown in the figure, the times to set recovery configurations for 100 (=50+50) current PWs, 500 (=250+250) current PWs, and 1000 (=500+500) current PWs by both protections are respectively about 0.8, 2.2, and 4.7 seconds.

7) Recovery-ID distribution time for changing operation plane

The times taken to distribute the recovery ID to related PTNs and recover after the last area-based network failure is detected in the case of 100 (=50+50) current PWs, 500 (=250+250) current PWs, and 1000 (=500+500) current PWs are plotted in Figure 18. Three area-based network-failure patterns, namely, failures of network areas (1) and (6), failures of network areas (1), (6), and (4), and failures of network areas (1), (6), (4), and (7), were evaluated. As shown in the figure, in the case of 100 (=50+50) current PWs, the times taken to recover from the last failure for the three area-based network-failure patterns are respectively about 167, 177, and 167 milliseconds. In the case of 500 (=250+250) current PWs, the times taken to recover from the last failure for the three area-based network-failure patterns are respectively about 533, 569, and 564 milliseconds. In the case of 1000 (=500+500) current PWs, the times taken to recover from the last failure for the three area-based network-failure patterns are respectively about 1227, 1134, and 1205 milliseconds. As a result, tables that are used for data transmission on 1000 (=500+500) PWs are reconfigured by changing an operation plane in about 1.2 seconds.

In Figure 18, the proposed method is compared with a conventional restoration method in terms of the time taken to calculate and configure PWs. With the conventional method, the times to set recovery configurations for 100 (=50+50) current PWs, 500 (=250+250) current PWs, and 1000 (=500+500) current PWs are respectively about 177, 900, and 2002 milliseconds.

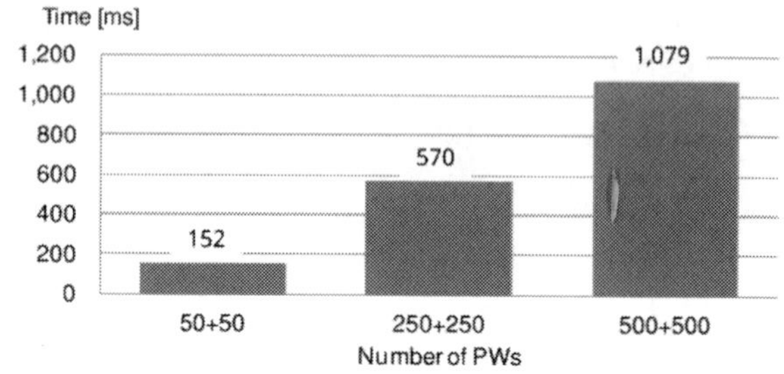

Figure 12. Calculation time for current paths

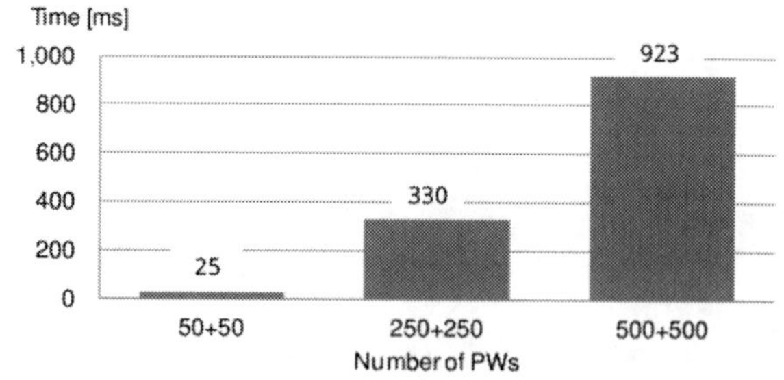

Figure 13. Distribution time for current-path configuration

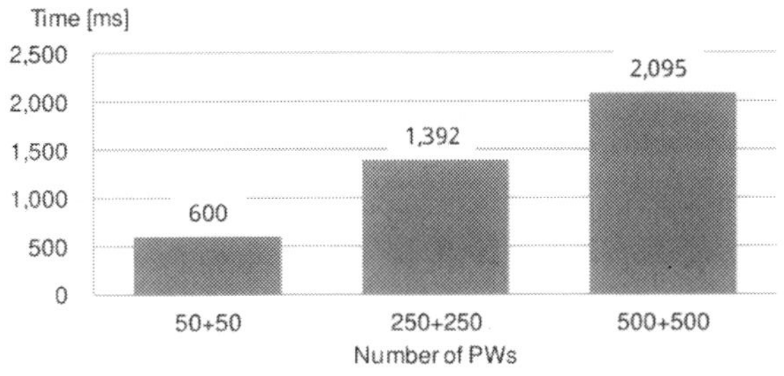

Figure 14. Calculation time for protection paths in each area

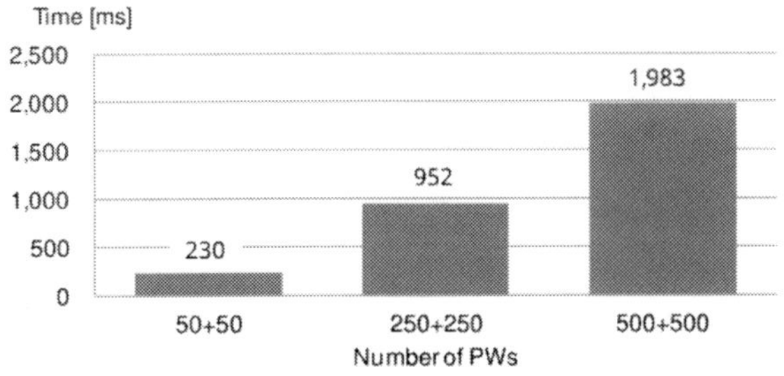

Figure 15. Calculation time for end-to-end protection paths

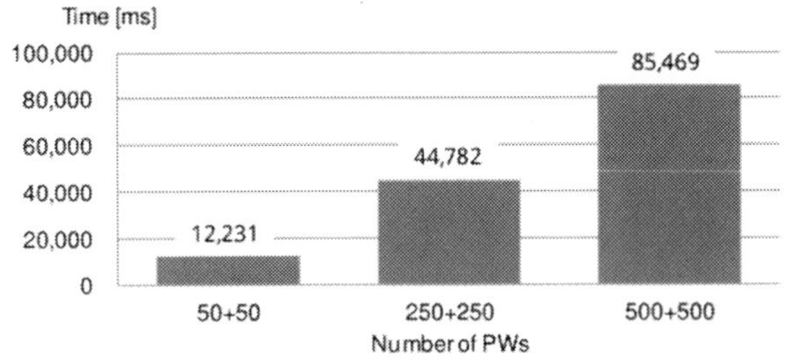

Figure 16. Calculation time for changing operation plane

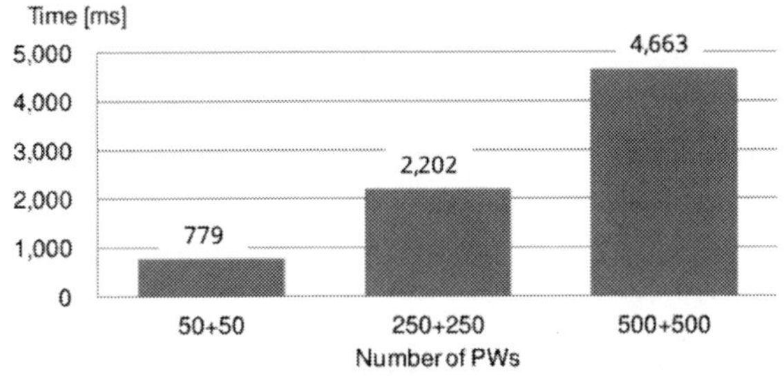

Figure 17. Recovery-configuration time in the cases of using protection paths in NW areas and end-to-end protection paths

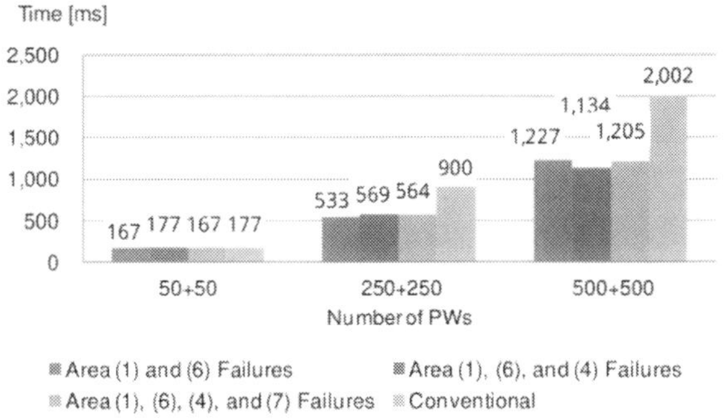

Figure 18. Recovery-configuration time in the case of changing operation plane

D. Discussion

The times taken to recover from failures, such as disconnection of paths, are plotted in Figure 17. In this evaluation, a PTN failure was intentionally invoked in area (5). As a recovery procedure, inside-area protection is expected to be appropriate, since the failure was invoked in area (5). However, end-to-end protection was also used. As for the proposed system, updated PWs and LSPs are always stored after changing data-transmission paths by one of the recovery procedures, such as inside-area protection. In addition, if a failure that is not recovered by the inside-area protection for 100 milliseconds occurs, it is recovered by the end-to-end protection. Over 100 milliseconds were taken to store the PWs and LSPs updated by the inside-area protection; therefore, the PTN failure in area (5) was recovered by both the inside-area protection and the end-to-end protection. The PTN failure was recovered in about 5 seconds for 1000 (=500+500) current PWs, which is a little longer than expected recovery times as a protection, since recovery paths are sequentially configured one by one by using emulated nodes on a server. In addition, a configured network topology was detected and stored. Therefore, the times taken by both protection schemes to recovery are a little longer compared to the recovery time by changing an operation plane. In future work, the times taken to manage multiple updated PWs and LSPs should thus be shortened.

The times taken to distribute the recovery ID and store updated PWs and LSPs are shown in Figure 18. As shown in the figure, the times taken to recover are almost independent of the number of area-based network failures, although they are dependent on the number of setup PWs. In the case of 96 PTNs, tables for data transmission on 1000 (=500+500) current PWs were reconfigured in about 1.2 seconds. The times for recovery are short because the times for setting up real PWs are not included; instead, the times for configuring tables to transmit data are included. In addition, all tables for data transmission are changed at once by switching the operation plane. According to the results of this evaluation, the proposed system can provide a faster recovery procedure than recalculating and transmitting recovery paths to PTNs (since it omits the recalculation process).

In summary, a transport-network-recovery management system, which can recover from both a small network failure and a major network disaster, was proposed and evaluated. Specifically, for small failures, inside-area protection and end-to-end protection were proposed. In addition, for major failures, an area-based recovery procedure was proposed. As described above, updated data-transmission paths of PWs and LSPs are always stored in a database. Therefore, transmission paths composed of PWs and LSPs updated by changing the operation plane are also stored in the database. As a result, the times taken to recover from the network disaster by changing the operation plane depend on the number of PWs. However, as shown in Figures 16 and 17, the proposed system could promptly recover from both a small network failure and a catastrophic network failure (which is not covered by conventional network-recovery schemes).

VII. Conclution

A system for managing transport-network recovery based on the degree of network failures is proposed. Under this management scheme, an entire network is separated into multiple areas. A network-management server executes a three-step recovery procedure. In the first step, an inside-area protection scheme is applied to the current data-transmission path in each area. In the second step, an end-to-end protection scheme is applied to the current data-transmission path. In the third step, the operation plane is changed. Each assumed operation plane is composed of recovery configurations for restoring failure paths under the assumption of area-based network failures. If a small network failure occurs, it is recovered and localized by the inside-area protection and end-to-end protection schemes. If a catastrophic network failure (due to a disaster) that is not recovered by the protection schemes occurs, it is recovered by changing the operation plane according to damaged areas.

A prototype system composed of a network-management server and 96 emulated packet-transport nodes was developed and evaluated by configuring 1000 (=500+500) data-transmission paths. In the case of a small network failure, 500 data-transmission paths composed by LSPs and PWs were damaged and reconfigured by the inside-area protection and end-to-end protection schemes in about 5 seconds. If a network failure was not recovered by the protection schemes, all tables for 1000 (=500+500) data transmission paths were reconfigured to recover from the failure by changing the operation plane in about 1.2 seconds. As a result, the proposed system could provide a faster recovery procedure than recalculating and transmitting recovery paths to PTNs. In addition, it could localize and recover a network failure according to the degree of network failures.

Although the protection scheme could recover 500 data transmission paths from a small network failure, it took the network-management server about 5 seconds to configure and store changed-data transmission paths. If numerous current paths exist, it will take too much time to assess changed paths. Accordingly, the protection scheme will be further developed so that it can promptly manage a large number of recovered paths.

Acknowledgments

Part of this research was done within research project O3 (Open, Organic, Optima) and programs, "Research and Development on Virtualized Network Technology," "Research and Development on Management Platform Technologies for Highly Reliable Cloud Services," and "Research and Development on Signaling Technologies of Network Configuration for Sustainable Environment" supported by MIC (The Japanese Ministry of Internal Affairs and Communications).

References

[1] T. Suzuki et al., "A system for managing transport-network recovery according to degree of network failure," *The Fourth International Conference on Communications, Computation, Networks and Technologies (INNOV 2015)*, Nov. 2015, pp. 56-63.

[2] T. Suzuki et al., "A network-disaster recovery system using multiple-backup operation planes," *International Journal on Advances in Networks and Services*, vol. 8 nos. 1&2, July 2015, pp. 118-129.

[3] E. Mannie and D. Papadimitriou, "Recovery (Protection and Restoration) Terminology for Generalized Multi-Protocol Label Switching (GMPLS)," IETF RFC 4427, Mar. 2006.

[4] International Telecommunication Union - Telecommunication Standardization Sector (ITU-T) http://www.itu.int/en/ITU-T/Pages/default.aspx [retrieved: Nov. 2016].

[5] The Internet Engineering Task Force (IETF), http://www.ietf.org/ [retrieved: Nov. 2016].

[6] B. Niven-Jenkins, D. Brungard, M. Betts, N. Sprecher, and S. Ueno, "Requirements of an MPLS transport profile," IETF RFC 5654, Sept. 2009.

[7] M. Bocci, S. Bryant, D. Frost, L. Levrau, and L. Berger, "A Framework for MPLS in transport networks," IETF RFC 5921, July 2010.

[8] T. Busi and D. Allan, "Operations, administration, and maintenance framework for MPLS-based transport neworks," IETF RFC 6371, Sept. 2011.

[9] N. Sprecher and A. Farrel, "MPLS transport profile (MPLS-TP) survivability framework," IETF RFC 6372, Sept. 2011.

[10] P. Pan, G. Swallow, and A. Atlas, " Fast reroute extensions to RSVP-TE for LSP tunnels," IETF RFC 4090, May 2005.

[11] J. Zhang, J. Zhou, J. Ren, and B. Wang, "A LDP fast protection switching scheme for concurrent multiple failures in MPLS network," *2009 MINES '09. International*

Conference on Multimedia Information Networking and Security, Nov. 2009, pp. 259-262.

[12] Z. Jia and G. Yunfei, "Multiple mode protection switching failure recovery mechanism under MPLS network," *2010 Second International Conference on Modeling, Simulation and Visualization Methods (WMSVM)*, May 2010, pp. 289-292.

[13] M. Lucci, A. Valenti, F. Matera, and D. Del Buono, "Investigation on fast MPLS restoration technique for a GbE wide area transport network: A disaster recovery case," *12th International Conference on Transparent Optical Networks (ICTON)*, Tu.C3.4, June 2010, pp. 1-4.

[14] T. S. Pham, J. Lattmann, J. Lutton, L. Valeyre, J. Carlier, and D. Nace, "A restoration scheme for virtual networks using switches," *2012 4th International Congress on Ultra Modern Telecommunications and Control Systems and Workshops (ICUMT)*, Oct. 2012, pp. 800-805.

[15] X. Wang, X. Jiang, C. Nguyen, X. Zhang, and S. Lu, "Fast connection recovery against region failures with landmark-based source routing," *2013 9th International Conference on the Design of Reliable Communication Networks (DRCN)*, Mar. 2013, pp. 11-19.

[16] E. Rosen, A. Viswanathan, and R. Callon, "Multiprotocol lable switching architecture," IETF RFC 3031, Jan. 2001.

[17] S. Bryant and P. Pate, "Pseudo wire emulation edge-to-edge (PWE3) architecture," IETF RFC 3985, Mar. 2005.

A Scalable and Dynamic Distribution of Tenant Networks across Multiple Provider Domains using Cloudcasting

Kiran Makhijani, Renwei Li and Lin Han

Future Networks, America Research Center
Huawei Technologies Inc., Santa Clara, CA 95050
Email: kiran.makhijani, renwei.li, lin.han@ {huawei}.com

Abstract—**Network overlays play a key role in the adoption of cloud oriented networks, which are required to scale and grow elastically and dynamically up/down and in/out, be provisioned with agility and allow for mobility. Cloud oriented networks span over multiple sites and interconnect using Virtual Private Network (VPN) like services across multiple domains. These connections are extremely slow to provision and difficult to change. Current solutions to support cloud based networks require combination of several protocols in data centers and across provider networks to implement end to end virtual network connections using different overlay technologies. However, they still do not necessarily meet all the above requirements without adding operational complexity or without new modifications to base protocols. This paper discusses a converged network virtualization framework called Cloudcasting, which is a single technology for virtual network interconnections within and across multiple sites. The protocol is based on minimal control plane signaling and offers a flexible data plane encapsulation. The biggest challenge yet for any virtual network solution is to distribute and inter-connect virtual networks at global scale across different geographies and heterogeneous infrastructures. Data center operators are faced with the predicament to re-design networks in order to support a specific virtualization approach. Cloudcasting technology can be easily adopted to interconnect or extend virtual networks with in a massive scale software defined data centers, campus networks, public, private or hybrid clouds and even container environments with no change to physical network environment and without compromising simplicity.**

Keywords–Network Overlay; Network Virtualization; Routing, Multi-Tenancy Virtual Data Center; VXLAN; BGP; EVPN.

I. Introduction

The Cloud adoption continues to grow; there is an upward trend of applications and services being built in platform independent manner and the scope of connectivity is no longer limited to a single site or a fixed location. As the cloud based applications evolve, the isolated operation and management of tenant networks (sharing common network access) that host these application becomes extremely complex and is different than the underlying physical networks. While infrastructure networks focus on delivering basic functions to ensure that the physical links are reliably available and reachable; the tenants concern with mechanisms to allocate and/or withdraw resources on-demand from different sites and network resource pools. The leading requirement for tenants is to use the networks in the most economical manner and still have sufficient resources available when needed.

The above mentioned motivation was first mentioned in the original Cloudcasting paper [1], which described a network virtualization framework that addresses many shortcomings of existing solutions. The present paper expands on concepts described in the original paper and covers details about prototype experiences, applications and advanced concepts of using Cloudcasting. Since the original work, we have observed that the Cloudcasting architecture applies to almost all virtualization scenarios and can be considered as a generalized framework for infrastructure indepedent virtual networking. The later sections of this paper further validates our observation.

The key characteristics of Cloud-oriented network architectures are resource virtualization, multi-site distribution, scalability, multi-tenancy and workload mobility. These are typically enabled through network virtualization overlay technologies. Initial network virtualization approaches relate to layer-2 multi-path mechanisms such as, Shortest Path Bridging (SPB) [2] [3] and Transparent Interconnection of Lots of Links (TRILL) [4] to address un-utilized links and to limit broadcast domains. Later, much of the focus was put into the data plane aspects of the network virtualization, for example, Virtual eXtensible Local Area Networks (VXLAN) [5], Network Virtualization using Generic Routing Encapsulation (NVGRE) [6], and Generic Network Virtualization Encapsulation (GENEVE) [7]. These tunneling solutions provide the means to carry layer-2 and/or layer-3 packets of tenant networks over a shared IP network infrastructure to create logical networks. Though, due to their lack of corresponding control plane schemes, the overall system orchestration and configuration becomes complex for virtual network setup and maintenance [8].

Even more recently, MultiProtocol-Border Gateway Protocol (MP-BGP) based Ethernet VPN (EVPN) [9] has been proposed as a control plane for virtual network distribution, and has foundations of the VPN style provisioning model. This requires additional changes to an already complex protocol that was originally designed for the inter-domain routing. The deployment of MP-BGP/EVPN in data center networks also brings in corresponding bulky configurations, for example, defining Autonomous System (AS), that are not really relevant to the data center infrastructure network. The solutions like TRILL, SPB and MP-BGP are a class of virtual network architectures that consume data structures of physical (substrate) network protocols, therefore, we refer to them as Embedded Virtual Networks. The term substrate network henceforth will be used to describe a base, underlying, or an infrastructure network upon which tenant networks are built as virtual network overlays. Whereas Cloudcasting protocol is referred to as Extended Virtual Network because it inter-connects different types of virtual networks through its own routing scheme. It can be organized over any substrate network topology and routing arrangements. As a note to the reader, with in the scope of this document, a virtual, customer or tenant network are used interchangeably and mean the same. A cloud is a location and infrastructure network. A virtual network is an entity that shares physical network resources and access with other similar entities; virtual networks are isolated from each other. In the context of this paper agility is understood as being able to responds to the changes in virtual network in real time or as quickly as needed to best serve the customer experience. Whereas elasticity refers to an ability to grow or shrink resource requirements on-demand.

Even though Embedded Virtual Network (the term is inspired from [10]) solutions mentioned above are quite functional, they are faced with several limitations. Of which the most significant and relevant to cloud-scale environments is their dependence on the substrate networks. In addition to being scalable and reliable, a cloud scale network must also be elastic, dynamic, agile, infrastructure-independent, and capable of multi-domain support. There has not been any converged architecture for network virtualization yet. In [1], we proposed Cloudcasting, an Extended Virtual Network framework that operates on top of any substrate network and offers primitives for cloud auto-discovery, dynamic route distribution as needed. As an extension to original paper, several operational concepts have been described. We have provided details of the prototype but most important section deals with the scalable distribution of virtual networks across geographically remote sites.

The rest of the paper is organized as follows. We have kept Section II and III intact from original paper to introduce the reference model and its major functions. Section IV explains different deployment scenarios where cloudcasting applies to. While Section V discusses scalability at global level of the solution, Section VI introduces the Cloudcasting policy framework where in constraints on virtual networks may be specified. Section VII has the qualitative analysis and implementation details and in Section VIII comparison with a few most common already existing solutions are made. Lastly, Section IX briefly lays out an interesting extension of cloudcasting combining services and mobile networks.

II. Cloudcasting Model

A converged virtual routing scheme can be described by two primary factors; an infrastructure-independent virtual network framework, and a unified mechanism to build an overlay of various types of tenant networks with different address schemes. On these basis, a new virtual routing scheme called Cloudcasting, is proposed with the following characteristics

1) ***Auto discovery:*** A signaling scheme that enables us to add, delete, expand and virtualize a tenants network with minimum configuration.
2) ***Auto distribution:*** A signaling scheme that connects multiple virtual networks with each other or asymmetrically as needed.
3) ***Auto Scale:*** The ability to provide and serve high scale of tenants in a location-agnostic manner.

A cloudcasting network is an IP network, which is shared and used by multiple tenant clouds to route traffic within a single virtual network or between different virtual networks. We use the terminology of tenant cloud to emphasize that a tenant or

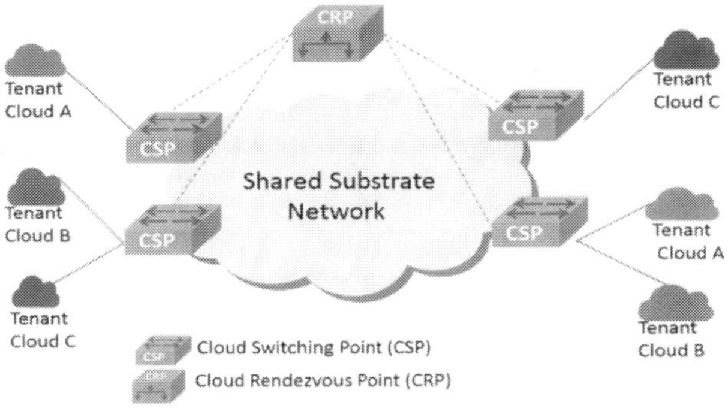

Figure 1: Cloudcasting Reference Model.

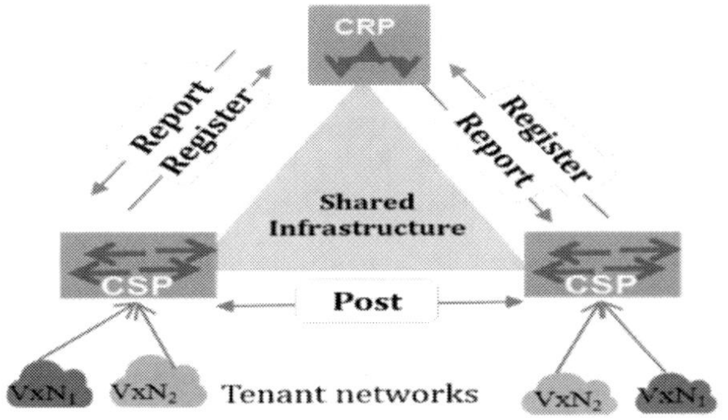

Figure 2: Cloudcasting Framework.

a user network may reside anywhere on the substrate network with a highly dynamic routing table. The IP address space in one tenant cloud may overlap with that in another cloud and these are not exposed to the shared IP infrastructure network. The cloudcasting reference model, is shown in Fig. 1. Each customer has its own network shown as Tenant Cloud A, B and C, a shared substrate IP network that was built independently and can encompass multiple administrative domains. This model describes a centralized conversational scheme, in which tenant clouds or Virtual Extensible Networks (VXNs) announce their presence as well as membership interests to a centralized designated authority, called Cloudcasting Rendezvous Point (CRP), via a cloudcasting network virtualization edge element called Cloudcasting Switching Point (CSP). To communicate among the network elements, a new signaling protocol, called CloudCasting Control (CCC) protocol is defined with three simple primitives facilitating cloud auto-discovery and cloud route distribution. The protocol primitives are defined as below and are further illustrated in Fig. 2.

- *Register message*: A virtual network interest and self-identifying announcement primitive from CSP to CRP.
- *Report message*: A response from CRP to all CSPs with similar virtual network interests.
- *Post message*: A CSP to CSP virtual network route distribution primitive.

The details of aforementioned cloudcasting network elements and their properties in cloudcasting framework are discussed as below.

A. Virtual Extensible Network

A Virtual Extensible Network is a tenant cloud or a user network. It is represented by a unique identifier with a global significance in cloudcasting network. Using this construct, it is possible to discover all its instances on the substrate IP fabric via CRP. VXN identifiers are registered with CRP from CSPs to announce their presence. There are various possible formats to define the VXN, for instance, an alphanumeric value, number or any other string format. In the preliminary work we have defined it as a named string that is mapped to a 28-bit integer identifier, thus enabling support for up to 256 million clouds.

B. Cloud Switch Point

A Cloud Switch Point is a network function that connects virtual networks on one side to the substrate IP network on the other side. It can be understood as an edge of a virtual network that originates and terminates virtual tunnels. A CSP holds mappings of L3 routes or L2 MAC forwarding information of a virtual network. A CSP is cloudcasting equivalent of a Virtual Tunnel End Point (VTEP) [5] in VXLAN networks or an Ingress/Egress Tunnel Router (xTR) in the LISP domain [11] and may similarly be co-located with either on a service providers edge (PE) router, on a top of rack (ToR) switch in a data center, or on both. A CSP participates in both auto-discovery and auto-route distribution. In order to establish a forwarding path between two endpoints of a virtual network or of two different virtual networks, a CSP first registers with the CRP its address and VXN identifiers it intends to connect to. Then the CRP will report to all CSPs that have interest in same VXN. Finally, the CSP will communicate with those other CSPs and exchange their routing information. On the data forwarding plane, a CSP builds a virtual Forwarding Information Base (vFIB) table on per VXN basis and route/switch traffic to the destination virtual networks accordingly.

C. Cloud Rendezvous Point

A Cloud Rendezvous Point is a single logical entity that stores, maintains and manages information about CSPs and their VXN membership. The CRP maintains the latest VXN to CSP membership database and distributes this information to relevant CSPs so that they can form peer connection and exchange virtual network routes automatically. A report message is always generated whenever there is a change in the virtual network membership database. However, CRP is oblivious to any change in vFIB (described above in CSP).

III. Cloudcasting Communication Primitives

Now, we describe cloudcasting communication primitives used among CRP and CSPs. Fig. 3 illustrates the layering of the virtual routing over any substrate layer and overlay control messages between CSP and CRP. The encapsulation message format is shown above in Fig. 4. A predefined TCP destination port identifies the cloudcasting protocol and CCC header contains the specification for the register, report and post messages.

A. Cloudcasting Register Message

An auto-discovery of virtual networks involves two messages. The first message is the Cloudcasting Register that originates from CSPs to announce CSP is interested in a VXN

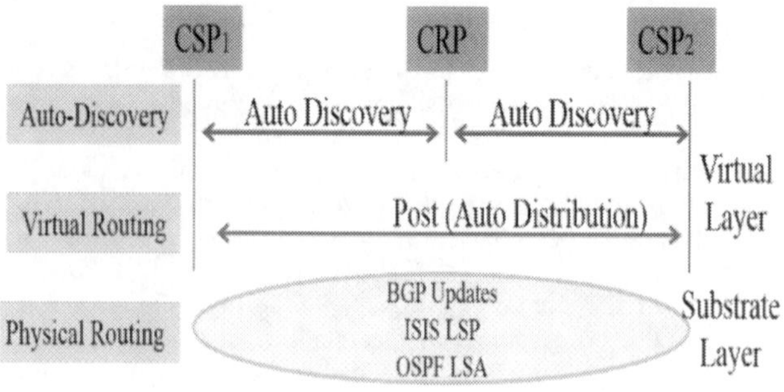

Figure 3: Cloudcasting Protocol Primitives

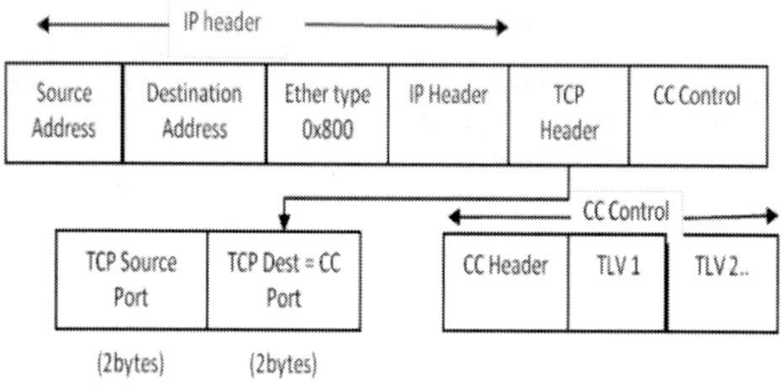

Figure 4: Cloudcasting Control Message Format

with the CRP. A Register message specification includes the CSP address and list of VXNs it is interested in. An interest is defined as an intent to participate in a specific virtual network. For example, a vxn_{red} on csp_1 expresses interest to join vxn_{red} on csp_2. As an example, consider virtual networks vxn_{red} and vxn_{green} are attached to csp_1. Then, the register message contains a tuple as follows

Register{*sender:* csp_1, [vxn_{red}, vxn_{green}]}

After the CRP receives a cloudcasting register message, it scans its CSP membership database to look for the same VXN identifiers. If it finds one (or more), a cloudcasting report message is generated and sent to all the CSPs with same interest, otherwise, it simply logs the VXN in its CSP database.

B. Cloudcasting Report Message

The CRP generates cloudcasting report messages in response to a cloudcasting register message to inform CSPs of other CSPs address and their associated VXN identifiers. If the CRP finds other CSP(s) with the same VXN membership (or interested VXNs), then the Report messages are generated for that CSP as well as the other found CSPs. A Report message is sent to each CSP, that contains other CSP addresses for the shared VXNs. As an example, consider CRP already has csp_2 with interest in vxn_{red}. Upon receiving a cloudcasting register message from csp_1 as described earlier, two report messages are generated as below for csp_2 and csp_1, respectively:

Report (csp_2) {*to:* csp_1, [*interest:* vxn_{red}]}
Report (csp_1) {*to:* csp_2, [*interest:* vxn_{red}]}

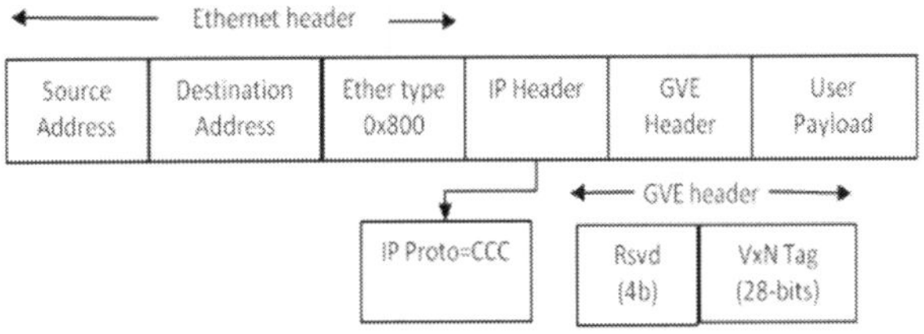

Figure 5: Cloudcasting GVE Protocol Encapsulation

In this manner, auto-discovery of virtual network locations is accomplished that is based on interest and announcement criteria.

C. Cloudcasting Post Message

The cloudcasting post messages facilitate route distribution as needed. As a cloudcasting report message is received, the CSP will connect with other CSPs to exchange their routing information that includes VXN identifiers, a Generic VXN encapsulation (GVE) tag and the network reachability information within the VXN along with the address family. The list of network reachability information type includes but not restricted to IP prefixes (such as, IPv4, IPv6), VLANs, MAC addresses or any other user defined address scheme. As an example, when a report as described earlier is received, the following Post will originate from csp1. Post (csp1, csp2) vxnred, gve: i, [AF: IPv4, prefix list] In the example above, it is shown that csp1 sends a post update to csp2 stating that vxnred will use encapsulation tag i; and that it has certain ipv4 prefixes in its IP network. The routing (network reachability) information has the flexibility to support various address families (AF) defined by Internet Assigned Numbers Authority (IANA) as well as certain extensions not covered under the IANA namespace.

D. Cloudcasting Transport - Generic VXN Encapsulation

In a cloudcasting network, all network devices will work exactly the same as before on the data plane except the Cloud Switch Points (CSP). A CSP will perform encapsulation and decapsulation by following the VXN vFIB table. A VXN vFIB table includes the routing information for a virtual network on a remote CSP where a packet should be destined to. The route information was learned by exchanging Post messages between CSPs.

The format for VXN encapsulation is shown in Fig. 5 above in which IP protocol is set to GVE and following IPv4 header is the 32-bit GVE-header. If and when Cloudcasting dataplane is adopted by IETF, the protocol number for GVE will be assigned by IANA.

IV. Use Cases

The cloudcasting architecture can be used to deploy tenant networks under many different scenarios. As the cloud based architectures become more prevalent, it will be far more efficient to use a single virtualization technology (at least in control plane) both within a site and for interconnection across multiple sites. The cloudcasting protocol can be deployed for the following use cases

1) Multi-Tenancy Virtualized Data Centers
2) Multi-Site Interconnection of Data Centers
3) Interconnection of Hybrid Clouds
4) VPN Accesses in service provider environments

In the following sections, these deployments are described in more details, note that the same concept is easily extensible to any environment that requires infrastructure network to provide connectivity for tenant networks.

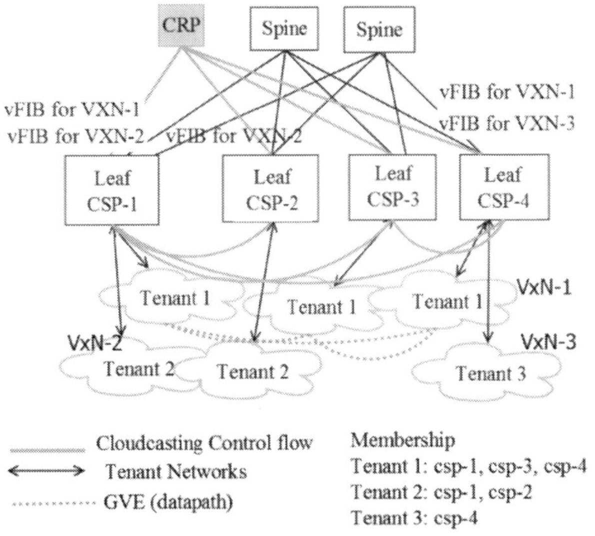

Figure 6: Cloudcasting Enabled Deployment

A. Cloudcasting in virtualized data center

Fig. 6 shows a cloudcasting-enabled virtualized data center. As discussed earlier in Section I, the CRP is a logically centralized node that is accessible by all the CSPs.

A leaf-spine switch architecture is used as a reference to explain cloudcasting deployment. A plausible co-location for CRP could be with the spine node, however, it may be anywhere in the substrate network as long as CSPs can reach it with the infrastructure address space. In Fig. 6, several tenant networks are shown as connected to different CSPs and CSP function itself is co-resident with the leaf switches. Each CSP has a virtual FIB table for both encapsulation and decapsulation of traffic along with the tenant network to CSP memberships (dynamically learned through auto-discovery).

The cloudcasting control protocol flow is shown in lighter color lines between CRP and CSPs and among CSPs.

At the bottom of Fig. 6 only the logical GVE data path tunnels with dotted lines for tenant 1 on CSP-1, CSP-3 and CSP-4 are shown.

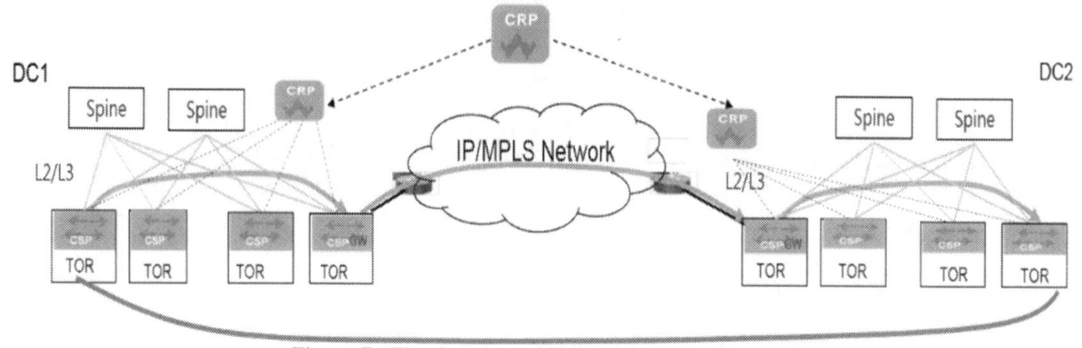

Figure 7: Cloudcasting with Data Center Interconnect

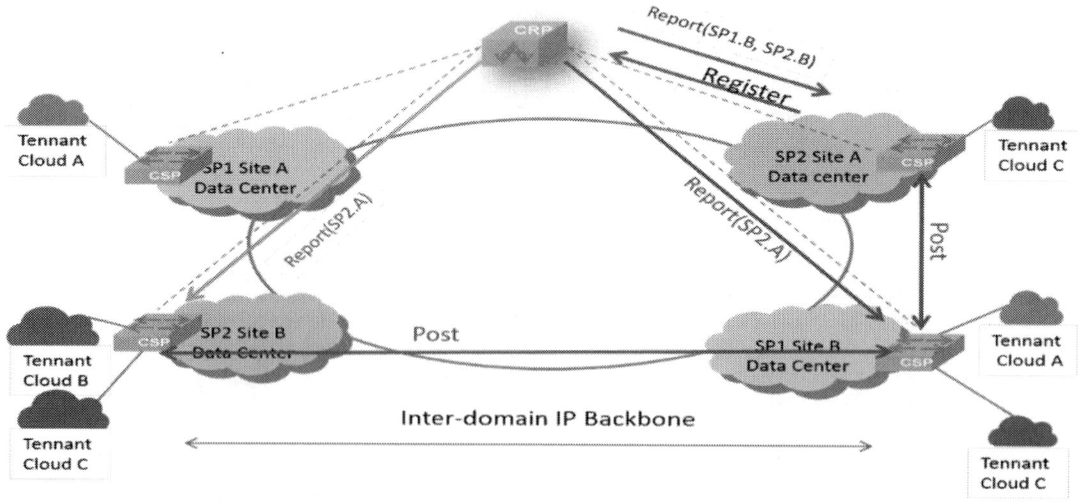

Figure 8: Cloudcasting for multi-site virtual private networks access to Data Centers

B. Cloudcasting As Data Center Interconnect

In a data center inter connect situation, typically data center operator leases MPLS circuits or dedicated link from the service provider. There are several different protocols to provide interconnection between the two data centers such as TRILL, SPB, EVPN, and L3VPN depending upon what is supported by the provider. Instead, cloudcasting can enable all these interconnections very easily without requiring to wait for service provider enabled circuits. In Fig. 7, there are two data centers; both running spine-leaf topologies along with cloud casting enabled network. There are 2 cases shown in this figure. First case is an example that the CSPs in either data centers that need interconnection across data center has infrastructure spaces public IP address. This address is globally routable and therefore, it is possible to directly setup a GVE tunnel in the following manner. Both the CSPs with global space IP address send a CC Register to logical CRP, which facilitates CC Reports. Since CSPs can reach each other, a GVE tunnel can be directly established and CC Post updates may be exchanged as well. This case implements scenario where cloud networks are hosted in two different public clouds, if there are CSPs with global space IP address, the communication between the 2 networks can take place. Often distribution and maintenance of public IP address in not feasible; then a CSP gateway on either data centers can provide a straight forward functionality to translate internal VXNS and bundle multiple GVEs over a single service provider connection.

C. Cloudcasting as VPN in service provider networks

Fig. 8 shows a multi-site VPN connection through cloudcasting. Extending the same concept of CSPs being hosted on each site and they connect to a single logical CRP, cloudcasting enabled VPNs can be formed in the similar manner as described in previous sections. The flexibility of cloudcasting allows to carry layer 2, VLAN, VXLAN, IP or any other network address family through a single virtual routing scheme in a topology independent manner. There is an additional discussion on cloudcasting vs existing technologies in the later section.

V. Scalability And Extensibility In The Cloud

The vision of cloudcasting protocol is many-fold. Firstly, it envisions geographically dispersed Internet-wide multi-tenancy enabled over global infrastructure at a massive scale through a single control signaling mechanism. Secondly, it aims to integrate the data-plane methods in order to normalize the tenant networks forwarding paths.

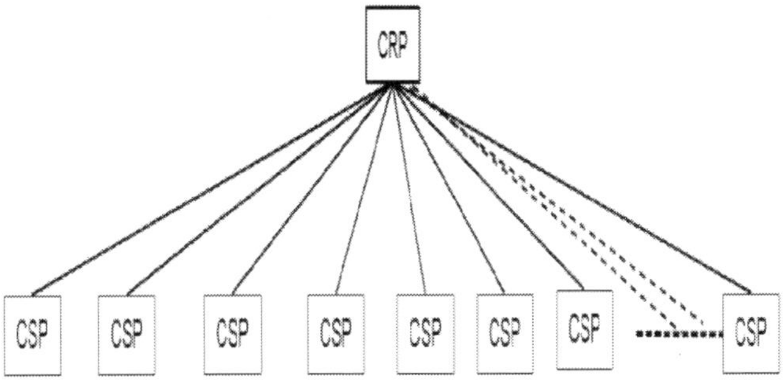

Figure 9: Growth in CRP-CSP connections at scale

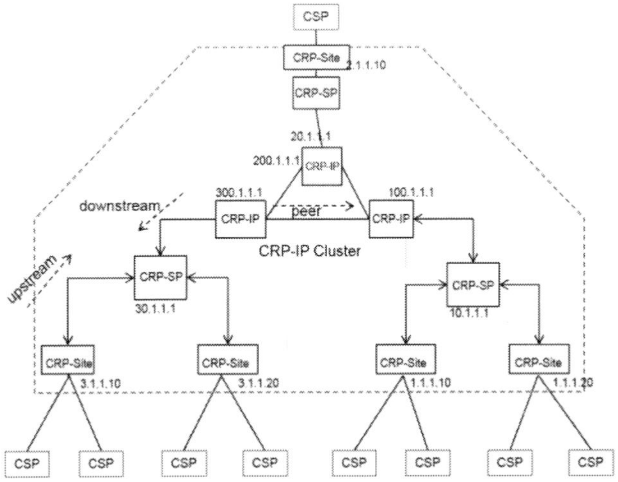

Figure 10: Hierarchical CRP System

A. *Scalability in Controlplane*

Cloudcasting is a virtual routing scheme for cloud based environments that maybe hosted across multiple service provider networks or at multiple sites. In the preceding section, it is assumed that the CRP is a single centralized entity.

1) Hierarchical CRP-system: Cloud networks are expected to be distributed beyond a local site, for example, a tenant network is not scoped with in a single provider domain, but needs to communicate with entities residing behind multiple provider domains. Assuming there are millions of such tenants, then a single CRP managing high number of sessions with as many CSPs in the Internet becomes unmanageable with a flat architecture as shown above in Fig. 9. A centralized CRP node can cause severe performance bottlenecks when servicing large number of CCC messages such as Register and Reports originating from high number of CSPs simultaneously.

The ability to scale is the most important requirement for cloudcasting routing scheme, otherwise, it does not provide a converged deployable solution. With in the cloudcasting protocol a distributed and hierarchical system of CRPs is proposed to exchange CRP control plane signaling. The system builds a connected graph of CRP instances across service provider domains. In order to create a hierarchy, a CRP node is associated with a scope. The scope maybe up to a local site (CRP-site), provider-specific (CRP-SP) or inter-provider (CRP-IP). The definition of cloud networks is also extended now to have scope with in (a) local site, (b) a single provider or (c) multiple providers.

An example of a 3-tier CRP hierarchical system is shown in Fig. 10. In this figure, the CRPs inside the dashed lined box connected together form a CRP system. A CRP-Site (nodes with IP address 3.1.1.10, 3.1.1.20, 1.1.1.10, 1.1.1.20 and 2.1.1.10) is an instance of a local CRP where CSPs from a physical location or a site connect to and is at the lowest level node in CRP system hierarchy. A CRP-SP (nodes with IP address 30.1.1.1, 10.1.1.1, 20.1.1.1) corresponds to a middle-tier CRP in a provider specific space and has a role of interconnecting multiple CRP-Sites in a given region in a single administrative domain. Finally, at the highest-tier of CRP hierarchy is a CRP-IP that supports inter-provider communication. The communication between CRP-Site to CRP-SP and CRP-SP to CRP-IP respectively is required to exchange discovery of cloud networks that are scoped to extend beyond a specific site, administrative domain respectively. In Fig. 10, it is shown multi-provider CRPs, CRP-IPs form a cluster together. Each node (IP address 300.1.1.1, 200.1.1.1, 100.1.1.1) cluster has equal status of cloud network Cloudcasting Information Base (CCIB).

2) CC Protocol Extensions: In order to extend cloudcasting signaling to Hierarchical CRP the following additions to the base protocol are proposed

- *Originating CRP TLV*: It identifies the source of a CC Register in a CRP system hierarchy. It is used maintain mapping of CRP-Site and cloud networks or VXNs in CRP-SP. In addition, CRP Role Attribute (local, provider, global) is also included to determine the scope of CRP.
- *VXN Scope Attribute*: It is used to describe the scope of a cloud network.
- *Cloudcasting Information Base (CCIB)*: The CCIB is the control information base maintained at each CRP is aware of the scope of a signaling and originating source of the request. It is a stateful table that is learnt and looked at upon receiving Register and Reports from neighboring CRPs. Additionally, the CCIB state in each CRP may be stored separately for upstream and downstream in CRP-SP. A CC Report is generated and distributed in a similar manner.

3) Single provider scenario: Consider a scenario of single administrative domain on the left side of the Fig. 10 CRP-SP (30.1.1.1) and two CRP-Site with IP address 3.1.1.10 and 3.1.1.20. Further assume that a cloud network Cn is scoped in a single provider SP1 (30.1.1.1). As left CRP 3.1.1.10 receives a Register message from one of connected CSPs, it finds scope to be provider specific and relays message to CRP-SP (30.1.1.1). Before doing so, TLV extensions as per previous sections are added. Receiving CRP-SP maintains (3.1.1.10, Cn) mapping in its information base. At a later time if another CRP say 3.1.1.20 sends a CC Register for cloud network Cn, CRP-SP, 30.1.1.1 generates a CC Report for both CRPs 30.1.1.10 and 30.1.1.20. Finally, CSPs receive Register from their respective CRPs and can continue with route distribution.

4) Multi-provider scenario: A more elaborate collaboration is required to distribute cloud networks across multiple administrative domains, more so when these domains are geograph-

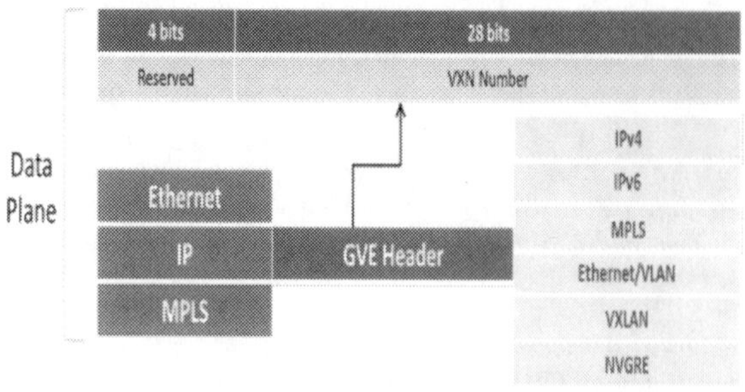

Figure 11: Normalized GVE Data Encapsulation

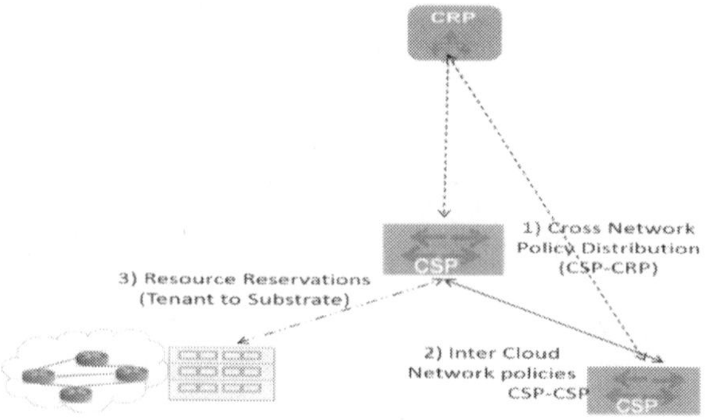

Figure 12: 3-Dimensional Policy Framework for Cloudcasting

ically distributed. Therefore, CRP-IP (CRPs for inter provider communications) are clustered to store identical Cloudcasting information base. In this scenario, all CRP-IPS have identical database of cloud networks that are to be distributed beyond administrative domains. A CC Register of scope global is sent from CRP-Site to CRP-SP to adjoining CRP-IP. The receiving CRP-IP distributed this information to all other CRP-IPs in the cluster. Each CRP-IP is then responsible for downstream distribution of CC-Register to attached CRP-SPs, if and only if it has some knowledge in its information base that a CRP-site has interest in same cloud network. For example, lets assume a new global-scoped cloud network C_n is created by CSP attached to CRP-site 3.1.1.20. This CRP sends CC Register with extended TLV to its attached CRP-SP, 30.1.1.1, which in turn relays it to its attached CRP-IP, 300.1.1.1 by replacing originating CRP as itself in the extended TLV. This CC Register is distributed everywhere in CRP-IP cluster. As this is a new cloud and no instances exist, the request stays in the cluster. Similarly, at a later time when a CSP attached to CRP-site, 1.1.1.10 generates a CC Register for C_n, it reaches CRP-IP 100.1.1.1, which determines from its information base that CC Registers need to be sent to 1.1.1.10, does so and also send CC Registers to 3.1.1.20. The CC Reports are generated in exactly the same manner and finally a GVE tunnel is established.

B. *Extensibility through normalized data plane*

The second important aspect of extensibility in cloudcasting protocol is related to the normalization of data plane encapsulation. In preceding section, the GVE encapsulation is defined and Fig. 11 further illustrates it to be highly flexible and scalable. GVE is extensible by virtue of connecting 2 heterogeneous clouds through the multi-protocol information it carries. The figure also illustrates that GVE expects flexibility in terms of its position in outer header. It maybe carried as layer-2, layer-3 or MPLS payload and is capable of translating multiple encapsulations for example IP, MAC, VLAN, VXLAN, NVGRE and so on. The protocol also allows that an instance of a cloud networks at a site may use NVGRE encapsulation and another site of the same cloud may continue to use VXLAN encapsulation. It is of great advantage to migration of connecting 2 islands of a cloud network transparently without changing anything on the local site except for enabling cloudcasting between the edges or gateways.

VI. Policy Framework for Cloud Networks

A smart policy framework can help build simple orchestration platforms that do not need to excessively interact with the infrastructure and can also adapt independently to policy changes within the virtual networks. Even in the cloudcasting framework, most traffic within and across the cloud networks is still required to be subjected to forwarding or application specific policies. In this section a brief discussion of a new policy model is presented that in general suits better with the cloud networks. The policies in any network of scale such as an enterprise or a campus tend to be fairly diverse, complex and yet quite similar from one tenant to the other. It is difficult to describe network policies because they are designed and created from a business logic perspective. The business logic itself is created centrallly but must be disaggregated and applied in parts across different network segments. In case of cloud-centric environments, it is further obscured because now the environment is virtualized and physical location agnostic. The state of art of policy framework is far too fragmented [12] [13] [14] [15] both in terms of policy description language and common specifications for policy distribution. There are several vendor specific approaches as well open policy frameworks as well. In our view, it is much simpler to break down network policies for cloud networks across three dimensions to address different aspects. In cloudcasting architecture, we separate policy-based interfaces as shown in Fig.12 associating CSP, CRP and the substrate network through 3 different types of policies and their scope. These are explained as below.

1) Cross-Network Policies: In this case, considerations are made to propagate rules that permit or disallow traffic across different cloud networks to the other through policies or Service Level Agreements (SLAs). These type of policies interface at higher level of abstraction. For example, it may also be necessary to specify if dev-test clouds can access the database from production clouds. Within cloudcasting, this is an interface between CRP and CSP. It is extremely simple to associate such policies on CRP, then when the Register request is made, CRP may deny or accept the request to join a certain cloud network. The dotted lines on right-hand side of the Fig.12 shows the scope of such policies.

2) Inter Cloud Network Policies: It is very common to setup policies in a network so that traffic must get steered through specific service chains. For example, traffic from an ingress port is first subjected to firewall then load balancer and finally to an application server. Such policies are not infrastructure related and are within a cloud network that may need distribution within a site or across multiple sites. Once tenant networks are discovered, CSPs have a path to distribute policies through CSP-CSP policy interface. This scope is shown as CSP-CSP through solid line on the bottom right of Fig.12.

3) Tenant to Substrate Network Policies: In section II, it is explained that cloud centric tenant networks borrow and consume resources from substrate networks and tenants do not own any physical resources themselves. Yet, it is necessary to allocate resources to support quality assurance and bandwidth guarantees. Since tenant network operators cannot reserve resources they do not own and any bulk pre-allocation does not align with infrastructure independence, a separate tenant to substrate network policy interface is mandatory. This interface is not related to cloudcasting and therefore, should not be part of cloudcasting. However, there is a need for generalized reservation and administration method, be it a protocol or API based that may be used between tenant and substrate networks. This scope is shown on the left-hand side of the Fig.12.

In previous two sections additional features of cloudcasting such as extensibility, scalability, normalization and policy interfaces were briefly explained to demonstrate that cloudcasting framework is entirely viable solution for interconnectivity of cloud networks. In this paper, emphasis is on core architecture extensions and many details relating to extended TLVs are omitted out. For the same reason, policy interface details are excluded from the paper.

VII. Evaluation And Analysis

The cloudcasting architecture and primitives have been implemented in our research laboratory. We have successfully used the cloudcasting architecture and control protocol to implement the above mentioned use cases. First and foremost, we emphasize that the cloudcasting architecture represents a paradigm shift. It is a truly converged technology for virtual networks, clouds, and VPNs. No matter what the structure of the underlying substrate network is, any/all types of virtual tenant networks can be constructed in the same way by using cloudcasting.

A. Qualitative Analysis

The Cloudcasting suitability and applicability can only be verified vis-a-vis characteristics of the cloud-scale environments. Therefore, we have laid importance on the primary characteristics of cloud centric networks that are elasticity, efficiency, agility, and distribution. The Cloudcasting control plane is elastic, because it can grow and shrink independently of (1) the heterogeneous protocols of the substrate network, (2) number of virtual network attachment points, the CSPs, (3) number of domains (autonomous systems), (4) number of routes within a users virtual network, and (5) mobile nature of the host stations. The Cloudcasting control plane is efficient, because (1) no CSP distributes routes to other CSPs that they are not interested in, (2) thus, no CSP receives and stores routes of virtual networks of non-interest or the ones it is not connected to. In addition, the control plane is fully distributed in such a manner that through a single primitive (post-update); change in the tenant networks can be announced immediately, from the spot of change without configuration changes. The Cloudcasting allows for agile networking. Every time when a new CSP is added, it is only required to configure the newly added CSP by using a few lines of commands. Every time when a CSP is deleted, no additional configuration change or for that matter nothing else needs to be done. This is because cloudcasting has a built-in auto-discovery mechanism that has not been seen in the embedded virtual networks. The Cloudcasting data plane scales as well. Its default GVE encapsulation protocol allows to support 256 million clouds. In other technology such as, VXLAN, it only up to 16 million clouds are supported. Due to the limitation of space, we wont discuss and describe other more desirable characteristics.

B. Prototype Implementation

In our lab, three small-scale data centers were implemented for the demonstration of functionality. Each data center had a CSP network element and also connected to the CRP in cloudcasting enabled network. In addition, each data center also comprised of one or two hosts; and each host had at least 2 VMs spawned with their own private IP addresses. All the traffic from VMs or hosts was default forwarded to the CSP, which performed the data plane encapsulation/decapsulation and forwarding between CSPs. One of the data centers served as media server center and others were clients. The purpose of this setup is to show isolation with in a virtual network domain and VM mobility from one data center to the other. The setup also has a network management system that provisions CSPs about virtual networks and VM hosted with in them. The development environment is entirely based on open source code or is in-house developed. The code is implemented in the following categories -

1) CSP control plane software: CSP software is based on quagga (0.99.24) [16] open source, because it provides an ideal and quick router/switch like development environment to use many features such as command line for configuration, message parsing, daemon and process communication features that are already build in quagga. A csp daemon was created in quagga base and new code was written to provide following functions

- CSP-CRP Connection: CSPs listen to a TCP port and connect to CRP, which is a configurable IP address. On this channel Register and Report messages are exchanged.
- CSP-CSP Communication: CSPs listen to another TCP port to connect to CSP IP addresses received in Report messages. This channel is used for Post updates for virtual route exchanges. Once the routes are learnt from peer CSPs, the datapath process is updated.
- CSP Network Management Interface: CSP also interfaces with a management entity to receive virtual network specifications or changes thereafter. These changes are pushed as an XML file and can easily be changes to REST APIs.

2) CSP datapath: CSP data plane is implemented as another daemon using pcap library [17] to perform tunneling functions for traffic between hosts and CSPs. It maintains two forwarding rules passed from CSP control process, viz. host-CSP and CSP-host. Since the aim was proof of concept and data plane is implemented in software, it is irrelevant to discuss the forwarding path throughput.

3) CRP control plane software: While, CSP control and data plane are developed in C; CRP code is entirely written in Java, consequently both Java and C code base for the CCC protocol exists. CRP uses neo4j [18] based highly scalable graph databases to store and visualize relationships between the virtual networks and CSPs.

4) Network Management Interface: The management system is in-house developed software for a network operator. Written using C# as a web application on IPAD, an operator is able to add or delete new virtual networks to a specific data center as well as add, delete and move VMs from one data center to the other.

The above code may be made available to those interesting in further research in cloudcasting. Due to lack of testbeds and other resources quantitative comparison has not been performed adequately and results are not available yet. It is our intent to demonstrate controlplane efficiency through analysis of bytes and messages transferred under several approaches.

VIII. Related Work

There are several works available that partially solve network virtualization problem; however, they do not provide a complete and consistent solution that sufficiently fulfills all basic requirements discussed earlier in this paper. In what follows, we discuss and compare a few prominent network-overlay approaches.

A. IETF NVO3

The cloudcasting architecture and protocol shares some goals chartered by the IETF working group NVO3 (Network Virtualization Overlays over Layer 3) [19]. The purpose of NVO3 is to develop a set of protocols and/or protocol extensions that enable network virtualization within a data center environment that assumes an IP-based underlay. Cloudcasting varies from NOV3 in that cloudcasting is not just restricted to the data center, and it does not expect a specific structure or protocol conventions in the underlay. The control plane of NVO3 may seem to be a reformulation of the BGP architecture, where NVEs (Network Virtualization Edge) and NVA (Network Virtualization Authority) resemble iBGP speakers and Route Reflectors, respectively, and NVO3-VNTP [20] resembles BGP update messages between an iBGP speaker and its Route Reflector. Therefore, NVA needs to learn and store routes from an NVE and then distribute those routes to other NVEs. In contrast, in Cloudcasting virtual route information is a function between CSPs, the routes are only distributed between the CSPs, the CRP is not involved in routes. CRP is used for cloud membership auto-discovery and thus enables agile provisioning. Auto-discovery functions are also missing from NVO3, where are they are natural to cloudcasting protocol. We should emphasize that CRP has no route database inside that has a significant impact on the size of the database in CSP. This differentiation is common with other related work discussed in the following sections. NVO3 suffers from the existence of multiple encapsulations, the working group has not been able to make progress on a native control plane design and most often resort to EVPN control plane. The group is also divided on the subject of data plane format whether the group shall support a single or multiple encapsulations. In this regard, Cloudcasting GVE supports multiple types of data plane encapsulations inherently as is discussed in earlier extensibility section V (B).

B. VXLAN and EVPN

VXLAN is a data plane format for network overlay encapsulation and decapsulation, and EVPN has been proposed as the control plane for VXLAN [21] [9] [22]. BGP was originally designed for inter-domain routing across service provider networks. Although, EVPN is the only IETF defined distributed control plane protocol, BGP in data center network virtualization leads to may operational overheads as explained in the following ways

1) In order to deploy EVPN, the network operator must configure something like an AS (autonomous system) in substrate networks, which is not really a data center design concept. In addition to this many other BGP-VPN related constructs such as route-targets (RT) are route-distinguisher (RD) must be defined. Configurations can be templatized to reduce complexity, yet to keep the network consistent these parameters must be carefully chosen and during network outages, trouble shooting is extremely difficult because an operator has to be aware of the mappings of RTs and RDs to virtual networks, not to mention that higher number of configuration parameters adds to management traffic. A sample configuration maybe found at [23].
2) Running BGP in a data center requires VTEPs to be iBGP speakers. This can also lead to serious scalability problems of a full-mesh of peering sessions between iBGP speakers (VTEP-BGP). Typically, to address this problem, deployment of Route Reflectors (RR) is recommended. RRs then speaks with every other VTEP-BGP to synchronize their BGP-RIB. As a result, no matter if a VTEP needs a route or not, all the other VTEPs will always send their routes to the VTEP through a Route Reflector, and the VTEP is required to filter out not needed routes through Route Target and other BGP policies. Distribution of not needed virtual routes from RR to VTEP-BGP levies an unnecessary overhead on the substrate network and burn CPU power, processing these BGP messages.
3) BGP in the data centers not only makes operational cost of data centers as high as that of a service providers network it also lacks the agility because BGP heavily relies on configurations (it is well known that configuration errors are a major cause of system failures [8]). For example, when a new BGP-VTEP is added/removed the operator has to configure all the BGP peering relationships by stating which BGP neighbors are peering among each other.

Observe that when BGP was first designed, some distribution and peering principles were built-in; for example, iBGP peers should have received and synchronized the same copies of routes. In the case of clouds, many such principles are not applicable and exceptions need to be added to BGP protocol to address requirements for the cloud networks. Cloudcasting architecture does not suffer from the drawbacks described above. By means of auto-discovery and route distribution, only specific routes of a virtual network are distributed. Moreover, the role of CRP does not require it to be an intermediate hop between two CSPs to distribute the routes. The detailed comparison and evaluation is still in progress and will be published at a later stage.

C. LISP based data center virtualization

Although Locator ID Separation Protocol (LISP) [11] is not an inherent data center virtualization technology, it has a framework to support network overlays. LISP achieves this by distributing encapsulated tenant (customer) routing information and traffic over provider (substrate) network through its control plane based on a mapping system. The LISP architecture includes Ingress/Egress Tunnel Routers (xTRs) and a mapping system (MS/MR) that maintains mappings from LISP Endpoint Identifiers (EIDs) to Routing Locators (RLOCs). LISP requires mapping information to be pulled on-demand and data-driven, xTRs also implement a caching and aging mechanism for local copies of mapping information. Cloudcasting CSPs and LISP xTRs are similar in that they are the virtualization tunnel endpoints performing encapsulation and decapsulation. But the VXN route database and LISP's mapping databases are different as below

1) LISPs mapping system [24] is a separate protocol element and is based on hierarchical design of Domain Name Server (DNS). The xTRs work in collaboration with mapping server (MS) and map resolvers (MR). First and foremost, an xTR must register its EIDs with the mapping system. When a remote xTR is ready to exchange data for an EID, it will query mapping system to find the xTR where EID is located, create the local mapping cache (is referred to as pull method) where entries are aged when not needed. In comparison, CSPs are able to discover each other on the basis of VXN, without registering any EIDs with CRP. Once CSPs and VXN mappings are formed vFIBs are built by post updates. Thus, routes are local and significant only to the CSP.
2) An xTRs local database is built on demand after receiving a data packet without knowing its mapping information, which may expose sender to security risks because the destination is unknown, while CSPs VXN CCIB is signaled through the cloudcasting control protocol over an authorized communication channel. The infrastructure can flexibly make the channel as secure as it prefers using security and encryption protocols.
3) A CSP can auto-discover other CSPs that join the same VXNs, while LISP xTR can only know about another particular xTR after querying the mapping database.

IX. Virtualization in Mobile Networks using Cloudcasting

During our research and study of policy based constraints in Cloudcasting, we came across Fifth Generation (5G) network slices. We concurred with the authors of Next Generation Mobile Networks (NGMN) [25] white paper that 5G networks will be a collection of service aware logical networks. It was obvious that a higher degree of automation is vital in 5G for services to be discovered, provisioned and resources to be apportioned/released. Authors have discussed using Cloudcasting as fundamental block in [26] for auto-discovery of services in mobile network supporting cloud hosted environments. In this work, a network slice corresponds to a VXN in cloudcasting, while service extensions (resource specifications) are newly added and associated with a network slice. The main idea in this paper deviates from symmetric VXN relationship of Cloudcasting. 5G services in [26] have asymmetric producer and consumer association. First, network segments participate in cloudcasting system and network slices are bound to those segments. Then in a producer role, the services announce themselves, their location in the system and their resource requirements. Thus services become available and discoverable with in those slices. Subsequently, in the consumer role, an end user or device attaches itself to the service; network resources are allocated across different network segments. The procedures just described are done dynamically that allows a mobile network system to be easily managed. The idea of auto-discovery is fairly advanced and prototyping of this approach is still being done.

X. Future Work

In this paper, we have presented several extensions to Cloudcasting protocol in terms of policy, services and scalability that makes it more complete. Cloudcasting can be thought of as a generalized virtual routing framework. Its validity, scalability and extensibility as a single mechanism for implementing cloud centric networks. There are several scenarios not explored yet include containers, microservices and SD-WAN.

Since the publishing of original paper, we have designed an integrated policy model as the basis of interface between substrate and virtual network. The model allows distribution of tenant policies using the base protocol. However, resource allocations over substrate network were not found to be as simple and in fact led to new work as an extension to cloudcasting protocol. The corresponding data structures and prototype implementation are an open for further research at the time of writing this paper.

Previous section alluded to Cloudcasting extensions for service distribution in mobile networks. The 5G network slice definition is still evolving, therefore, an opportunity lies in exploring this topic further both from prototyping and validation perspective. Finally, although the prototype for base protocol is available, further comparison study, assessment of control plane signaling overheads, robustness and datapath optimizations related work is not complete yet and we welcome contributions from interested research community.

XI. Conclusion

Cloud-scale networking environments require a technology where virtual networks are first class objects; such that the coarse policies and routing decisions can be defined and applied on the virtual networks. Cloudcasting is a routing system based on converged, unified network virtualization and will evolve better because of lower provisioning costs and enhanced agility through auto discovery. This paper presented several new concepts; it extended original idea from single data center to explain global scale distribution of VXNs across multiple providers, sites and domains. Many use cases are further discussed in great detail. We also shared our perspective on policy model, which plays an important role in interaction between virtual and physical infrastructures to provide operation and management functions. The prototype implementation is discussed at great length and interested readers are encouraged to contact the authors for code. As an interesting application, we have taken the idea of cloudcasting for virtual networks and extended it to the auto-discovery of services in the 5G network slicing context that further bolsters adaptability and flexibility of the framework.

ACKNOWLEDGMENT

The authors are thankful to the members of the Cloud-casting project, particularly those involved in the early design and proof of concept and prototype development for their collaboration and fruitful discussions.

REFERENCES

[1] K. Makhijani, R. Li, and L. Han, "Cloudcasting: A New Architecture for Cloud Centric Networks," in Proc. IARIA Int. Conf. on Comm. Theory, Rel., and Qual. of Serv. (CTRQ), Lisbon, Portugal, February 2016.

[2] D. Fedyk, P. Ashwood-Smith, Allan, A. Bragg and P. Unbehagen, "IS-IS Extensions Supporting IEEE 802.1aq Shortest Path Bridging," Internet Engineering Task Force (IETF), April 2012.

[3] IEEE, "IEEE Standard for Local and metropolitan area networksMe-dia Access Control (MAC) Bridges and Virtual Bridged Local Area NetworksAmendment 20: Shortest Path Bridging," June 2012.

[4] D. Eastlake, T. Senevirathne, A. Ghanwani, D. Dutt and A. Banerjee, "Transparent Interconnection Of Lots Of Links (Trill) Use Of Is-Is," Internet Engineering Task Force (IETF), April 2014.

[5] M. Sridharan et al., "Virtual eXtensible Local Area Network (VXLAN): A Framework for Overlaying Virtualized Layer 2 Networks over Layer 3 Networks," Aug. 2014.

[6] M. Mahalingam et al., "NVGRE: Network Virtualization using Generic Routing Encapsulation, draft-sridharan-virtualization-nvgre-08 (work in progress)," Internet Engineering Task Force (IETF), 2015, pp. 1–10.

[7] J. Gross, T. Sridhar et al., "Geneve: Generic Network Virtualization En-capsulation, draft-ietf-nvo3-geneve-0," Internet Engineering Task Force (IETF), April 2015.

[8] T. Xu, Y. Zhou, "Systems approaches to tackling configuration errors: A survey, article no.: 70, acm computing surveys (csur) volume 47 issue 4," July 2015.

[9] A. Sajassi et al., "A Network Virtualization Overlay Solution using EVPN," Internet Engineering Task Force (IETF), February 2015.

[10] M. Yu, Y. Yi, J. Rexford, and M. Chiang, "Rethinking virtual network embedding Substrate support for path splitting and migration,Computer Communication Review," vol. 38, 2008 2008, pp. 17–29.

[11] D. Farinacci, V. Fuller, D. Meyer, and D. Lewis, "The Locator/ID Separation Protocol (LISP)," Internet Engineering Task Force (IETF), January 2013.

[12] VMWare Micro segmentation. web:https://www.vmware.com/content/dam/digitalmarketing/vmware/en/pdf/products/nsx/vmware-microsegmentation-solution-overview.pdf. (2015)

[13] Simplified Use of Policy Abstractions (SUPA). web:https://datatracker.ietf.org/wg/supa/charter/. (2015)

[14] Opendaylight, Group based Policy. web:https://wiki.opendaylight.org/view/Group_Based_Policy_(GBP). (2015)

[15] Cisco Application Centric Infrastructure(ACI). http://www.cisco.com/c/en/us/solutions/data-center-virtualization/application-centric-infrastructure/index.html. (2015)

[16] Quagga Routing Software Suite, GPL licensed. http://download.savannah.gnu.org/releases/quagga/quagga-0.99.24.tar.xz.

[17] libpcap, a portable C/C++ library for network traffic capture. http://www.tcpdump.org/.

[18] Neo4j, a highly scalable native graph database. https://neo4j.com/.

[19] M. Lasserre et al., "Framework for Data Center (DC) Network Virtu-alization," Internet Engineering Task Force (IETF), October 2014.

[20] Z. Gu, "Virtual Network Transport Protocol (VNTP)," Internet Engi-neering Task Force (IETF), October 2015.

[21] E. Rosen and Y. Rekhter, "BGP/MPLS IP Virtual Private Networks (VPNs)," Internet Engineering Task Force (IETF), April 2006.

[22] Sami et al., "VXLAN DCI Using EVPN, draft-boutros-bess-vxlan-evpn-01.txt," Internet Engineering Task Force (IETF), January 2016.

[23] VXLAN Network with MP-BGP EVPN Control Plane Design Guide. http://www.cisco.com/c/en/us/products/collateral/switches/nexus-9000-series-switches/guide-c07-734107.html. [retrieved: April, 2016]

[24] V. Fuller et al. LISP-DDT: LISP Delegated Database Tree, Work in Progress. https://tools.ietf.org/html/draft-ietf-lisp-ddt-08. [retrieved: September, 2015]

[25] N. Alliance, "NGMN 5G White Paper," White paper, February 2015, pp. 1–125.

[26] K. Makhijani, S. Talarico, and P. Esnault. Efficient Service Auto-Discovery for Next Generation Network Slicing Architecture, presented at O4SDI, IEEE NFV-SDN 2016. Unpublished.

Device Quality Management for IoT Service Providers by Tracking Uncoordinated Operating History

Megumi Shibuya†, Teruyuki Hasegawa† and Hirozumi Yamaguchi‡

†KDDI Research, Inc.
Saitama, JAPAN
e-mail: {shibuya, teru}@kddi-research.jp

‡Osaka University
Osaka, JAPAN
e-mail: h-yamagu@ist.osaka-u.ac.jp

***Abstract*—According to the widespread of Internet of Things (IoT) services with a huge number of IoT devices, service providers will face the challenges how to grasp the product quality of the IoT devices by themselves in order to make IoT services highly reliable and dependable. The cumulative failure rate is an important reliability index for evaluating the product quality and service reliability of IoT devices. However, in the horizontal specialization business model, IoT service infrastructure is often operated by multiple players such as service providers and device vendors, and device management information that is necessary to obtain the cumulative failure rate is independently and uncoordinatedly owned by them. In this paper, we propose a method of calculating the cumulative failure rate in such environment. We design an algorithm to aggregate and organize such distributed, uncoordinated information to derive the device operating history, which is fed into the cumulative failure rate calculation formula. Through several simulation experiments, we show the effectiveness of our method in several realistic scenarios, where we also arrange several uncoordinated cases.**

Keywords - IoT; Service reliability; Cumulative failure rate; Operating history; Multiple players; Horizontal specialization business model

I. INTRODUCTION

Recently, the concept of Internet of Things (IoT) has been widely penetrating into our daily lives and IoT device reliability is one of fundamental, technical issues to achieve IoT-enabled world. We have been focusing on such IoT device reliability in reference [1] and this issue enhances the concept of IoT device reliability management for more realistic cases.

According to [2], the number of devices which are available for mobile access is expected to grow to approximately 50 billion units (6.58 units per user) by 2020. In IoT enabled systems, a huge number of *IoT devices* are being interconnected, and such infrastructure becomes more sophisticated and smarter to support our lives. Simultaneously, as it becomes more indispensable, it should be more reliable to achieve sufficient service availability [3]-[5]. This cannot be achieved without high reliability and dependability of IoT devices themselves.

In the research field of reliability engineering, there are several kinds of reliability-indexes such as Mean Time Between Failure (MTBF), Mean Time To Repair (MTTR), Mean Time To Failure (MTTF) and Failure in Time (FIT) [6]. In addition, *cumulative failure rate* is often utilized as a device reliability index [7]. It is a probability of failure occurrence in a certain time period starting from the time when the device becomes in operation. The cumulative failure rate is usually derived using the failure rate for every unit of time, which is defined as a ratio of the number of failed devices to the number of devices being in operation in the unit of time. Here, the devices being in operation may vary at every moment not only due to device failure but also due to operational activities such as new device installation, removal and replacement. Therefore, we need to trace the operating history of each device to calculate accurate cumulative failure rate.

However, in order to obtain the operating history of each device, it is required to obtain the dates of device-associated events such as installation of the device, suspension and resumption of device utilization and failure. If the device manufacturers, simply called *vendors*, themselves provide services (this way of service provision is called *vertically integrated business model* [8]), such information can be obtained easily as everything is managed at a single place. In contrast, in *horizontal specialization business model* [9]-[11] where service providers (simply called *providers*) purchase the devices from vendors and use them (this style is often seen in smart meter services and the Internet access services), device operating history is owned and managed partially and uncoordinatedly by multiple business operators called *players*. Furthermore, by changing business environment around the providers, e.g., the number of IoT devices is dramatically increased and demand for service reliability becomes much more severe, we believe each provider itself is required to expand the quality management of devices which the vendors have been dealing with and responsible for. Accordingly, the possibility of lack of information from the perspective of providers is newly exposed. Therefore, the horizontal specialization business model will causes a significant issue in building a single, consistent view of operating history.

We introduce an example case to explain how and why such a situation is seen in the horizontal specialization business model in the following. In smart meter services, an electric company (i.e., a provider) purchases power meters in bulk from a vendor, lends them to subscribers, and stocks the rest as spares. When a power meter becomes out of order, the provider supports to replace it. Since the provider entrusts the repair service to the vendor, the vendor receives the failed power meter directory from a user and repairs it in order to mitigate the provider's tasks. Then, the vendor is able to manage the product-related information such as the production date and the model number of the meter as well as the failure-related information such as the date and reason of failure and the repair process. However, the device operating status (e.g., operating start date) is not observed by the vendor. Meanwhile, the provider has to manage the subscriber information including the asset information (e.g., the current meter location). Hence, it is not necessary to trace back the information about failure and others. Consequently, in order to obtain a consistent history of meters, it is necessary to design a method of aggregating the management information that are separately and uncoordinatedly managed by multiple players to enable calculation of the cumulative failure rates.

In this paper, we propose a method of calculating the cumulative failure rate, which is an important reliability index that represents device reliability. We assume that services are provided (i) using a large quantity of homogeneous devices and (ii) following the horizontal specialization business model where multiple players are involved and management information are owned separately and uncoordinatedly by them. Then, the method aggregates and analyzes those distributed information to derive the operating history of each IoT device to enable the calculation of cumulative failure rates.

The contributions of this work are four-fold.

- We deal with a significant issue of IoT device management inspired by our business experience on how we grasp and measure the device reliability, which is mandatory to maintain the quality of large-scale IoT service infrastructure operated by multiple players in the horizontal specialization business model.
- We propose a method to obtain the operating history of each IoT device from various types of management information. We would like to emphasize that calculating the cumulative failure rate using complete device history is normally done in device management, but taking into account those devices that are often replaced, repaired and reused at different times and locations is not straightforward.
- We present the experimental result of measuring the accuracy of cumulative failure rates with realistic scenarios where a part of the information is missing. Such a situation often occurs in the real environment.
- To prove wide applicability of our proposed method, we further evaluate the additional but promising uncoordinated case in which additional information elements are added from the middle, i.e., after the service was launched, due to emerging new operational requirements.

This paper is organized as follows. Section II summarizes related work and Section III introduces a service scenario in IoT infrastructure with multiple players. Section IV presents our method and experimental results are shown in Section V. Section VI considers the additional uncoordinated case in which some information elements are added after the service launch. Finally, we conclude this work in Section VII.

II. Related Work

There have been various activities on evaluating product quality and device reliability [6][7][12]-[19] including the research field of reliability engineering [6][7]. Several studies on Operation And Management (OAM) issues of IoT devices in IoT service infrastructure [20]-[27]have also been conducted.

As the reliability terms, based on the methods and procedures for lifecycle predictions for a product, there are several kinds of reliability indexes [6]. Mean Time Between Failure (MTBF) is a reliability term in which the average time form the up time after the repair following a failure to the next failure. Mean Time To Failure (MTTF) is that the average length of time before failure of a device. While MTBF is used for repairable device, MTTF is used for non-repairable device. Mean Time To Repair (MTTR) is the term that the average length of time to repair a failed item. Furthermore, Failure in Time (FIT) reports the number of expected failure per one billion hours of operation for a device. Moreover, cumulative failure rate is often utilized as a device reliability index [7]. It is a probability of failure occurrence in a certain time period starting from the time when the device becomes in operation. The cumulative failure rate is usually derived using the failure rate for every unit of time, which is defined as a ratio of the number of failed devices to the number of devices being in operation in the unit of time.

References [12]-[14] present evaluation methods at the design or production phase of devices, where the cumulative failure rate is estimated by modeling the occurrence of major failures at the component level of devices. Reference [12] focuses on how to calculate the failure rate of N-channel Metal Oxide Semiconductor (NMOS) devices under Hot Carrier Injection (HCI) mechanism and Time Dependence Dielectric Breakdown (TDDB) failure mechanism. The failure rate models and hypothesis test are proposed for each HCI and TDDB. Reference [13] discusses how to determine a new parameter from failure factors observed in the field, e.g., electrostatic discharge inrush current, to integrate it into a conventional estimation method for more accurate cumulative failure rate at the product design phase. Reference [14] proposes how to use the failure statistics to obtain the failure rate of a particular component according to its real conditions. It also demonstrates how the proposed methodologies are applied for failure rate estimation of power circuit breakers. The methodologies can be used for condition-based reliability analysis for electric power networks, in order to obtain an optimized maintenance strategy. Reference [15] proposes an approach to estimating the failure rate for Time-varying Failure Rate (TFR) of the relay protection device with the field data using random failure and aging failure. These approaches assume that all information elements, which are necessary for calculating also the cumulative failure rate, are maintained by the vendor manufacturing the devices, and it is not considered that the number of devices varies by factors other than failures.

The bathtub curve is a common feature of product failure behavior [16]. It is a lifetime of a population of products using a graphical representation. The typical bathtub curve has three phases. The first part is the birth-in period, which is characterized by a high and rapidly decreasing failure rate. The second part is the useful period, when the failure rate remains almost constant. The third part has an increasing failure rate, known as the wear-out period. The bathtub curve can be useful for predicting the device failure if the age of each device is known, however only the characterizations are known.

Reference [17] proposes a one line prognostic algorithm for the power module devices using the operating history of the device to detect the time of failure quickly during operation. Reference [18] proposes the calculating probability of failure using an equipment age model that is relaxed the independence assumption of individual measurements of usage intensity and operating conditions. Moreover, it shows practitioners how to develop a more complete maintenance strategy that allows for both corrective maintenance (CM) and condition-based maintenance model (CBM) using the simple decision routine.

On the other hand, in the telecommunication network, it is difficult to calculate the failure rate accurately by reliability engineering methods because the failure rate is calculated by the number of devices and time differentiation of the cumulative number of failure devices at the given timing of elapsed time. References [19][20] propose evaluation methods for product reliability based on the observation of each device's operation history considering device changes due to non-failure, which is not taken into account in the existing work [7][21]. In reference [19], the instantaneous failure rate of a repairable device for the communication network is calculated as the limit of the average failure rate that is available for the increase and decrease of the number of devices. Namely, the number of cumulative failure rate and the number of devices are estimated as the continuing functions to times. In contrast in [20], they study the applicable condition of the mathematical model for the proposed method.

All the above assume a vertical integration structure in which all the information elements for calculating the cumulative failure rate (or a similar index) are maintained by only one player. In contrast, we are focusing on IoT service infrastructure in which multiple players (e.g., providers and vendors) are collaboratively involved. In such a horizontal specialization structure, which is expected to penetrate the IoT market in the future [11], the followings should be done to manage the product reliability of IoT devices for realizing dependable infrastructure; 1) coordinating the management information provided by each player, 2) extracting and deriving information elements and 3) reconstructing the device operation history from the information elements. As far as we know, this is the first activity focusing on IoT device management with multi-player issues.

Meanwhile, there have been many approaches so far toward IoT device applications [22]-[27], which basically focus on the management and configuration of remote sensor devices over the Internet. For example, Ref. [22] implements IPv6 over 6LoWPAN and RPL and provides CoAP-based control to facilitate sensor device management over the Internet. Reference [23] also takes a remote-management approach where MQ Telemetry Transport is utilized for IoT application and management. In Reference [24], the authors discuss the necessity of wireless sensor network management in a unified manner. They consider that the industrial authorities should be able to provide a network infrastructure supporting various WSN applications and services to facilitate the management of sensor devices, and industrial ecosystem and industrial device management standards have been introduced. Reference [26] is rather unique in the sense that a distributed approach is introduced for IoT device management from a social network point of view, where a social network theory is applied to model the services. Reference [27] discusses cloud-resource management for multi-agent IoT systems, which is also important for entire system coordination. However, they basically focus on the protocol and architecture issues and do not deal with the IoT device management processes and operations.

III. Service Scenario

In this paper, we assume IoT infrastructure with multiple players in the horizontal specialization business model. Under this assumption, we explain the device operating and management information that are separately and uncoordinatedly managed by multiple players. The scenario is based on our own experience, so cases hereafter are likely to be seen in the real world business.

As explained briefly in Section I, we target a service provider such as an electric company or a network provider that purchases the devices in bulk from an IoT device vendor and lends them to subscribers (users). If the IoT device fails, the provider lends an alternative IoT device that is stocked in their warehouse to the subscriber. After receiving it, the user sends the failed IoT device to vendor. As the provider service, it is a common business model that the user lends the device from the provider, such as STB [28].

Figure 1 illustrates the interactions between each player and user. We explain the service provision scenario using this figure.

<u>(1) IoT Device Purchase and Stocking:</u>

The provider purchases IoT devices from the vendor and stocks them as spares. Lending an IoT device from the provider to a user and returning it by the user due to cancellation is conducted via the provider's warehouse. The provider records the *current* location of the purchased IoT devices in asset management information. The vendor records the product-related information such as the shipping date and model number of IoT devices in shipment management information.

<u>(2) Service Startup:</u>

The provider creates the contract-related information for every user and manages it. The provider lends an IoT device to a user, starts the service and records the service start date in user contract information.

(3) IoT Device Failure and Replacement:

When an IoT device fails at a user location, the user contacts the provider to tell his/her device has been failed. The provider sends an alternative IoT device from their warehouse to the subscriber. After receiving it, the user sends it back to the vendor directly using a preprinted address label included with the alternative IoT device for optimizing the physical transport route. The vendor repairs the failed IoT device and records the failure-related information such as date and model number (or send-back date or receiving date as the date of failure). After the repaired IoT device is sent from the vendor to the provider, it is stocked in the warehouse. The provider updates the records related to these two devices (i.e., the current locations of failed and alternative devices). The vendor records the user's location ID from the address label as the evidence for the provider to check whether the user returns the failed IoT device.

(4) Service Cancellation:

When a user cancels its contract, he/she returns his/her IoT device to the provider. The provider re-stocks it in the warehouse and updates the current location information of the IoT device. Furthermore, the service end date of this user is recorded in the contract-related information.

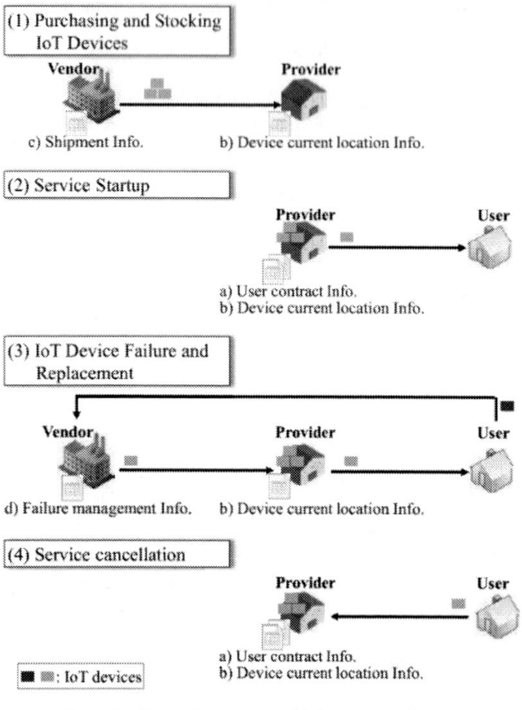

Figure 1. Interaction among multiple players and user.

In summary, the provider maintains a) contract information with users and b) asset management information of IoT devices, the vendor maintains c) shipment-related information of IoT devices and d) the failure-related information. Here, b) is usually sufficient for asset management by the provider. This is because the provider does not care about whether an IoT device was installed at different locations in the past.

On the other hand, as described in Section I, it is required to obtain the occurrence dates of device-associated events such as installation of the device, suspension and resumption of device utilization and failure to calculate the cumulative information such as the service start date and suspension and resumption of the device date in this scenario, and the provider does not observe the information such as the failure date. Therefore, each player cannot collect and build complete device-associated information. This is our motivation to provide a method to build complete operating history of each IoT device from such partial, distributed operating and management information as indicated by the above a) to d).

TABLE I. SERVICE OPERATING AND MANAGEMENT DATA

LIST-A) CURRENT DEVICE LIST (MANAGED BY PROVIDER)

List created date (=Today) (*Tc*) : 2016/09/01			
Location (*L*)	Service start date (*T1*)	Current device (*SN*)	Operating start date of current device at *L* (*T4*)
1	2016/01/01	a	-
3	2016/05/01	b	-
4	2016/03/01	c	-
:	:	:	:

LIST-B) FAILED DEVICE LIST (MANAGED BY VENDOR)

Location (*L*)	Failed date (*T2*)	Failed device (*SN*)	Operating start date of failed device at *L* (*T5*)
1	2016/02/01	a	-
3	2016/04/01	a	-
1	2016/04/01	b	-
:	:	:	:

LIST-C) RETURN DEVICE LIST (OUT OF MANAGEMENT BY PROVIDER)

Location (*L*)	Return date (*T3*)	Return device (*SN*)	Operating start date of return device at *L* (*T6*)
3	2016/03/01	c	-
5	2016/06/01	d	-
2	2016/07/01	e	-
:	:	:	:

(▒ : unknown)

Firstly, from a) and b), we try to obtain List-A of Table I with its created date *Tc*. Each pair of the sequence number *SN* and its location *L* can be obtained from b). This *L* is matched with that in a) to associate this pair with the service start date *T1* contained in a). If this device has not been failed since the day of initial installation at a user, we can obtain the history indicating that device *SN* has been working without failure between *T1* and *Tc*, which results in the fact that the operation start date *T4* is *T1* (*T4*=*T1*). Meanwhile, if there was a failure, *T1* is set to the date when an alternative device is started working at location *L*. In this case, *T4*, the operating start date of the original device *SN*, is left *unknown*.

Secondly, we try to obtain List-B of Table I from a) and d). In this scenario, the vendor records the location where the failure occurred (this kind of information is generally useful for such vendors which need some statistics of failure occurrence patterns). Here, we should consider how we will obtain column *T5*, which is the operation start date of each failed device. To do this, we associate date *T2* of failure, the sequence number *SN* and location *L* with contract information of a). Then, we obtain *T5* and the history indicating that device *SN* installed at location *L* had been working from *T5* until *T2* and then failed at *T2*.

In addition, from Figure 1 (3), the provider might maintain the information corresponding to d) that is maintained by the vendor. However, we consider that such information is not necessary for the provider's asset and the provider may not be motivated to maintain it. In other case, the provider might start maintaining it later. However, the information before starting cannot be obtained. Hence, we assume the worst case that the provider does not maintain it.

Moreover, a) contains the service end date *T3* and the service start date *T1*. If we have sequence number *SN* of the device that was returned from location *L*, we can obtain List-C of Table I containing *T6*, the operation start date of the returned device. We note that the provider may not be motivated to record sequence number *SN*. Similarly with the List-A case, from this List-C, we can obtain the history indicating that the returned device *SN* had been working from *T6* until *T3* without failure. Under a certain condition, *T6* is equal to *T1*.

In the next sections, we present how *T4*, *T5* and *T6* are obtained using List-A, B and C, and how the cumulative failure rate is calculated using the history.

IV. Proposed Method

A. Overview

In this section, we explain how to obtain the cumulative failure rate of IoT devices whose management information is maintained separately and uncoordinatedly by multiple players. Our proposed method consists of the following three Steps;

Step1: Reconstructing the operating history of each IoT device,
Step2: Counting the operating days, and
Step3: Calculating the cumulative failure rate.

Specifically, our proposed method basically uses List-A and B for reconstructing the operating history, and List-C as well as (if exists). Note that even without List-C, the method can reconstruct the history but some error may occur because *T3*, and *T6* in List-C are not plotted on the time-sequence diagram (See Figure 2 in Section IV-B). We numerically evaluate the impact of such error in Section V.

B. Design Details

Step1: Reconstruct the operating history of IoT device.

Step1-1) Create time-sequence diagram per location.

(1) First, the time-sequence diagram per location is created as shown in Figure 2 (i) where x- and y-axes are # of days passed (denoted as *T*) from the reference date "0" and location *L* (1, 2, ...), respectively. Current date *Tc*, failed date *T2* and return date *T3* in List-A, B, and C are plotted as square boxes on the diagram at (*x*,*y*)=(*Tc*/*T2*/*T3*, relevant *L*), respectively. Note that for easy understanding, in Figure 2, we assign a numeral number *j* to each plot as ID. It is denoted inside the square box corresponding to the plot.

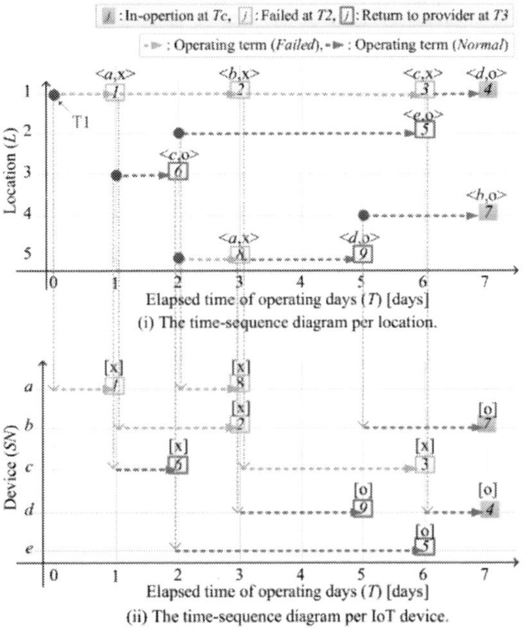

Figure 2. Time-sequence diagrams for reconstructing the operating history of each IoT device.

(2) For each plot j, device SN and device operating status x="*Failed*" or o="*Normal*" at the relevant date are associated as its attribute. For instance in Figure 2 (i), plot j=8 with <a,x> (at T=3 and L=5) means that the device a was "*Failed*" at location L=5 (then it was sent back to the vendor for repair). Plot j=7 with <b,o> means that the device b was "*Normal*" at L=4 (therefore, it is in-operation now (T=7)). Plot j=9 with <d,o> means that the device d was "*Normal*" at L=5 (because it was returned to the provider without failure due to user cancellation at T=5).

(3) Service start date $T1$ at location L in List-A is plotted on the diagram.

(4) We assume that the failed device is replaced to another device on the same day for non-stop service. Along the time-sequence of each location L, the plots on it are traced back from the current date Tc (T=7) to the reference date (T=0) in order to determine the start date (referred to as S_j) of each plot j at the location. The date of j's previous plot is regarded as the start date of j. For example, the start date of device b at plot j=2 ((x,y)=(3,1)) is determined as S_2=1 because its previous plot (j=1) is at T=1 ((x,y)=(1,1)).

(5) The operating term for each plot j can be extracted as the term from S_j to T of plot j. For example, device b at plot j=2 is operated from S_2=1 to T=3 so the term is 2 days. As another example, device b at j=7 ((x,y)=(7,4)) is operated from S_7=5 to T=7 (now in-operation) so the term is also 2 days.

Step1-2) Transform time-sequence diagram per location to per IoT device.

(1) The time-sequence diagram per IoT device (see Figure 2 (ii)) is transformed from Figure 2 (i). At first, each plot j in Figure 2 (i) is re-plotted on Figure 2 (ii) according to the device SN in its attribute. Note that the device operating status x/o in its attribute is inherited. For instance, plot j=2 with <b,x> ((x,y)=(3,1)) in Figure 2 (i) is re-plotted to j=2 with [x] ((x,y)=(3,b)) in Figure 2 (ii).

(2) For each plot j, the relevant operating term from S_j to T of the plot j is drawn on Figure 2 (ii). It is easy to obtain each IoT device's operating history by collecting operating terms per device from Figure 2 (ii). For instance, the operating history of device b includes two operating terms, i.e., S_2=1 to T=3 (*Failed*) and S_7=5 to T=7 (*Normal*).

Step2: Counting the operating days.

Two types of operating days are counted per IoT device from the operation histories. The first type is referred as "*Failed days*" (P) which is ended with a plot derived from $T2$, i.e., failed date. The second type is referred to as "*Normal days*" (Q) which is ended with a plot derived from $T3$ or Tc, i.e., return or current date without failure. For counting the operating days of each IoT device, an operation term of the device is selected in chronological order and checked whether the term is ended by $T3$ or not. If so, the term should be concatenated to the next operating term (if any) as a single piece of operating days. For example in Figure 2 (ii), the device b is set P=2 and Q=2, while the device c is set P=4(=1+3), and the device d is set Q=3(=2+1). P and Q of each device are shown in Table II.

TABLE II. THE OPERATING DAYS FOR EACH SN IN FIGURE 2 (ii)

SN	# of operating days (# of terms)	Operating days [days]	
		1st	2nd
a	2 (2)	P=1	P=1
b	2 (2)	P=2	Q=2
c	1 (2)	P=4 (=1+3)	-
d	1 (2)	Q=3 (=2+1)	-
e	1 (1)	Q=4	-

Step3: Calculating the cumulative failure rate.

From both *Failure days* and *Normal days* in Step2, the cumulative failure rate is calculated. Let $f(x)$ denote the failure density function, the failure occurrence probability until time i has passed, i.e., the cumulative failure ratio $F(i)$, is expressed in equation (1) [6].

$$F(i) = \int_0^i f(x)dx \tag{1}$$

We can approximately obtain the following difference equation by differentiating equation (1) and substituting infinitesimal di to the unit time (a day).

$$F(i) - F(i-1) = f(i) \tag{2}$$

Here, let $\lambda(i)$ denote the failure rate of i-th unit time. Since $f(i)$ is expressed as

$$f(i) = (1 - F(i-1)) \cdot \lambda(i), \tag{3}$$

we can obtain the following equation:

$$F(i) = F(i-1) + (1 - F(i-1)) \cdot \lambda(i), \tag{4}$$

where

$$F(0) = 0, \quad \lambda(i) = \frac{n(i)}{N(i)+n(i)} \quad (i = 1, 2, \ldots). \tag{5}$$

Note that $n(i)$ and $N(i)$ are the number of failed devices (P = i-1) at day i, and the number of in-operation devices at the end of day i, respectively. From the above discussions, the cumulative failure rate can be calculated from the operating history.

In addition, $m(i)$ denotes the number of returned devices, which is suspended at day i, is given by the following equation:

$$m(i) = N(i-1) - \big(N(i) + n(i)\big). \qquad (6)$$

Assuming that $\lambda(i)$ is the same regardless of the devices, the cumulative failure rate is not affected even if suspended devices exist.

V. Experimental Evaluation

We verify that the proposed method expressed in Section IV can reconstruct operating histories and calculate the cumulative failure rate. In addition, we evaluate the accuracy of the cumulative failure rate when some information elements are missing.

A. Experimental Setup

In order to validate the effectiveness of our proposal, we develop the simulator implementing the proposed method. The input data set for this simulator consists of List-A, B, and C (if any) without *T4, T5*, and *T6*. From these input data sets, the simulator complements the unknown fields (*T4, T5*, and *T6*), then reconstructs operating histories and calculates the cumulative failure rate. This simulator is a Ruby program with approximately 17,000 lines, executing on a PC whose specification is shown in Table III.

TABLE III. Specification of PC for Simulation

Parameters		Values
PC	CPU	E5-2650L v2@1.70GHz
	Memory	126GBytes
	OS	CentOS 6.6
Program		Ruby 1.9.3

TABLE IV. Parameters of Creating Evaluation Data

Parameters	Values
Failed rate U [%/day]	0.2, 0.5, 0.8
Return rate R [%/day]	0, 0.2, 0.4, 0.6, 0.8, 1.0
The number of simulation days T [days]	1,826 (= 5 years)
The number of devices [units]	15,000 ~ 70,000
The number of locations [locations]	100 ~ 10,000

Evaluation data sets as shown in Table IV are arranged with various return rates R and failure rates U, both of which follow uniform distribution irrespective of T. Simulation days T is 1,826 days (= 5 years), the maximum number of devices is 70,000 [units], and the maximum number of locations is 10,000. We assume no IoT devices are in-operation at T=0, and the replacement of failed device is finished on the same day as the failure occurs. In addition, we assume the followings to simplify the simulation.

- Just after a user cancels his/her contract at location L, a new user at Location L' starts his/her contract and uses another device.
- Through the simulation, we regard L and L' are equivalent, i.e., the total number of devices and that of locations are never changed by return events.

TABLE V. Verification Cases

Case #	List-C management / non-management	unknown data
Case1	Management (=use List-C)	*T4, T5, T6*
Case2	Non-management (=not use List-C)	*T4, T5*, List-C*

**T6*: unknown because of List-C unmanaged

For accurate evaluation results, we arranged 180 data sets in total, because 18 *R/U* pairs are specified and 10 random data sets are generated per *R/U* pair. Note that these data sets are given as List-A, B and C. At first, a data set consists of all the information elements in List-A, B and C are generated (we call it "reference data set"). Then, an evaluation data set is created from it by omitting unknown fields, i.e., *T4, T5* and *T6* or *T4, T5* and whole List-C, according to the case in Table V.

B. Verification of proposed method

We verify that the proposed method can complement the unknown fields in List-A, B, and C in Case1 and Case2 by comparing with the reference data sets. We also reconstruct operating histories and calculate cumulative failure rates from all the evaluation data sets.

As a result, we confirm that the simulator successfully completes the above processes for any data sets in any cases. In Case1, all *T4, T5* and *T6* of event start dates are completely matched with those in the reference data sets. In contrast, in Case2, *T4* and *T5*, which are operating start dates of failed and current devices respectively, are unmatched from those in the reference data sets due to the lack of List-C. Here, let K denote the unmatched rate of start dates. In percentage terms, K is given by the following equation:

$$K = ((v1 + v2)/(w1 + w2)) \times 100,$$

where $v1$ and $v2$ denote the number of unmatched *T4, T5*, respectively, while $w1$ and $w2$ denote the total number of failure events and in-operation events, respectively.

Figure 3 shows the unmatched rate of the start dates K where the failure rate U varies from 0.2 to 0.8. From this figure, we can easily find that K is increased as R does, and decreases in proportion to U. For example, K becomes 77.3%, 62.2% and 52.2% at R=1.0 of U=0.2, 0.5 and 0.8, respectively. Note that K is 0% irrespective of U when R=0.0 (no return event occurs) because there is no influence due to lack of List-C.

On the other hand, the example computation time to obtain the operating history and the cumulative failure rate are approximately 3 [min] and 1 [min], respectively, in the case of U=0.8 and R=1.0 with 70,000 IoT devices.

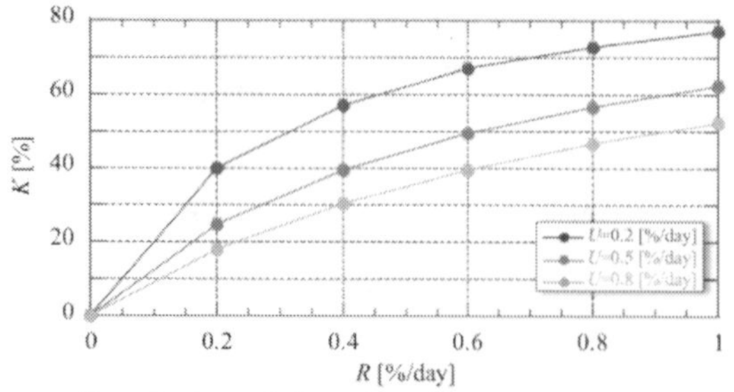

Figure 3. Unmatched rate of start date K vs. return rate R.

C. *Effect of cumulative failure rate by return rate R*

We evaluate the reliability by calculating the cumulative failure rate $F(i)$ various rerun rate R. Figure 4 shows the cumulative failure rate $F(i)$ in each failure rate U where the return rate R varies from 0.0 %/day to 1.0 %/day at 0.2 %/day intervals. Each plot indicates the average of $F(i)$ values individually calculated from 10 random data sets arranged per R/U pair.

It is clear in Figure 4 that $F(i)$ increases in proportion to R irrespective of U and that the larger R becomes, the more rapidly the cumulative failure rate $F(i)$ increases. As for the errors of $F(i)$ (referred to as α) between R=0.0 and 1.0, α =0.143 at i=400, α=0.138 at i=159, and α=0.130 at i=105, respectively. So the error α decreases with increase of U.

Figure 4 also indicates that our method conservatively underestimates the cumulative failure rate. In the case hat List-C is unmanaged, the operating terms of return events, such as device d at S_9=3 to T=5 and device c at S_6=1 to T=2 in Figure 2 (ii), are lost. As a result, $N(i)$ in equation (5) can be smaller so that $F(i)$ in equation (4) tends to be increased in a short time as R increases. From the provider's perspective, the calculated rate can be still useful when the provider discloses it to the vendor for encouraging more improvement on the product quality and reliability of IoT devices.

However, in the reverse direction from the vendor to the provider, such underestimation may mislead the vendor, e.g., vendor may consider he need not do anything next. Conversely, the vendor should recognize that the actual failure rate may be higher. Meanwhile if multiple vendors exist, the cumulative failure rate can be still used as an important index for comparing device qualities between these vendors.

Therefore, the calculated failure rate should be interpreted carefully according to the player's role.

VI. Additional Uncoordination Case

Practically there could be wide variations on what management information is maintained by each player. In the scenario described in Section III, we assume that each player is dedicated to playing his role and does not have any incentive to maintain extra management information beyond his role. However, in the real world, it is probable that players may add some management information due to emerging new operational requirements after the service starts. For example, similar service infrastructures and their providers are often unified in real cases.

Here, we qualitatively discuss how to handle such management information change, especially in the case that some useful information elements can be obtained after a certain date. For example, in Sec. III, it is considerable that the service is started with a very small number of users and it is not so important for the provider to improve product reliability of IoT devices at this moment. However, the number of IoT devices increases as the service grows, and the provider wants to improve the product reliability of IoT devices so that the provider starts maintaining List-C on a certain date (T=Y).

In such a case, return date $T3$ in List-C is on and after the date Y and there are no previous records before it, i.e., from T=0 to Y-1. For calculating the cumulative failure rate, we can choose one of the following three options.

Option 1)

The calculation is conducted using recorded $T3$ ($T3 \geq Y$) only, assuming that no return event (service cancelation), occurs at any T where $T<Y$.

Option 2)

The calculation is conducted after complementing $T3$ at T ($T<Y$) based on R calculated from recorded $T3$ ($T3 \geq Y$).

Option 3)

The calculation is conducted without List-C.

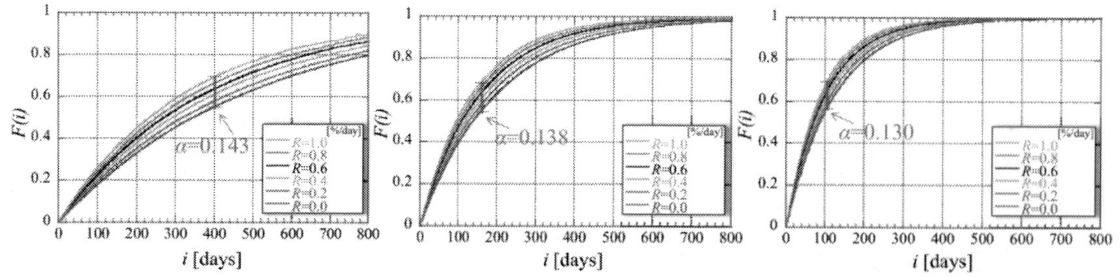

(1) U=0.2 %/day (2) U=0.5 %/day (3) U=0.8 %/day

Figure 4. Cumulative failure rate $F(i)$ vs. operating days i with different return rates R.

Among above three options, Option 3 is equivalent to the result of $R=0.0$ in each U in Figure 4. According to the results in Figure 4, it is expected qualitatively that the cumulative failure rate $F(i)$ in Option 2 is the most increasing trend, i.e., seems the worst product quality, followed in order by $F(i)$ in Option 1 and $F(i)$ in Option 3. Hereafter, we describe it as "Option 2 > Option 1 > Option 3".

To verify the above qualitative analysis, we conduct the quantitative evaluation of the three options. At each option, the evaluation data are emulated as follows, then the cumulative failure rate $F(i)$ is calculated.

Option1)
Return events occurring at $T<Y$ are deleted from reference data. Then, the start dates of all events (return, failure, and current) are calculated.

Option2)
Return events occurring at $T<Y$ are deleted from reference data, and return rate R' at T ($T \geq Y$) is calculated. Then, the return events are inserted at T ($T<Y$) based on R'. Finally, the start dates of all events are calculated.

Option3)
All the return events are deleted. Then, the start dates of all events are calculated.

Evaluation data sets are arranged with different return rates R (0.2, 0.5, and 0.8) and failure rates U (0.0 to 1.0 at 0.2 intervals), and other parameters are set as shown in Table IV. In addition, Y is set to 365, 730, 1,095 or 1,460 [days] considering one year as a unit. For accuracy of evaluation results, we arrange 1,620 data sets in total. Concretely, 72 $R/U/Y$ sets are specified and 10 random datasets are generated per $R/U/Y$ sets in Options 1 and 2. In Option 3, 18 R/U pairs are specified and 10 random data sets are generated per R/U pairs. Note that at Option 3, the calculation is conducted without List-C regardless of T.

TABLE VI. MAXIMUM ERROR RATE (ABSOLUTE VALUE) OF R' IN OPTION 2 AT EACH Y

Y [days]	365	730	1,095	1,460
Max. $\lvert R'-R \rvert / R$	0.023	0.029	0.026	0.028

Before presenting the evaluation results, we confirm the error rate of the estimated return rate R' to the ground truth at each Y in order to verify whether or not R' was given accurately when the data sets of Option 2 are created. The maximum error rates (absolute values) of R' for different Y's in 24 data sets are shown in Table VI. Consequently, the errors are between 0.023 and 0.029, which are negligibly small. Hence we conclude that R' can be regarded as R in Option 2.

Figure 5 shows the cumulative failure rate $F(i)$ in each option, where failure rates U are 0.2, 0.5 and 0.8 and return rates R are between 0.0 and 1.0 at 0.2 %/day intervals. We note that only $F(i)$ in Y=730 case is shown in Figure 5 for better visualization. In all options, $F(i)$ increases rapidly as U becomes larger. In Options 1 and 2, $F(i)$ increases proportionally to R. On the other hand, in case of Option 3, $F(i)$ is almost same[i] for the different R values.

Next, we evaluate the cumulative failure rate $F(i)$ in each option quantitatively. $F(i)$ where return rates R are 0.0 and 1.0 at Y=730 is shown for each U in Figure 6. It is clear in each case of U, the cumulative failure rate $F(i)$ at R=1.0 increases rapidly where the increasing rates of three options are: Option 2 > Option 1 > Option 3. As for the errors of $F(i)$ between Options 2 and 1 (referred to as β) and between Options 2 and 3 (referred to as γ) where the values of U are 0.2, 0.5, and 0.8, we obtain β=0.05, 0.04 and 0.03, γ=0.13, 0.13 and 0.12, respectively.

[i] Only negligible difference caused by failure events generated randomly in each data set is observed.

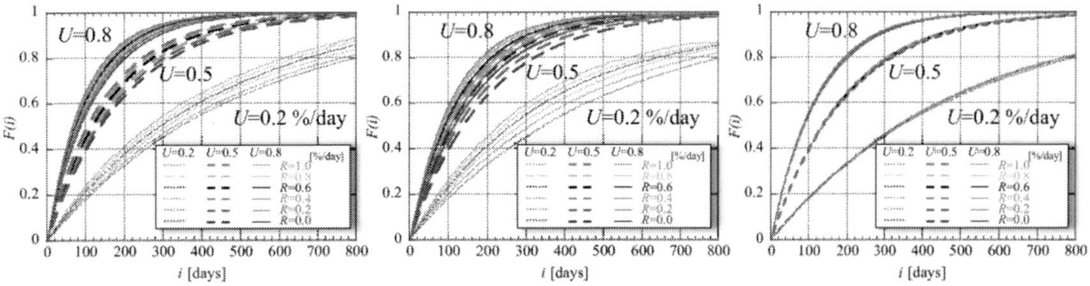

(1) Option 1 (2) Option 2 (3) Option 3

Figure 5. Cumulative failure rate $F(i)$ vs. operating days i with different return rate R and failure rate U in each Option (Y=730). (thin dot, thick dot and solid lines correspond to U=0.2, 0.5 and 0.8 cases, respectively)

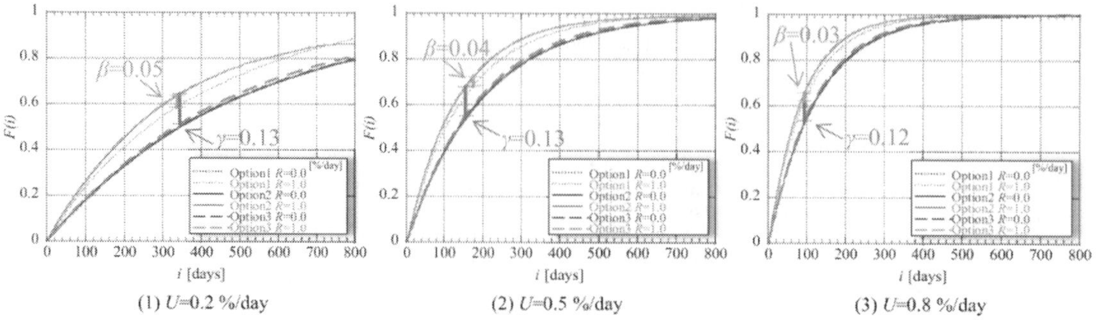

Figure 6. Cumulative failure rate $F(i)$ vs. operating days i with differenet Option/R pairs in each U value (Y=730).

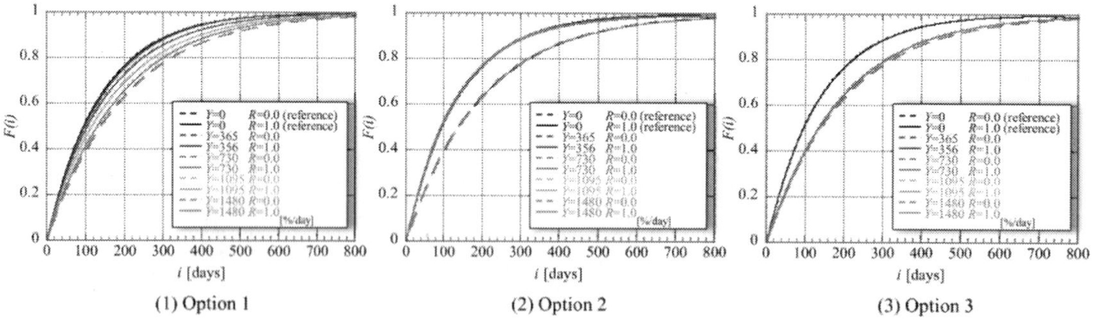

Figure 7. Cumulative failure rate $F(i)$ vs. operating days i with different Y/R pairs in each Option (U=0.5).

Furthermore, we confirm the impact of starting the maintenance of List-C at Y on the cumulative failure rate $F(i)$. Figure 7 shows $F(i)$ at each Y when U is 0.5. For comparing the results, in all figures, we plot Y=0 (black solid and dotted lines) as the references in which List-C is maintained from the beginning as well as List-A and List-B. In Option 2 at R=1.0, $F(i)$ is almost the same irrespective of Y. On the other hand in Option 1, $F(i)$ becomes larger as Y decreases. In addition, $F(i)$ at Y>0 is smaller than that at Y=0. Furthermore, as for comparison of Options 1 and 2, $F(i)$ in Option1 is smaller than that in Option 2 at Y=365 (the smallest value of Y in this evaluation).

These results prove the correctness of our qualitative expectation for the cumulative failure rate $F(i)$, i.e., Option 2 > Option 1 > Option 3 (see Section VI). Note that the above order is not changed irrespective of Y, the date for starting the maintenance of List-C.

VII. Conclusion

In this paper we proposed a method of calculating the cumulative failure rate in IoT service infrastructure operated by multiple players such as service providers and device vendors in the horizontal specialization business model. According to changing business environment around providers such as massive numbers of IoT devices and strenuous demand on its service availability, we believe each provider itself is also required to expand the quality management of devices instead of or together with vendors.

We revealed the possibility on lack of information from the provider's perspective, and proposed the method which aggregates and analyzes distributed information to derive the operating history of each IoT device to enable calculation of cumulative failure rates. We also verified that the proposed method can derive operating histories and calculate the cumulative failure rate. In addition, we evaluated the accuracy of the derived cumulative failure rates when some information about device operation are missing. From the experimental evaluation, our method conservatively underestimates the cumulative failure rate. So, the calculated failure rate should be interpreted carefully according to the player's role. Even if such underestimation exists, from the provider's perspective, it is considered to be useful because it becomes some evidence to encourage the vendor to improve the product quality and reliability of IoT devices more.

Furthermore, to prove wide applicability of our proposed method, we also evaluated the additional but promising uncoordinated case in which additional information elements are added after the service was launched, due to emerging new operational requirements. We quantitatively analyzed the cumulative failure rate using three types of options for calculating methods.

We are now planning to apply our method to further different cases. We believe that we have shown the applicability of our method by introducing well-seen, representative cases in this paper, but examination of our approach in a variety of scenarios is part of our future work.

REFERENCES

[1] M. Shibuya, Y. Hasegawa, and H. Yamaguchi, "A Study on Device Management for IoT Services with Uncoordinated Device Operating History," Proc. International Conference on Networks (ICN 2016), pp.72-77, Feb. 2016.

[2] Cisco Systems Inc., "Cisco Visual Networking Index: Global Mobile Data Traffic Forecast Update, 2013-2018," http://www.cisco.com/c/en/us/solutions/collateral/service-provider/visual-networking-index-vni/white_paper_c11-520862.html, accessed Jan. 8, 2016.

[3] M. Ahamad, "Reliability Models for the Internet of Things: A Paradigm Shift," Proc IEEE International Symposium on Software Reliability Engineering Workshops, pp.52-59, Nov. 2014.

[4] M. Ahamad, "Designing for the Internet of Things: A paradigm Shift in reliability," Proc. Electribuc Cioibebts & Technology Conference, pp.1758-1766, May 2015.

[5] M. N. Sahana, S. Anjana, S. Ankith, K. Matarajam, K. R. Shobha, and A. Paventhan, "Home energy management open IoT protocol stack," Proc. IEEE Recent Advances in Intelligent Computational Systems (RAICS), pp.370-375, Dec. 2015.

[6] S. Stanley, "MTBF, MTTR, MTTF & FIT Explanation of Terms," http://imcnetworks.com/wp-content/uploads/2014/12/MTBF-MTTR-MTTF-FIT.pdf, accessed Sep. 16, 2016.

[7] W. Zheng, W. Zengquan, and W. A-na, "Failure Rate Calculating Method of Components Based on the Load-strength Interference Model," Proc. IEEE Industrial Engineering and Engineering Management (IEEM 2010), pp.783-787, Dec. 2010.

[8] OPS rules, "Vertical vs. Horizontal Integration: Which is a better Operations Strategy?," Sep. 2012, http://www.opsrules.com/supply-chain-optimization-blog/bid/241648/Vertical-vs-Horizontal-Integration-Which-is-a-Better-Operations-Strategy, accessed Jan. 8, 2016.

[9] Z. Yu, "IT, Production Specialization, and Divison of Labor: A Smith-Ricardo Model of International Trade," Carleton Economic Paper, Jun. 2003, http://carleton.ca/economics/wp-content/uploads/cep03-06.pdf, accessed Jun. 8, 2016.

[10] R. Suoranta, "New Directions in Mobile Device Architectures," Proc. Euromicro Conference on Digital System Design (DSD'06) , pp.17-26, Aug. 2006.

[11] Fujitsu Limited, "Management Direction Briefing," Oct. 2015, http://pr.fujitsu.com/jp/ir/library/presentation/pdf/en/md-20151029note.pdf, accessed Aug. 8, 2016.

[12] Z. Zhou, X. Liu, Q. Shi, Y. En, and X. Wang, "Failure Rate Calculation for NMOS Devices under Multiple Failure Mechanisms," Proc. International Symposium on the Physical and Failure Analysis of Integrated Circuits (IPFA), pp.362-365, Jul. 2013.

[13] T. Tekcan, G. Kahramanoglu, and M. Giinduzalp, "Determining Reliability by Failure Rate Estimation via a New Parameter," Proc. Reliability and Maintainability Symposium (RAMS), pp.1-7, Jan. 2012.

[14] J. Pan, Z. Wang, amd D. Lubkeman, "Condition Based Failure Rate Modeling for Electric Network Components," Proc. Power Systems Conference andExposition (PSCE '09), pp.1-6, Mar. 2009.

[15] R. Wang, A. Xue, S. Huang, X. Cao, Z. Shao, and Y. Luo, "On the Estimation of Time-Varying Failure Rate to Protection Devices Basedon Failure Pattern," Proc. Electric Utility Deregulation and Restructuring and Power Technologies (DRPT), pp.902-905, Aug. 2011.

[16] Q. Duan and J. Liu, "Modelling a Bathtub-Shaped Failure Rate by a Coxian Distribution," Proc. IEEE Transactions on Reliability, vol. 65, issue 2, pp.878-885, Jun. 2016.

[17] P. James and A. Forsyth, "Real time, on line, age calculation of IGBT power modules," Proc. Power Electronics, Machines and Drives (PEMD 2010), pp.1-4, Apr. 2010.

[18] A. J. Henry and J. A. Nachlas, "An equivalent age model for condition-based maintenance," Proc. Reliability and Maintainability Symposium (RAMS), pp.1-6, Jan. 2012.

[19] H. Funakoshi and T. Matsukawa, "A failure Rate Estimation Considering the Change in the Number of Equipments," IEICE Trans. B Vol. J93-B No.4, pp.681-692, 2010 (in JAPANESE).

[20] H. Funakoshi and T. Matsukawa, "A Failure Rate Estimation Considering the Change in the Number of Equipments - Applicable condition of mathematical model for proposed method -," IEICE NS2009-17, pp.1-6, 2009 (in JAPANESE).

[21] M. Xie, Y. Tang, and T. N. Goh, "A modified Weibull extension with bathtub-shaped failure rate function," Reliability Engineering and System Safety, 2002, 76(3): 279-285.

[22] Z. Sheng, H. Wang, C. Yin, X. Hu, S. Yang, and V. C. M. Leung, "Lightweight Management of Resource-Constrained Sensor Devices in Internet of Things," in IEEE Internet of Things Journal, vol.2, no.5, pp.402-411, Oct. 2015.

[23] C. Zhou and X. Zhang, "Toward the Internet of Things application and management: A practical approach," in IEEE WoWMoM 2014, pp.1-6, 2014.

[24] S. N. Han, S. Park, G.M. Lee, and N. Crespi, "Extending the Devices Profile for Web Services Standard Using a REST Proxy," in IEEE Internet Computing, vol.19, no.1, pp.10-17, Jan.-Feb. 2015.

[25] Z. Sheng, C. Mahapatra, C. Zhu, and V. C. M. Leung, "Recent Advances in Industrial Wireless Sensor Networks Toward Efficient Management in IoT," in IEEE Access, vol.3, pp.622-637, May 2015.

[26] G. Chen, J. Huang, B. Cheng, and J. Chen, "A Social Network based Approach for IoT Device Management and Service Composition," Proc. IEEE World Congress on Services 2015, pp.1-8, Jun. 2015.

[27] B. Manate, T. Fortis, and V. Negru, "Infrastructure Management Support in a Multi-Agent Architecture for Internet of Things, " Proc. Modelling Symposium (EMS), pp.372-377, Oct. 2014.

[28] Freepress, "That Box Your Cable Company Forces You to Rent," May 2016, http://www.freepress.net/blog/2016/05/20/box-your-cable-company-forces-you-rent, accessed Nov. 22, 2016.

SDN Solutions for Switching Dedicated Long-Haul Connections: Measurements and Comparative Analysis

Nageswara S. V. Rao

Oak Ridge National Laboratory
Oak Ridge, TN 37831, USA
Email: raons@ornl.gov

Abstract—**We consider a scenario of two sites connected over a dedicated, long-haul connection that must quickly fail-over in response to degradations in host-to-host application performance. The traditional layer-2/3 hot stand-by fail-over solutions do not adequately address the variety of application degradations, and more recent single controller Software Defined Networks (SDN) solutions are not effective for long-haul connections. We present two methods for such a path fail-over using OpenFlow-enabled switches: (a) a light-weight method that utilizes host scripts to monitor application performance and dpctl API for switching, and (b) a generic method that uses two OpenDaylight (ODL) controllers and REST interfaces. For both methods, the restoration dynamics of applications contain significant statistical variations due to the complexities of controllers, north bound interfaces and switches; they, together with the wide variety of vendor implementations, complicate the choice among such solutions. We develop the impulse-response method based on regression functions of performance parameters to provide a rigorous and objective comparison of different solutions. We describe testing results of the two proposed methods, using TCP throughput and connection rtt as main parameters, over a testbed consisting of HP and Cisco switches connected over long-haul connections emulated in hardware by ANUE devices. The combination of analytical and experimental results demonstrate that the dpctl method responds seconds faster than the ODL method on average, even though both methods eventually restore original TCP throughput.**

Keywords–Software defined networks; OpenFlow; Opendaylight; controller; long-haul connection; impulse-response; testbed.

I. Introduction

We consider scenarios where two remote sites are connected over a dedicated long-haul connection with hundreds of millisecond latency, such as a transcontinental fiber or satellite link [1], as illustrated in Figure 1(a). Different client-server application pairs are executed at different times on host systems located at the sites, which range from data transfers to on-line instrument monitoring to messaging. Applications may incorporate different methods to account for network losses and jitter; for example, they may utilize TCP or UDT for guaranteed delivery, UDP for loss tolerant cases, custom buffering methods and others at application level to account for jitter. Furthermore, their performance may be optimized or customized to connection parameters such as latency, jitter and loss rate; for example, TCP parameters may be tuned for long-haul connections and buffers of interactive codes may be tuned for long latencies and jitter of satellite links. The connection quality can degrade due to a variety factors such as equipment failures, weather conditions, and geographical events, which may be reflected in host-to-host application performance. Indeed, the client-server application pairs may respond differently to various degradations, such as decreased throughput of file transfers, increased jitter in streaming, loss

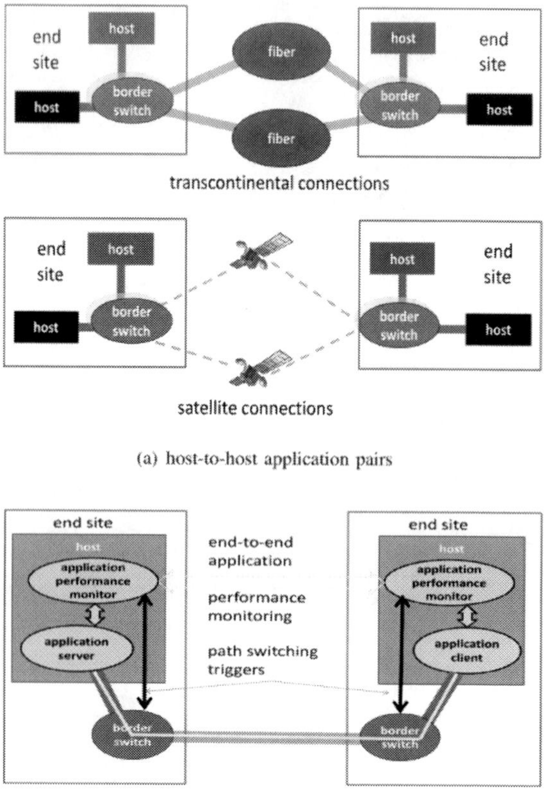

(a) host-to-host application pairs

(b) two connection modalities

Figure 1. Two sites connected over long-haul connections.

of end-to-end control in computational steering, and in some cases (such as messaging) having very little effect. As a mitigation strategy, a physically diverse and functionally equivalent *standby* path is switched to when the performance of currently running application pairs degrades.

The performances of application pairs are continuously monitored on host systems, and the current *primary* path is switched out when needed, for example, by modifying Virtual Local Area Networks (VLAN) and route tables on border switches and routers, respectively. In our use cases, human operators watch host-level performance monitors, and invoke Command Line Interface (CLI) commands or web-based interfaces of network devices for path switching. Typically, the path fail-overs are accomplished either by manual configuration or through device-specific scripts. Since triggers for path switching are dynamically generated by application pairs, they are not adequately handled by conventional hot standby layer-2/3 solutions that solely utilize connection parameters. For example, certain losses may be tolerated by messaging applications but not by monitoring and control applications of instruments and sensors. Currently, the design and operation of such application-driven fail-over schemes require a detailed knowledge of host codes, and the specialized interfaces and APIs of switches, such as custom TL1, CURL and python scripts, which currently vary significantly among vendor products. Furthermore, in our use cases such fail-over operations must be coordinated between two physically-separated operations centers located at the end sites. The combination of recent advances in host and network virtualization technologies [2] offers very promising and potentially game changing solutions to seamlessly automate the dynamic fail-over workflows that integrate diverse application monitors and network elements.

We are interested in exploiting the network and host virtualization layers to unify and automate such monitoring and path switching operations. Automated scripts for these tasks provide the following advantages over current practices: (i) improved response time, since scripts can be executed much faster than manual configurations, (ii) reductions in performance degradations due to human errors in application monitoring and path switching, and (iii) reductions in site operations costs of host systems and network devices.

A. SDN Solutions

The rapidly evolving *Software Defined Networks* (SDN) technologies [3], [4] seem particularly well-suited for automating the path switching tasks, when combined with host monitoring codes. In particular, the northbound interfaces of SDN controllers can be used to communicate the path degradations information to trigger path switching; then, the path can be switched by installing flow entries that divert traffic onto the standby path using the southbound controller interfaces [5]. Thus, SDN technologies provide two distinct advantages over current network operations:

(a) trigger modules of new applications can be "dropped in place" with no no major software changes by using communications via generic northbound interfaces, and
(b) switches from different vendors with virtual interfaces can be simply be swapped, avoiding the re-work often needed to account for custom interfaces and operating systems.

While the problem space of our use cases is somewhat straightforward, their SDN solution space is much more complex: due to the rapid developments in underlying technologies, these is a wide array of choices for controllers and switches, which in turn leads to a large number of solution combinations. Indeed, their complexity and variety requires systematic analysis and comparison methods to assess their operational effectiveness and performance, such as recovery times. In addition, compared to certain data-center and network provisioning scenarios for which SDN technologies have been successfully applied, these long-haul scenarios present additional challenges. First, single controller solutions are not practical for managing the border switches at end sites due to the large latency. Second, solutions that require a separate control-plane infrastructure between the controllers and switches are cost prohibitive, in sharp contrast to the connection-rich data-center or Internet scenarios.

B. Outline of Contributions

In this paper, we present automated software solutions for path fail-over by utilizing two controllers, one at each site, that are coordinated over a single connection through measurements. We first describe a light-weight, custom designed *dpctl method*[1] for OpenFlow border switches that uses host Linux bash scripts to: (i) monitor the connection parameters, such as rtt or TCP throughput, at the host-level and detect degradations that require a fail-over, and (ii) utilize dpctl API to install and delete flow entries on the border switches to implement path fail-over when needed. This script is about hundred lines of code, which makes it easier to analyze for its performance and security aspects. We then present a more generic *ODL method* that utilizes two OpenDaylight Hydrogen (ODL) controllers [6] located at the end sites. We use REST interface of ODL controller to communicate the trigger information for path switching in the form of new OpenFlow entries to be installed on border switches. We also utilize Linux bash scripts to monitor the connection performance to generate fail-over triggers, and invoke python REST API scripts to communicate new flow entries to ODL controllers. The executional path of this approach is more complex compared to the dpctl method since it involves communications using both northbound and southbound ODL interfaces and invoking several computing modules within ODL software stack. Thus, a complete performance and security analysis of this method requires a closer examination of much larger code base that includes both host scripts and corresponding ODL modules, including its embedded http server.

We present implementation and experimental results using a testbed consisting of Linux hosts, HP and Cisco border switches, and ANUE long-haul hardware connection emulation devices. We utilize TCP throughput as a primary performance measure [2] for the client-server applications, which is effected by the connection rtt and jitter possibly caused by path switching, and the available path capacity. Experimental results show that both dpctl and ODL methods restore the host-to-host TCP throughput within seconds by switching to the standby connection after the current connection's RTT is degraded (by external factors). However, the restoration dynamics of TCP throughput show significant statistical variations, primarily as a result of interactions between the path switching dynamics of controllers and switches, and the highly non-linear dynamics of TCP congestion control mechanisms [7]–[9]. As a result, direct comparisons of individual TCP throughput time traces corresponding to fail-over events are not very instructive in reflecting the overall performance of the two methods.

To objectively compare the performance of these two rather dissimilar methods, we propose the *impulse-response*

[1]Note that dpctl is originally intended for diagnosis purposes, which we utilize as a controller.

[2]The overall approach is applicable to other application-level performance measures such as response times, which typically degrade under connection disruptions and recover when connection is restored. Our choice of TCP is based on its widespread use for guaranteed packet delivery and its rich dynamics.

method that captures the average performance by utilizing measurements collected in response to a train of path degradation events induced externally. We establish a statistical basis for this method using the finite-sample theory [10] by exploiting the underlying monotonic properties of performance parameters during the degradation and recovery periods. This analysis enables us to objectively conclude that on the average the dpctl method restores the TCP throughput several seconds faster than the ODL method for these scenarios. This paper is an expanded version of an earlier conference paper [1] with additional explanations and details of SDN implementations, and it also provide a complete derivation of the performance equations for the impulse response method using finite sample statistical analysis.

The organization of this paper is as follows. Two-site scenarios with dedicated long-haul connections are described in Section II. A coordinated controllers approach for connection fail-over, and its implementation using dpctl and ODL methods are described in Section III. An experimental testbed consisting of Linux servers and HP and Cisco switches is described in Section IV-A, and the results of experiments using dpctl and ODL methods using five different configurations are presented in Section IV-B. The impulse response method to assess the overall fail-over performance is presented in Section V-A, and its statistical basis is presented in Section V-B. Conclusions are presented in Section VI.

II. LONG-HAUL CONNECTION SWITCHING

We consider scenarios consisting of two sites connected over a long-haul connection such as transcontinental fiber routes or satellite connections as shown in Figure 1(a). The sites house multiple workstations on which server and client applications are executed, which form the client-server application pairs over the long-haul connection as shown in Figure 1(b). The client-server application performance depends on the quality of the connection specified by parameters such as latency, loss rate, and jitter. These connection parameters may degrade due to external factors such as equipment failures, fiber cuts and weather events. Such factors will be reflected in the degradation in client-server performance, which may be detected by the performance monitoring software implemented at application-level, for example, using Linux scripts. To protect against such factors, a parallel standby path is provisioned that can be switched-over to when performance degradations are detected. The border switches or routers at the sites are connected to both the primary long-haul connection that carries the traffic, and the stand-by connection whose traffic can be activated as needed. In our case, these connections are implemented as layer-2 VLANS at the border switches, which can be modified to implement the fail-over. All traffic between the sites is carried by the single long-haul connection, including client-server communications and other traffic needed for coordinating network operations; in particular, it is not cost-effective to provision a separate "control" connection for supporting the network configuration operations unlike in other cases, such as in UltraScienceNet [11] a decade ago and more recently in SDN based solutions.

Application codes on host systems continually monitor the client-server performance, such as iperf for TCP throughput and UDP loss rate. Under path degradations, these parameters would be out of normal range, and such events are detected

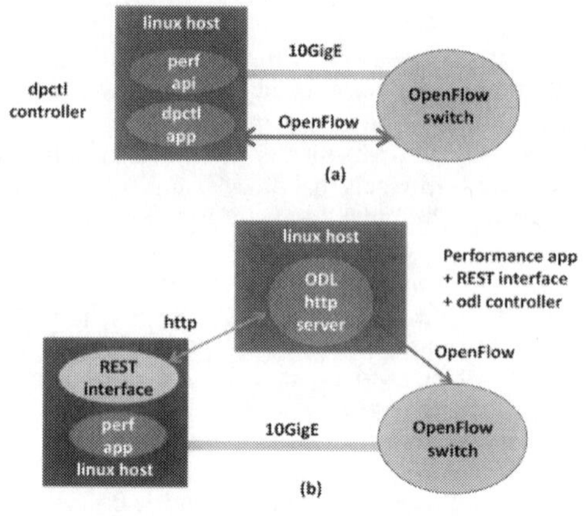

Figure 2. Configurations of dpctl and ODL controllers.

and alerts are sent to network operations. Typically, human operators receiving the alerts modify the VLANS on border switches to implement path switching, for example, by invoking CLI or TL1 or curl scripts, or manually making the changes through CLI or web interfaces. Due to different organizational zones at the sites and the long separation between them, it is not practical for a single network operations center to handle connection switching at both sites, particularly, if the same "degraded" connection is used for these communications as well. Instead, such tasks are typically coordinated between the two site organizations using other means such as telephone calls. Due to the multi-step process needed here, the fail-over operation can take anywhere between few minutes to hours. Thus, it is highly desirable to automate the entire fail-over work flow that includes application-level monitoring and network-level switching as described in Introduction section.

III. COORDINATED SDN CONTROLLERS

For the long-haul scenarios considered here, a single controller solution is not effective, although such approaches with stable control-plane connections have been effective in path/flow switching over local area networks using OpenFlow [12], [13] and cross-country networks using customized methods [11], [14]. Since the controller has to be located at a site, when primary connection degrades, it may not be able to communicate effectively with the remote site. Our approach is to utilize two controllers, one at each site, which are "indirectly" coordinated based on the monitored application-level performance parameters. When path degradation is inferred by a host script, the controller at that site switches to the fail-over path by installing the appropriate flow entries on its border switch. If the primary path degrades, for example, resulting in increased latency or loss rate, its effect is typically detected at both hosts by the monitors, and both border switches fail-over to the standby path approximately at the same time. If border switch at one site fails-over first, the connection loss will be detected at the other site which in turn triggers the fail-over at the second site. Also, one-way failures lead to path switching at one site first, which will be seen as a connection loss at the other site, thereby leading to path switching at that site as well. Due to recent developments in SDN technologies, both in open software [3], [4], [15] and specific vendor implementations [16], [17], there are many different ways such a solution can be implemented. We restrict here to OpenFlow solutions based on open standards and software [12].

A. dpctl Method

As a part of OpenFlow implementation, some vendors support dpctl API which enables hosts to communicate with switches to query the status of flows, insert new flows and delete existing flows. It has been a very useful tool primarily for diagnosing flow implementations by using simple host scripts; however, some vendors such as Cisco do not provide dpctl support. We utilize dpctl API in a light-weight host script that constantly monitors the connection rtt and detects when it crosses a threshold and invokes dpctl to implement the fail-over as shown in Figure 2(a). The OpenFlow entries for switching to the standby path are communicated to the switch upon the detection of connection degradation. This script consists of under one hundred lines of code and is flexible in that the current connection monitoring module can be replaced by another one such as TCP throughput monitor using iperf. Compared to methods that use separate OpenFlow controllers, this method compresses both performance monitoring and controller modules into one script, and thereby avoids the northbound interface altogether; for ease of reference, we refer to this host code as the *dpctl controller*. This small footprint of the code makes is easier to analyze both from performance and security perspectives. Also, the executional path of this code is very simple since it involves application monitoring directly followed by communications with the switch; in particular, this method does not require a separate controller that is constantly running at the end sites.

B. OpenDaylight Method

We now present a method that utilizes two ODL Hydrogen controllers and REST interfaces to implement fail-over functionality using OpenFlow flows as shown in Figure 2(b). ODL is an open source controller [6] that communicates with OpenFlow switches [3], and is used to query, install and delete flow entries on them using its southbound interface. The applications communicate with ODL controller via the northbound interface to query, install and delete flows. ODL software in our case runs on linux workstations called the controller workstations, and the application monitoring codes can be executed on the same workstation in the *local* mode or can be executed on a different workstation in the *remote* mode.

The same performance monitoring codes of the dpctl method above are used in this case to detect path degradations but are enhanced to invoke python code to communicate new flows for switching paths to ODL controllers via REST interfaces; the content of these flow entries are identical to previous case. Thus, both the software and executional paths of this method are much more complicated compared to previous case, and also the ODL controllers are required to run constantly on the servers at end sites. Also, this Hydrogen

[3]ODL provides interfaces to much broader classes of switches and applications, but we limit our discussions to the functionalities that are directly related to long-haul scenarios described in Section II.

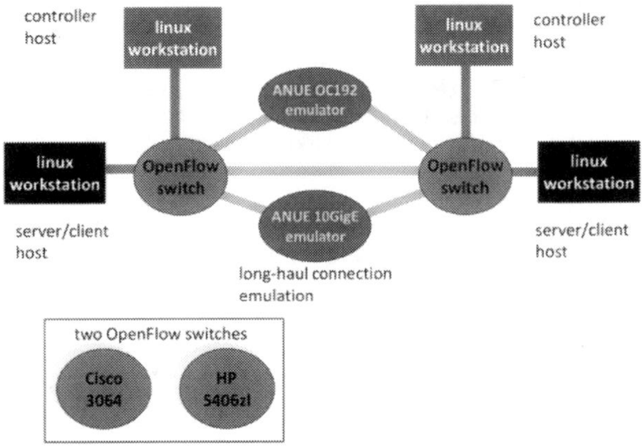

Figure 3. Testbed of two sites connected over local fiber and emulated connections.

ODL code[4] is much more complex to analyze since it involves not only the REST scripts but also the ODL stack which by itself is a fairly complex software. The execution path is more complex since it involves additional communication over both northbound and southbound interfaces of ODL controllers.

The dpctl and ODL methods represent two different fail-over solutions, and the choice between them depends on their recovery performance in response to triggers. In the next section, we describe a set of experiments using HP and Cisco switches that highlight the performances of controllers and switches. However, a direct comparison of the measurements between various configurations is complicated by their statistical variations, which we account for using the impulse response method described in Section V.

IV. Experimental Results

In this section, we first describe the details of testbed and tests using dpctl and ODL controllers, and then describe the experimental results.

A. Emulation Testbed

The experimental testbed consists of two site LANs each consisting of multiple hosts connected via 10GigE NICs to the site's border switch. The border switches are connected to each other via local fiber connection of few meters in length and ANUE devices that emulate long-haul connections in hardware, as shown in Figure 3. Tests are performed in configurations that use pairs of HP 5064zl and Cisco 3064 devices as border switches. These switches are OpenFlow-enabled but only HP switches support dpctl interface. We only utilize OC192 ANUE device in our tests, which can emulate rtts in the range of [0-800] milliseconds with a peak capacity of 9.6 Gbps. These devices are utilized primarily to emulate the latencies of long-haul connections, both transcontinental

[4]Later ODL releases starting with Helium, including Lithium and Beryllium, support more agile code builds wherein only the needed service modules are loaded (as karaf features [6]), thereby significantly reducing its size. However the execution path remains the same as in Hydrogen.

fiber and satellite connections, to highlight the overall recovery dynamics. However, no efforts are made to highlight their capacity differences, for example, by limiting the latter to typical satellite connection capacities, which could have resulted in somewhat muted dynamics. The conversion between 10GigE LAN packets from the border switches and long-haul OC192 ANUE packets is implemented using a Force10 E300 switch, which provides 10GigE LAN-PHY and WAN-PHY conversion as shown in Figure 4.

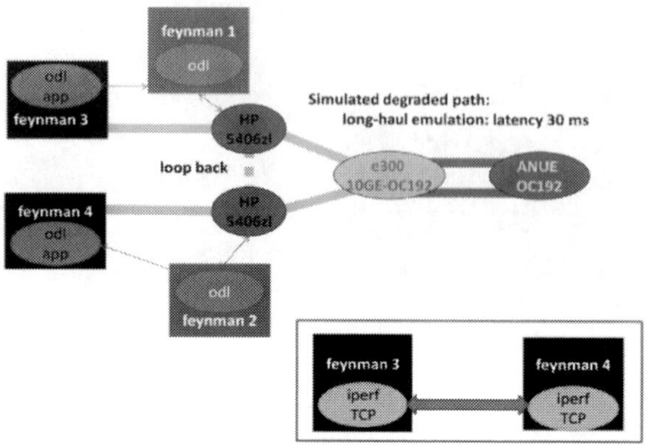

(a) Configurations C-E: remote

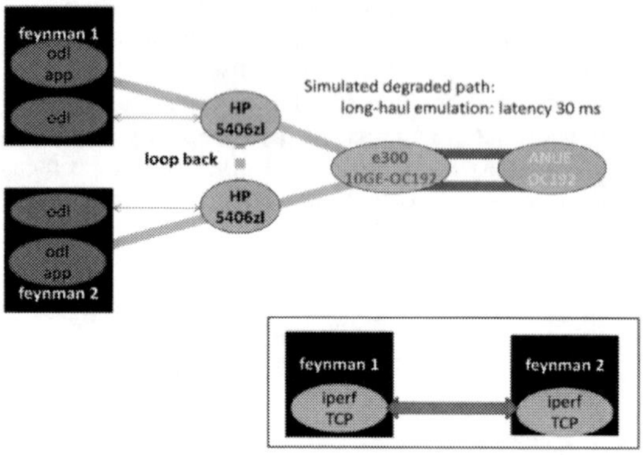

(b) Configuration B: local

Figure 4. Remote and local modes of ODL controller configurations.

Two classes of Linux hosts are connected to the border switches. The controller hosts (feynman1 and feynman2) are utilized to run ODL controllers, and client and server hosts (feynman3 and feynman4) are used to execute monitoring and trigger codes along with client server codes, for example iperf clients and servers. Five different configurations are employed in the tests as shown in Table I. The *dpctl* tests utilize only the client and server hosts to execute both monitoring and switching codes. In these tests, dpctl is used to communicate flow modification messages between the hosts and HP 5064zl switches, and Cisco switches are not used. Configuration A corresponds to these tests with the monitoring and dpctl

Table I. Five test configurations with two controllers, two connection degradation methods and two switch vendors.

test configuration	controller method	path degradation	switch vendor
A	dpctl	path switch	HP
B	ODL local	path swith	HP
C	ODL remote	path switch	HP
D	ODL remote	rtt extension	HP
E	ODL remote	rtt extension	Cisco

scripts running on server/client hosts, and it uses HP border switches. For *ODL remote mode* tests, the monitoring codes on client/server hosts utilize REST interface to communicate flow message needed for fail-over; both HP and Cisco switches are used in these tests. Configurations C-E implement these tests, which employ ODL controllers running on controller hosts and monitoring scripts running on server/client hosts. In *ODL local mode* tests, the monitoring and client/server codes are executed directly on control hosts. Configuration B implements these tests, and it is identical to Configuration C except its scripts are executed on controller hosts. The measurements in Configurations B and C are quite similar, and hence we mostly present results of the latter.

In the experiments, connection degradation events are implemented by external codes using two different methods:

(a) *Path switching using dpctl:* The current physical path with a smaller rtt is switched to a longer emulated path, whose rtt is sufficient to trigger the fail-over. This switching is accomplished by using dpctl or ODL by installing OpenFlow entries on the border switches to divert the flow from the current path to longer path. The packets enroute on the current path will be simply be dropped and as a result the short-term TCP throughput becomes zero. After the fail-over, the path is switched back to the original path, and the TCP flow recovers gradually back to previous levels.

(b) *RTT extension using curl scripts:* The current connection's rtt is increased by changing the setting on ANUE device to a value above the threshold to trigger the fail-over. This is accomplished using http interface either manually or using curl scripts. Unlike the previous case, the packets enroute on the current path are not dropped but are delayed; thus, the instantaneous TCP throughput does not always become zero but is reduced significantly. After the fail-over, the original rtt is restored, and TCP throughput recovers gradually to previous levels.

The first degradation method using dpctl to switch the paths is only implemented for configurations with HP border switches in Configurations A - C. The second method is used for both HP and Cisco system in Configurations D and E, and since the curl scripts are used here to change delay settings on ANUE devices, and border switches are not accessed.

B. Controller Performance

TCP throughput measurements across the long-haul connection are constantly monitored using iperf. The default CUBIC congestion control module [18] for Linux hosts is used in all tests. The rtt between end hosts is also constantly monitored using ping, and path switching is triggered when it crosses a set threshold; this module can be replaced by a more general application-based trigger module, for example, to detect when throughput falls below or jitter exceeds thresholds. The path degradations are implemented as periodic impulses and the responses are assessed using the recovery profiles of TCP throughput captured at one second intervals. Also, the ANUE dynamics in extending the rtt affect the TCP throughput recovery, and we obtain additional baseline measurements by utilizing a direct fiber connection that avoids packets being routed through ANUE devices. Thus, TCP throughout traces in our tests capture the performances of: (a) controllers, namely, dpctl and ODL, in responding to fail-over triggers from monitoring codes, and in modifying the flow entries on switches, typically by deleting the current flows and inserting the ones for standby path, and (b) border switches in modifying the flows entries in response to controller's messages and re-routing the packets as per new flow entries.

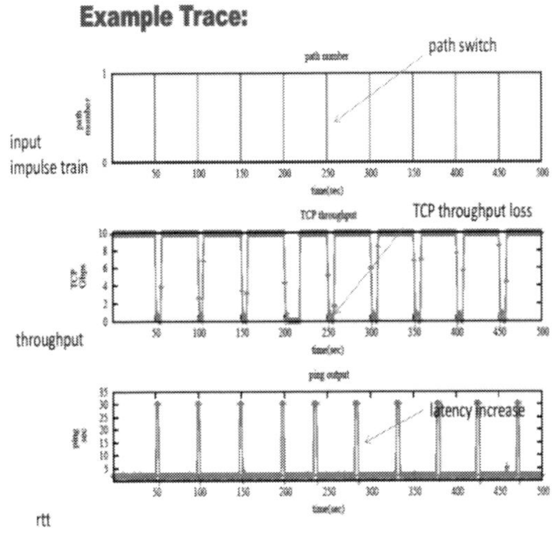

Figure 5. Trace of impulse response of TCP throughput for dpctl method with local primary path and path switching degradation.

An example TCP throughput trace of a test run in Configuration A is shown in Figure 5 for the dpctl method, with fiber connection as the primary path, and using the path switching degradation method. The connection rtt is degraded at the periodicity of 50 seconds by externally switching to the longer ANUE path, and the change is detected as shown in the bottom plot, which in turn triggers the fail-over. TCP throughput parameters on the hosts are tuned to achieve 10Gbps for the default rtt, and it degrades once the connection rtt is increased to 30ms after path switching. Upon the detection of increased rtt, the default path is restored, which in turn restores TCP throughput to the original value as shown in the middle plot of Figure 5. Note that throughput trace shows significant variations during the recovery periods following the fail-over, even in this simplest among the test configurations.

The restoration profiles of TCP throughput in these tests reflect the detection of connection degradation and fail-over, followed by the recovery response of the non-linear dynamics of CUBIC congestion control mechanism. Three different TCP recovery profiles from the tests are shown in Figure 6: (a)

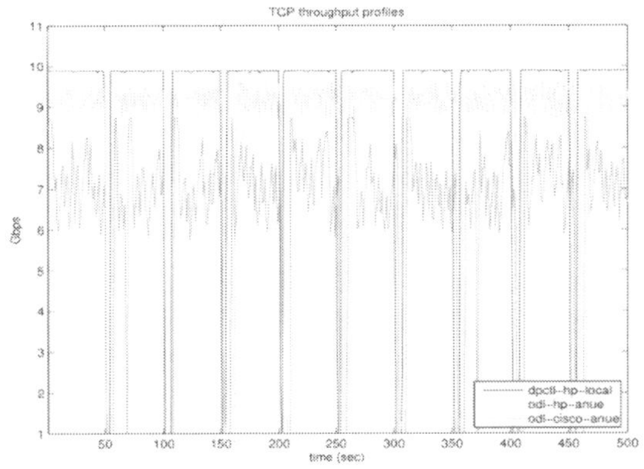

Figure 6. TCP throughput for dpctl method for configuration A and ODL methods for configuration D and E.

Configuration A: dpctl method using HP switches with connection degradation by path switching, (b) *Configuration D*: ODL method using HP switches with connection degradation by rtt extension, and (c) *Configuration E*: ODL method using Cisco switches with connection degradation by rtt extension. As seen in these plots, TCP response dynamics contain significant variations for different degradation events of the same configuration as well as between different configurations.

The individual TCP throughput recovery responses to single path degradation events reveal more details of the difference between configurations as shown in Figure 7. The delayed response of ODL method compared to dpctl method can be seen in Figure 7(a) for Configurations A and B. Since the packets in transit during the switching are simply lost during path switching, the instantaneous TCP throughput rapidly drops to zero for Configuration A. On the other hand, some of the packets in transit when rtt is extended are delivered, and as a result TCP throughput may be non-zero in some cases, as shown in Figure 7(b). Another aspect is that, TCP throughput recovers to 10Gbps when the direct fiber connection is used between the switches, but only peaks around 9 Gbps when packets are sent via ANUE connection with zero delay setting as shown in Figure 7(b). Also, the recovery profiles are different between HP and Cisco switches in otherwise identical Configurations E and F as shown in Figure 7(c). Thus, TCP dynamics depend both on the controller primarily in terms of recovery times, and on the switches in terms of the peak throughput achieved and its temporal stability.

We now consider more details of the dpctl and ODL methods using HP switches with path switching degradation shown in Figure 7(a) with the primary fiber connection. Here, the TCP throughput becomes zero and rtt crosses the threshold immediately following the path switching degradation, and both controllers respond to the fail-over triggers and switch the path back to original fiber connection. Since these configurations are identical except the controllers, the recovery time of ODL method is a few seconds slower than dpctl method. However, the complex dynamics and statistical variations of TCP profiles make it harder to draw general conclusions about their comparative performance based on such single degradation events.

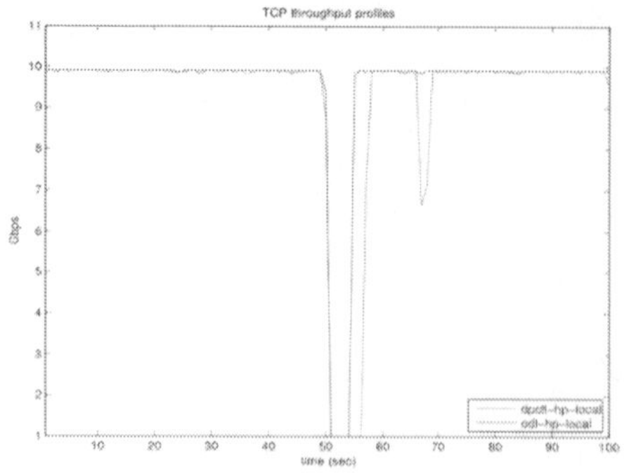

(a) Configurations A and B

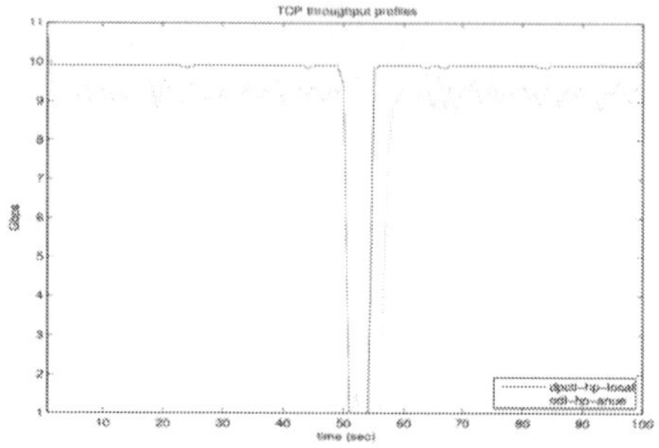

(b) Configurations A and D

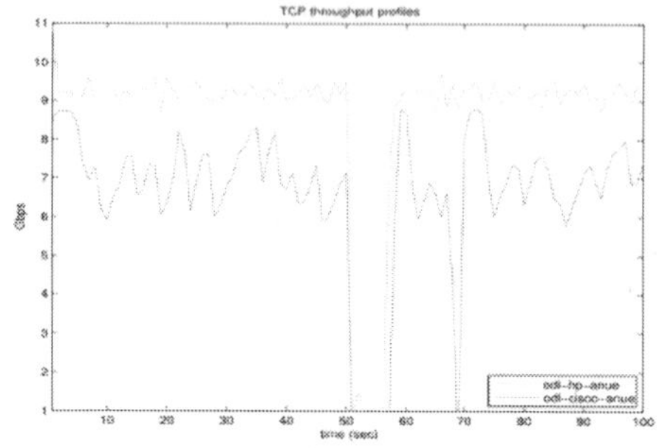

(c) Configurations D and E

Figure 7. Trace of impulse response of TCP throughput for dpctl method with local primary path and path switching degradation.

C. Switch Performance

TCP performance is effected by the path traversed by the packets between the border switches, in addition to its dependence on dpctl and ODL methods as described in the previous section (Figure 7(b)), thereby indicating the effects of the connection modality on client-server performance. In configurations A and B, the primary connection is few meters of fiber between the switches, and TCP throughput is restored to around 10 Gbps after the fail-over as shown in Figure 7(a). In Configurations D and E, the packets are sent through the emulated connection, which consists of long-haul Force10 E300 switch and OC192 ANUE emulator with the peak capacity of 9.6 Gbps. In this case, both peak value and the dynamics of TCP throughput are effected as shown in Figure 7(b); as expected, the peak is below 9.6 Gbps but there are significant variations in the throughput. Furthermore, the connection modality effects HP and Cisco switches differently as shown in Figure 7(c) in that the latter reached somewhat lower peak throughput and exhibited larger fluctuations [5].

Although we focussed on TCP throughput measurements in this section, the overall approach is applicable to other performance parameters such as latency in reporting sensor measurements, response times of remote control operations, and loss of quality in voice and video transmissions. In general, we consider that the chosen performance parameter degrades when the current connection properties degrade, and it recovers when stand-by connection is restored. This overall characterization is used to develop a method to systematically compare the measurements under different configurations.

V. Impulse Response Method

We present the *impulse response method* in this section that captures the overall recovery response by "aggregating" generic (scalar) performance measurements (such as TCP throughput as in previous section) collected in response to periodic connection degradations. It enables us to objectively compare the performances of different methods and devices by extracting the overall trends from measurement traces of multiple fail-over events. While our discussion is centered around TCP measurements described in the previous section, the overall approach is more generically applicable for comparing configurations with different controllers and switches, and it is particularly useful when the recovery throughput traces are not amenable to simple, direct comparisons.

A. Response Regression Function

A configuration X that implements the fail-over is specified by its SDN controller and switches that implement the fail-over, and also the monitoring and detection modules that trigger it. Let $\delta(t - iT), i = 0, 1, \ldots, n$ denote the input impulse train that degrades the connection at times $iT + T_D$, where t represents time, T is the period between degradations and $T_D < T$ is the time of degradation event within the period. Let $\mathbf{T}^X(t)$ denote the parameter of interest at time t, such as TCP throughput, as shown in Figure 6 for configurations X=A,D,E. Let $R^X(t) = \mathbf{B} - \mathbf{T}^X(t)$ denote the response that captures the "unrealized" or "unused" portion of the peak performance level $\mathbf{B}$. For example, over a connection with capacity $\mathbf{B}$ it is the residual bandwidth at time t above TCP throughput $\mathbf{T}^X(t)$; it is close to zero when throughput is close to the peak and it is close to $\mathbf{B}$ during the fail-over period when throughput is close to zero. We define the *impulse response function* $R^X(t)$ such that

$$R_i^X(t) = R^X(t - iT), t \in [0, T)$$

is the response to ith degradation event $\delta(t - iT)$, for $i = 0, 1, \ldots, n$. An ideal impulse response function is also an

[5]No connection-specific TCP optimizations are performed in these tests, and it is quite possible that different optimizations may be needed to achieve comparable throughput in these two configurations.

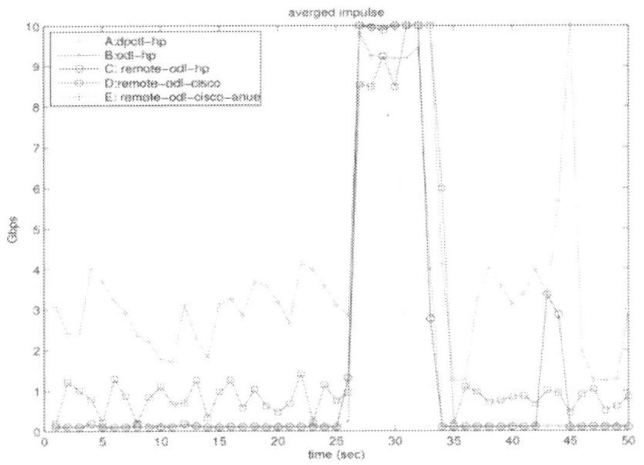

Figure 8. Examples of impulse response functions for Configurations A-E for a single path degradation.

impulse train that matches the input, wherein each impulse represents the instantaneous degradation detection, fail-over and complete recovery the parameter. But in practice, each $R_i^X(t)$ is a "flattened" impulse function whose shape is indicative of the effectiveness of the fail-over. In particular, its leading edge represents the effect of degradation and its trailing edge represents the recovery, and the narrower this function is the quicker is the recovery. Examples of $R_1^X(.)$ are shown Figure 8 for configurations A-E; these TCP measurements show significant temporal variations that persist across the different degradation events, which make it difficult to objectively compare these single-event time plots. In general, such variations are to be expected in other performance parameters such as latency and response time associated with sensor and control applications. Nevertheless, certain general trends seem apparent such as the faster TCP response of the dpctl method compared to the ODL method.

We define the *response regression* of configuration X as

$$\bar{R}^X(t) = E\left[R_i^X(t)\right] = \int R_i^X(t) d\mathbf{P}_{R_i^X(t)},$$

for $t \in [0,)$, where the underlying distribution $\mathbf{P}_{R_i^X(t)}$ is quite complex in general since it depends on the dynamics of controllers, switches, end hosts, application stack and monitoring and detection modules that constitute X. It exhibits an overall decreasing profile for $t \in [0, T_D + T_I]$ followed by an increasing profile for $t \in (T_D + T_I, T]$, where T_I is the time needed for the application to react to connection degradation. After the fail-over, TCP measurements exhibit an overall increasing throughput until it reaches its peak as it recovers after becoming nearly zero following the degradation. We consider that a similar overall behavior is exhibited by the general performance parameters of interest.

We define the *response mean* $\hat{R}_i(t)$ of $\bar{R}_i(t)$ using the discrete measurements collected at times $t = j\delta$, $j = 0, 1, ..., T/\delta$, as

$$\hat{R}^X(j\delta) = \frac{1}{n}\sum_{i=1}^{n}\left(R_i^X(j\delta)\right)$$

which captures the average profile. Examples of $\hat{R}_i^X(.)$ for TCP throughput are shown Figure 9 for different configurations

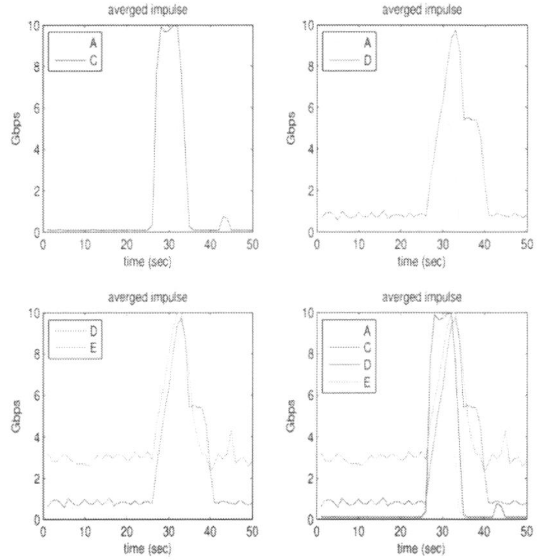

Figure 9. Impulse response regressions for $n = 10$ and $T = 50$ sec: (a) top-left: A and C, (b) top-right: A and D, (c) bottom-left: D and E , and (d) bottom-right: all.

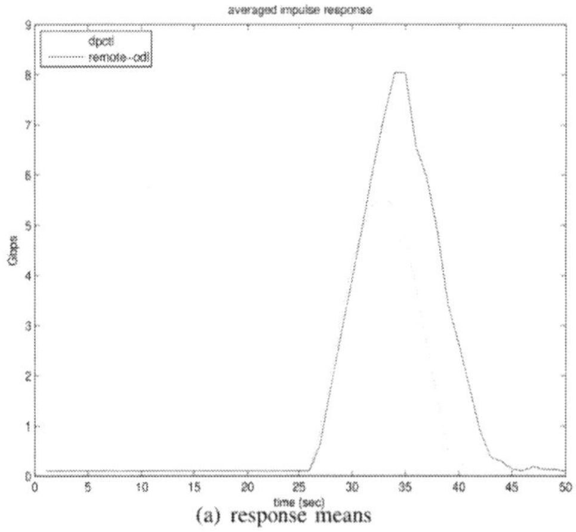

(a) response means

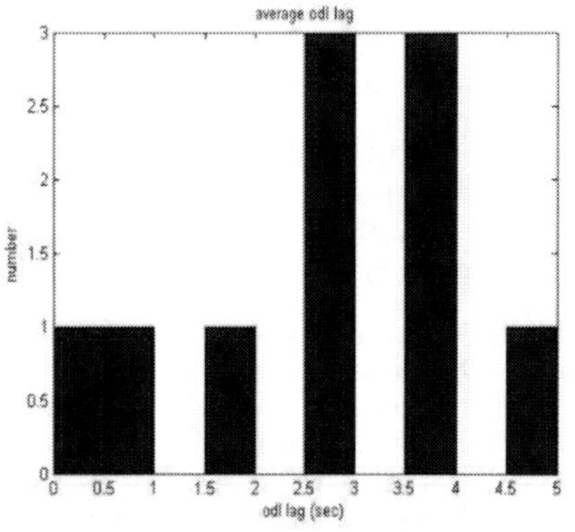

(b) delay histogram

Figure 10. Comparison of response means of dpctl (configuration A) and ODL (configuration C) methods using 100 path degradations with $T = 50$ seconds.

based on 10 path degradations with $T = 50$ seconds between them, which show the following general trends.

- The dpctl method responds seconds faster than ODL method as indicated by its sharper shape although their leading edges are aligned as shown in Figure 9(a).
- The connection degradation implemented by the rtt extension has a delayed effect on reducing the throughput compared to the path switching degradation method as indicated by its delayed leading edge in Figure 9(b).
- The dynamic response of regression profiles of HP 5604zl and Cisco 3064 switches are qualitatively quite similar as shown in Figure 9(c), but the latter achieved somewhat lower peak throughput overall; note that the larger throughput variations at individual switching events of the latter case are "averaged" in these plots.

In view of the faster response of dpctl method, we collected additional measurements in configurations A and C using 100 path degradations, and the resultant response means are somewhat smoother compared to 10 degradations as shown in Figure 10 (a) for both dpctl and ODL methods. Furthermore, the response mean of ODL method remained consistent with more measurements, and a histogram of the relative delays of ODL method compared to dpctl method is plotted in Figure 10(b), and they are in the range of 2-3 seconds in majority of cases. These measurements clearly show the faster response of the dpctl method for these scenarios. Such performance is expected because of its much simpler code and execution path, both in terms of computation and communication.

In general, dpctl is primarily intended for diagnostic purposes and has not been used for control, and as a result its performance for the latter has not been investigated much, in particular, its scalability with respect to the number of flow entries. We tested the effectiveness of dpctl method with respect to the number of flow entries used for path switching; in above tests, for each path fail-over, two flow entries are used by both dpctl and ODL methods on each border switch. We increased the number of additional flow entries to 10 and 100 for each fail-over in dpctl method, and the resultant TCP throughput measurements are shown in Figure 11(a), along with those of the original ODL method. The impact of additional flow entries in dpctl method is not apparent from a visual inspection of these plots, primarily due to TCP throughput variations. The response means for these cases are plotted in Figure 11(b) which show no significant differences due to the additional flow entries. But, they show that the response of dpctl method is still 2-3 seconds faster than ODL method on average even with the additional flow entries.

From an engineering perspective, the above performance comparisons based on the measurements seem intuitively justified, but the soundness of such conclusions is not that apparent. In the next section, we provide a statistical justification for the use of response mean $\hat{R}(t)$ as an estimate of the response regression $\bar{R}(t)$ by exploiting the underlying monotonic properties of the performance parameter, namely its degradation followed by recovery, as illustrated by TCP throughput measurements. Due to the somewhat technical nature of the derivations, these details are relegated to separate next section.

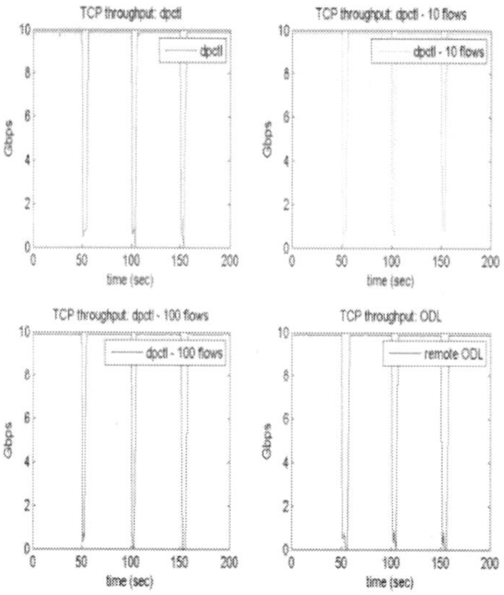

(a) TCP traces

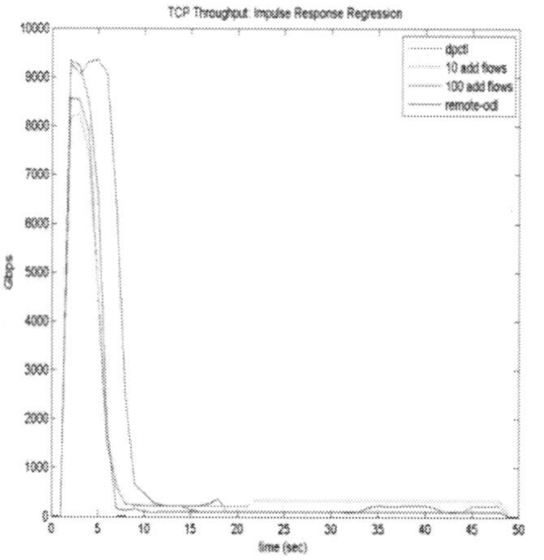

(b) response means

Figure 11. Comparison of response means of dpctl (configuration A) with 10 and 100 additional flows and original ODL (configuration C) methods using 100 path degradations with $T = 50$ seconds.

B. Finite Sample Statistical Analysis

A generic empirical estimate $\tilde{R}^X(t)$ of $\bar{R}(t)$ based on discrete measurements collected at times $t = j\delta$, $j = 0, 1, ..., T/\delta$, is given by

$$\tilde{R}^X(j\delta) = \frac{1}{n}\sum_{i=1}^{n}\left[g\left(R_i^X(j\delta)\right)\right]$$

for an estimator function g. We consider that the function class $\mathcal{M}$ of $\tilde{R}^X(.)$ consists of unimodal functions, each of which consists of degradation and recovery parts when viewed as a function of time. For ease of notation, we also denote $\tilde{R}^X(.)$ by f in this section such that it is composed of a degradation function f_D and a recovery function f_R as follows:

$$f(R_i(t)) = \begin{cases} f_D(R_i(t)) & \text{if } t \in [0, T_D + T_I] \\ f_R(R_i(t)) & \text{if } t \in (T_D + T_I, T] \end{cases} \quad (1)$$

where $f_D \in \mathcal{M}_D$ and $f_R \in \mathcal{M}_R$ correspond to the leading and trailing edges of the response regression. The *expected error* $I(f)$ of the estimator f is given by

$$\begin{aligned} I(f) &= \int [f(t) - R_i^X(t)]^2 d\mathbf{P}_{R_i^X(t),t} \\ &= \int_{[0,T_D+T_I]} [f_D(t) - R_i^X(t)]^2 d\mathbf{P}_{R_i^X(t),t} \\ &\quad + \int_{(T_D+T_I,T]} [f_D(t) - R_i^X(t)]^2 d\mathbf{P}_{R_i^X(t),t} \\ &= I_D(f_D) + I_R(f_R). \end{aligned}$$

The *best expected estimator* $f^* = (f_D^*, f_R^*) \in \mathcal{M}$ minimizes the expected error $I(.)$, that is

$$I(f^*) = \min_{f \in \mathcal{M}} I(f).$$

The *empirical error* of an estimator f is given by

$$\hat{I}(f) = \frac{\delta}{Tn} \sum_{i=1}^{n} \sum_{j=1}^{T/\delta} \left[f(j\delta) - \left(R_i^X(j\delta)\right)\right]^2.$$

The *best empirical estimator* $\hat{f} = (\hat{f}_D, \hat{f}_R) \in \mathcal{M}$ minimizes the empirical error $\hat{I}(.)$, that is,

$$\hat{I}(\hat{f}) = \min_{f \in \mathcal{M}} \hat{I}(f).$$

Since the response mean $\hat{R}(t)$ is the mean at each observation time $j\delta$, it achieves zero mean error, which in turn leads to zero empirical error, that is, $\hat{I}\left(\hat{R}\right) = 0$; thus, it is a best empirical estimator. By ignoring the minor variations for the smaller values of n, we assume that $\hat{R}$ is composed of a non-decreasing function $\hat{R}_D$ followed by a non-increasing function $\hat{R}_R$ that correspond to decreasing and increasing parts of the performance parameter (such as TCP throughput), respectively. This assumption is valid for the response means of dpctl and ODL methods in Configurations A and C, respectively, shown in Figure 10. In both cases, the response mean is composed of an increasing part followed by a decreasing part once the small variations in the tail of ODL method are ignored.

We will now show that Vapnik-Chervonenkis theory [19] guarantees that the response mean $\hat{R}(t)$ is a good approximation of the response regression $\bar{R}(t)$, and furthermore its performance improves with more measurements from connection degradation events. Such performance guarantee is a direct consequence of the monotone nature of the underlying f_D and f_R functions. Furthermore, this performance guarantee is distribution-free, that is, independent of the underlying joint distributions of controllers and switches, and is valid under very general conditions [10] on the variations of performance parameter (such as TCP throughput) measurements. We note that the underlying distributions could be quite complicated and generally unknown, since they depend on complex interactions between controller software and switches, which are individually complex.

We now provide a complete proof of the above performance result which was briefly outlined in [1]. Let $\hat{R} = \left(\hat{R}_D, \hat{R}_R\right)$ such that the estimator is decomposed into two monotone parts, namely non-decreasing $\hat{R}_D$ and non-increasing $\hat{R}_R$ such that

$$\hat{I}(\hat{R}) = \hat{I}_D(\hat{R}_D) + \hat{I}_R(\hat{R}_R).$$

We now apply Vapnik-Chervonenkis theory [10] in the following to show that the error of estimator $\hat{R}$, given by $I\left(\hat{R}\right)$, is within ϵ of the optimal error $I(f^*)$ with a probability that improves with the number of observations n. More precisely, we show that the probability

$$\mathbf{P}\left\{I\left(\hat{R}\right) - I(f^*) > \epsilon\right\}$$

decreases with n independent of other factors related to controller and switch distributions. We will establish this result in the following three basic steps. In the first step, we have the basic inequality

$$\begin{aligned} &\mathbf{P}\left\{I\left(\hat{R}\right) - I(f^*) > \epsilon\right\} \\ &\quad\leq \mathbf{P}\left\{I\left(\hat{R}_D\right) - I(f_D^*) > \epsilon/2\right\} \\ &\qquad + \mathbf{P}\left\{I\left(\hat{R}_R\right) - I(f_R^*) > \epsilon/2\right\}, \end{aligned}$$

which follows from the observation that the negation of the condition in either right term implies the negation of the condition in left term. Then, by applying the uniform convergence property of the expected and empirical errors over function classes $\mathcal{M}_D$ and $\mathcal{M}_R$ corresponding to the first and second terms on the right hand side [10], respectively, we obtain

$$\begin{aligned} &\mathbf{P}\left\{I\left(\hat{R}\right) - I(f^*) > \epsilon\right\} \\ &\quad\leq \mathbf{P}\left\{\max_{h \in \mathcal{M}_D} |I_D(h) - \hat{I}_D(h)| > \epsilon/4\right\} \\ &\qquad + \mathbf{P}\left\{\max_{h \in \mathcal{M}_R} |I_R(h) - \hat{I}_R(h)| > \epsilon/4\right\}. \end{aligned}$$

Then, by applying the uniform bound ([20], p. 143) provided by Vapnik-Chervonenkis theory to both right hand side terms, we obtain

$$\begin{aligned} &\mathbf{P}\left\{I\left(\hat{R}\right) - I(f^*) > \epsilon\right\} \\ &\quad\leq 16\mathcal{N}_\infty\left(\frac{\epsilon}{2\mathbf{B}}, \mathcal{M}_D\right) ne^{-\epsilon^2 n/(8\mathbf{B})^2} \\ &\qquad + 16\mathcal{N}_\infty\left(\frac{\epsilon}{2\mathbf{B}}, \mathcal{M}_R\right) ne^{-\epsilon^2 n/(8\mathbf{B})^2} \end{aligned}$$

where $\mathcal{N}_\infty(\epsilon, \mathcal{A})$ is the ϵ-cover size of function class $\mathcal{A}$ under L_∞ norm. Detailed properties of the ϵ-cover can be found in [20], and for our purpose, we note that the ϵ-cover size is a deterministic quantity that depends entirely on the function class. Consequently, the above probability bounds are distribution-free in that they are valid for any joint distribution of controllers and switches at the sites, since the ϵ-covers here depend entirely on the function classes $\mathcal{M}_D$ and $\mathcal{M}_R$.

Then, the monotonicity of functions in $\mathcal{M}_D$ and $\mathcal{M}_R$ establishes that their total variation is upper bounded by $\mathbf{B}$. This property in turn provides the following upper bound for the ϵ-cover sizes of both function classes [20]: for $\mathcal{A} = \mathcal{M}_D, \mathcal{M}_R$, we have

$$\mathcal{N}_\infty\left(\frac{\epsilon}{2\mathbf{B}},\mathcal{A}\right) < 2\left(\frac{4n}{\epsilon^2}\right)^{(1+2\mathbf{B}/\epsilon)\log_2(2\epsilon/\mathbf{B})}.$$

By using this bound, we obtain

$$\mathbf{P}\left\{I\left(\hat{R}_i\right) - I(f^*) > \epsilon\right\} < 64\left(\frac{4n}{\epsilon^2}\right)^{(1+2\mathbf{B}/\epsilon)\log_2(2\epsilon/\mathbf{B})} ne^{-\epsilon^2 n/(8\mathbf{B})^2}.$$

This bound provides qualitative insights into this approach when "sufficient" number of measurements are available. The exponential term on the right hand side decays faster in n than the growth in other terms, and hence for sufficiently large n it can be made smaller than a given probability α. Thus, the expected error $I(\hat{R})$ of the response mean used in the previous section is within ϵ of the optimal error $I(f^*)$ with a probability that increases with the number of observations, and is independent of the underlying distributions. An indirect evidence of this artifact is noticed in the increased stability of the response mean as we increase the number of connection degradation events from 10 to 100 in Figures 9(a) and 10, respectively.

The above probability estimates are not necessarily very tight in part due to the distribution-free nature of the performance guarantee. Nevertheless, this analysis provides a sound statistical basis for using the response mean $\hat{R}$ as an approximation to the underlying response regression $\bar{R}$ for comparing different controllers and configurations.

VI. CONCLUSIONS

We considered scenarios with two sites connected over a dedicated, long-haul connection, which must fail-over to a standby connection upon degradations that affect the host-to-host application performance. Current solutions require significant customizations due to the vendor-specific software of network devices and applications, which often have to be repeated with upgrades and changes. Our objective is to exploit the recent network virtualization technologies to develop faster and more flexible software fail-over solutions. The presence of a single long-haul connection and application-level triggers in these scenarios necessitate a solution that is different from usual single controller methods commonly used in many SDN solutions.

We first presented a light-weight method that utilizes host scripts to monitor the connection rtt and dpctl API to implement the fail-over. We then presented a second method using two OpenDaylight (ODL) controllers and REST interfaces. We performed experiments using a testbed consisting of HP and Cisco switches connected over long-haul connections emulated in hardware by ANUE devices. They show that both methods restore TCP throughput, but their comparison was complicated by the restoration dynamics of TCP throughput which contained significant statistical variations. To account for them, we developed the impulse-response method based on statistical finite-sample theory to estimate the response regressions. It enabled us to compare these methods under different configurations, and conclude that on the average the dpctl method restores TCP throughput several seconds faster than the ODL method.

It would be of future interest to generalize the proposed methods to trigger fail-overs based on parameters of more complex client-server applications that utilize TCP for reliable delivery. The performance analysis of such methods will likely be much more complicated since the application dynamics may be modulated by the already complicated TCP recovery dynamics. Our test results are based on using CUBIC congestion control mechanism [18] which is the default on Linux systems, and it would of future interest to test the performance of other congestion control mechanisms, including high-performance versions for long-haul [21] and satellite [22] connections.

Currently there seems to be an explosive growth in the variety of SDN controllers including open source products, such as Helium, Lithium and Beryllium versions of ODL, Floodlight [23], ONOS [24] Ryu [25] and others, and also vendor specific products and adaptations. Furthermore, there is a wide variety of implementations of OpenFlow standards by switch vendors, ranging from building additional software layers on existing products to developing completely native implementations. It would be of future interest to develop general performance analysis methods that enable us to compare various SDN solutions (that comprise of controllers, switches, docker containers and application modules) for more complex scenarios such as data centers and cloud services distributed across wide-area networks. In particular, it would be of interest to develop methods that directly estimate the performance differences between different configurations from measurements using methods such as the differential regression method [26].

It would be of future interest to generalize the approach of this paper to develop a baseline test harness wherein a controller or a switch can be plugged into a known, fixed configuration. The general approach is to develop canonical configurations each with fixed components of the harness, such as application trigger modules, physical network connections and others. Then, impulses responses of different controllers, switches or other SDN components can be generated in these configurations, and they can be objectively compared to assess their relative performance.

ACKNOWLEDGMENTS

This work is funded by the High-Performance Networking Program and the Applied Mathematics Program, Office of Advanced Computing Research, U.S. Department of Energy, and by Extreme Scale Systems Center, sponsored by U. S. Department of Defense, and performed at Oak Ridge National Laboratory managed by UT-Battelle, LLC for U.S. Department of Energy under Contract No. DE-AC05-00OR22725.

REFERENCES

[1] N. S. V. Rao, "Performance comparison of SDN solutions for switching dedicated long-haul connections," in Proceedings of International Symposium on Advances in Software Defined Networking and Network Functions Virtualization, 2016.

[2] Y. D. Lin, D. Pitt, D. Hausheer, E. Johnson, and Y. B. Lin, "Software-defined networking: Standardization for cloud computing's second wave," IEEE Computer: Guest Editorial, November 2014, pp. 19–21.

[3] D. Kreutz, F. M. V. Ramos, P. E. Verissimo, C. E. Rothenberg, S. Azodolmolky, and S. Uhlig, "Software-defined networking: A comprehensive survey," Proceedings of the IEEE, vol. 103, no. 1, 2015, pp. 14–76.

[4] W. Xia, Y. Wen, C. H. Foh, D. Niyato, and H. Xie, "A survey on software-defined networking," IEEE Communication Surveys & Tutorials, vol. 17, no. 1, First Quarter 2015, pp. 27–51.

[5] T. D. Nadeau and K. Gray, Software Defined Networks. OReilly publishers, 2013.

[6] "Opendaylight." [Online]. Available: www.opendaylight.org

[7] Y. Srikant, The Mathematics of Internet Congestion Control. Birkhauser, Boston, 2004.

[8] W. R. Stevens, TCP/IP Illustrated. Addison Wesley, 1994, volumes 1-3.

[9] N. S. V. Rao, J. Gao, and L. O. Chua, "On dynamics of transport protocols in wide-area internet connections," in Complex Dynamics in Communication Networks, L. Kocarev and G. Vattay, Eds. Springer-Verlag Publishers, 2005.

[10] V. N. Vapnik, Statistical Learning Theory. New York: John-Wiley and Sons, 1998.

[11] N. S. V. Rao, W. R. Wing, , S. M. Carter, and Q. Wu, "Ultrascience net: Network testbed for large-scale science applications," IEEE Communications Magazine, vol. 43, no. 11, 2005, pp. s12–s17.

[12] J. Tourrilhes, P. Sharma, S. Banerjee, and J. Pettit, "SDN and OpenFlow evoltion: A standards perspecitve," IEEE Computer, November 2014, pp. 22–29.

[13] C. E. Rothenberg, R. Chua, J. Bailey, M. Winter, C. N. A. Correa, S. C. de Lucena, M. R. Salvador, and T. D. Nadeau, "When open source meets network control planes," IEEE Computer, November 2014, pp. 46–53.

[14] N. S. V. Rao, S. E. Hicks, S. W. Poole, and P. Newman, "Testbed and experiments for high-performance networking," in Tridentcom: International Conference on Testbeds and Research Infrastructures for the Development of Networks and Communities, 2010.

[15] "Open networks foundation." [Online]. Available: www.opennetworking.org

[16] "Software defined networks," cisco Systems. [Online]. Available: www.cisco.com

[17] "Software defined networking," hP. [Online]. Available: www.hp.com

[18] I. Rhee and L. Xu, "Cubic: A new tcp-friendly high-speed tcp variant," in Proceedings of the Third International Workshop on Protocols for Fast Long-Distance Networks, 2005.

[19] V. N. Vapnik, The Nature of Statistical Learning Theory. New York: Springer-Verlag, 1995.

[20] M. Anthony and P. L. Bartlett, Neural Network Learning: Theoretical Foundations. Cambridge University Press, 1999.

[21] T. Yee, D. Leith, and R. Shorten, "Experimental evaluation of high-speed congestion control protocols," Transactions on Networking, vol. 15, no. 5, 2007, pp. 1109–1122.

[22] J. Cloud, D. Leith, and M. Medard, "Network coded tcp (ctcp) performance over satellite networks," in SPACOMM 2014, 2014.

[23] "Project floodlight." [Online]. Available: www.projectfloodlight.org

[24] "Onos overview." [Online]. Available: www.onosproject.org

[25] "Build SDN agilely." [Online]. Available: osrg.github.io/ryu/index.html

[26] B. W. Settlemyer, N. S. V. Rao, S. W. Poole, S. W. Hodson, S. E. Hicks, and P. M. Newman, "Experimental analysis of 10gbps transfers over physical and emulated dedicated connections," in International Conference on Computing, Networking and Communications, 2012.

A Model for Managed Elements under Autonomic Cloud Computing Management

Rafael de Souza Mendes*, Rafael Brundo Uriarte†, Carlos Becker Westphall*
*Federal University of Santa Catarina, Florianópolis, Brazil
emails: rafael.mendes@posgrad.ufsc.br, westphal@inf.ufsc.br
†IMT School for Advanced Studies Lucca, Italy
email: rafael.uriarte@imtlucca.it

Abstract—**Due to the scale and dynamism of cloud computing, there is a need for new tools and techniques for its management. This paper proposes an approach to quantitative modelling of cloud components' behaviour, using double weighted Directed Acyclic Multigraphs (DAM) through the different abstraction levels of components. With this formalism, it is possible to analyse load propagation and its effects on the cloud elements from an Anything as a Service (xAAS) perspective. Such model enables the comparison, analysis and simulation of clouds, which assist the cloud management with the evaluation of modifications in the cloud structure and configuration. The existing solutions either do not have mathematical background, which hinders the comparison and production of structural variations in cloud models, or have the mathematical background, but are limited to a specific area (e.g., energy-efficiency), which does not provide support to the dynamic nature of clouds and to the different needs of the managers. In contrast, our model has a formal mathematical background and is generic. Furthermore, we present formalisms and algorithms that support the load propagation and the metrics of *services*, *systems*, *third-parties* providers and resources, such as: *computing*, *storage* and *networking*. To demonstrate the applicability of our solution, we have implemented a software framework for modelling *Infrastructure as a Service*, and conducted numerical experiments with hypothetical loads and behaviours.**

Keywords-Autonomic Cloud Computing; Cloud Computing Management; Simulation; Multigraph.

I. Introduction

The management of pooled resources according to high-level policies is a central requirement of the *as a service* model, as fostered by Cloud Computing (CC). The two major functions in CC management, planning and decision making, are challenging and are still an open issues in the field. In our previous work [1], we have presented a formal model, based on Direct Acyclic Multigraphs (DAM) [2], to model the cloud elements' behaviour regarding loads and evaluations. This formal model intents to reduce the gap between Autonomic CC [3], [4] management and well-established approaches in *decision theory* [5] and *managerial science* [6]. In this regard, was presented a *managed elements model* which make easier the inference of states, actions and consequences. These states, actions and consequences are the bases for planning models and the core of our proposal to fulfil the lack between CC and decision methods. This lack of formal models is highlighted by our previous efforts to develop methods for CC autonomic management: [4][7][8] and formalisms based on Service Level Agreement (SLA) [9].

Currently, the existing solutions which provide CC models can be classified into two main groups: general models, usually represented by simulators; and specific models, devised for a particular field (e.g., energy saving). The former lacks a mathematical formalisation that enables comparisons with variations on the modellings. The latter usually have the formal mathematical background but, since they are specific, they do not support reasoning on different management criteria and encompass only cloud elements related to the target area.

The main obstacle to establish formal general models is to express the conversion of loads from abstract elements (i.e., services or systems) to their concrete components (i.e., physical machines or third-party services). However, such model is mandatory to simulate and analyse qualitatively and quantitatively the CC elements' behaviour, which facilitate the evaluation of managerial decisions, especially if the model deals with abstraction and composition of these elements. The need of this model do express managerial knowledge increases as concept of CC moves away from the concept of infrastructure and Anything as a Service (xAAS) providers build high level cloud structures. To address this gap in the literature, we analyse the domain elements and characteristics to propose the *Cloud Computing Load Propagation* (C_2LP) graph-based model, which is a formal schema to express the *load flow* through the cloud computing components, and the load's impact on them. This schema is required because the system analysis is performed in design time and focus on the behaviour of data when passing through the cloud structures, however, the cloud management requires a view about the behaviour of the structures when the *loads* are passing through them, in runtime. Therefore, we define a *load* as the type and amount of effort to process services' requests in systems or resources.

For example, the (C_2LP) model enables the comparison of different cloud structures, the distinction of load bottlenecks, the expression of conversion of loads units (change in type) between elements, the quantitative analysis of the load propagation and the evaluation of the effects of processing a load on the cloud structure. In more general terms, such solution unifies heterogeneous abstraction levels of managed elements into a single model and can assist the decision-making tasks in processes, such as: *load balance*, *resource allocation*, *scale up/down* and *migrations*. Moreover, simulations performed using our model can be useful to predict the consequences of managerial decisions and external events, as well as the evolution of baseline behaviour, in several abstraction levels.

More specifically, we model the basic components of CC:

(i) *services*; (ii) *systems*; (iii) *resources*, in which systems are deployed, that can be *computing*, *storage* and *networking*; and (iv) *third-party* clouds that deploy services. This taxonomy permits putting together, based on Directed Acyclic Multigraphs, the CC elements on different abstraction levels. It enables the manager to access consolidated graph analytical tools to, e.g., measure the components interdependencies, which is used to improve the availability and resource allocation. In order to demonstrate the applicability and advantages of the C_2LPmodel, we present a use case where our model is used to compare and evaluate different managerial configurations over several quantitative behaviour in load propagation and evaluation.

This article is organised as follows. Section II discusses the existing cloud models, the works that inspired the definition of this model and the background information necessary for the appreciation of this work. In Section III, we present an overview of the model, formalise it, the propagation algorithm, and the evaluation process. Section IV describes the implementation and the analysis performed on a use case. Finally, in Section V, we discuss the limitations and the future directions for the research.

II. Related Work

This section presents the related works that propose models to describe and simulate clouds. We have analysed them from a *cloud provider management perspective*, considering their capacity to: *express general* cloud models, define *components* of the managed cloud instance; *compare* structures; *simulate* behaviours and provide *formal* specifications with mathematical background. Table I summarises model's comparisons and the discussion about the survey is presented as follows.

We grouped the proposals into two classes: *general* and *specific*. General models, such as CloudSim [10], GreenCloud [12], iCanCloud [14], EMUSIM [15] and MDCSim [17], are usually associated with simulators and used to evaluate several criteria at the same time. On the other hand, specific models are commonly associated with particular criterion evaluation, such as performance [18], security [20][21], accounting [22][23] or energy [24].

CloudSim [10] was originally built on top of GridSim [11] and focus on modelling data centres. Its framework is Java based and loads are modelled through a class called "*CloudLet*", or an extension of it. Depiste its popularity, CloudSim does not have a strong mathematical background. This lack of formalism hinders the investigation of data crossing between states and configuration parameter, which limit the exploration of the cloud behaviours. Furthermore, the core classes of CloudSim model data centre elements as: physical machines, virtual machines (VMs), networks and storages; and requires customisations to deal with more abstract elements, e.g., services. Finally, also the comparison of simulation structures is not straightforward with CloudSim.

Kliazovich et al. in [12] presented GreenCloud, an extension of the network simulator NS2 [13] that offers a fine-grained modelling of the energy consumed by the elements of the data centre, such as servers, switches, and links. GreenCloud is a programmatic framework based in C++ and TCL scripts that, despite having the statistic background of NS2, does not have itself an underlying mathematical formalism. It also focuses on the data centres view and need extensions to consider abstract elements as services and systems. Even though the authors provided a comparison between data centre architecture in [12], the model does not favor the comparison of simulation structures.

The simulator iCanCloud, presented in [14], is also a general data centre simulation tool. Based in C++, it has classes as "Hypervisor", "Scheduler" and "VM" in the core class structure, which demonstrates its high level of coupling with infrastructure. Although the authors proposed iCanCloud as "targeted to conduct large experiments", it does not offer native support to compare structural changes between simulations. As the other general simulator, iCanCloud lacks of mathematical formalisms.

EMUSIM [15] is an emulator and simulator that enables the extraction of information from the application behaviour – via emulation – and uses the information to generate a simulation model. The EMUSIM has been built on top of two frameworks: Automated Emulation Framework (AEF) [16] (an emulation testbed for grid applications) and CloudSim [10]. The objective of EMUSIM understand application' behaviour profiles, to produce more accurate simulations and, consequently, to adapt the Quality of Service (QoS) and the budget required for hosting the application in the Cloud. Although EMUSIM partially addresses the lack of capacity to model application of CloudSim, adding higher level modelling layer, it still lacks mathematical formalisms as well as the support to compare simulation structures.

Finally, MDCSim presents a multi-tier data centre simulation platform. However, this multi-tier modelling works with concrete elements, in resource level, as a *front-end tier/web server*, a *mid tier*/application server, and a *back-end tier*/database server. The MDCSim also works with some metrics in a higher abstraction level on specific Java elements as EJBs and Tomcat. This approach still lacks a representation for abstract elements, such as services and systems, where metrics and parameters are related to groups of elements (e.g., availability of a service depending on several elements).

Overall, works proposing general models are data centre focused and have evolved from Grid Computing, which may hinders their usage on service orchestration level and with third-parties cloud infrastructures, where data centre concepts are not applicable. Designers of autonomic management methods require the generation of cloud architectures and behaviours in a combinatorial fashion, in order to test plans, decisions and consequences on a wide number cloud architectures, features that not supported in these models.

In the second group of proposals, that is, frameworks devised for a specific area, in-depth analysis based on robust formalisms are usually provided, such as queue theory [24] [18], probability [20], fuzzy uncertainty [23] and heuristics [22]. However, their models do not fit well in integrated management methods that intend to find optimal configurations considering several criteria of distinct types. Moreover, specific optimisation models are usually sensible to structural changes, having no robustness to support the dynamic nature of the clouds.

Vilaplana et al. in [18] presented a queue theoretic modelling for performance optimisation for scale CC. The model has a strong mathematical background and is able to evaluate jobs and VM scheduling policies using simulations. Nevertheless, this optimisation is dependent on strong assumptions, i.e., that the back-end tier is modelled as an Open Jackson network [19]. The model is focused on evaluation and it is only partially capable of performing simulation. In fact, in the paper the authors employed CloudSim to implement the simulations used in the experiments.

In [20], Silva et al. proposed a model, based on equations to quantify the degree of *exposure* to risk, *deficiency* in risk modelling, and *impact* on an information asset. The model is used to evaluate cloud service providers and has a mathematical background. Although in our previous work [1] we have considered that the ability to generate hypothetical scenarios and evaluate them as a "simulation" feature, we reconsidered and redefined it as "feature not supported" since the model does not support runtime simulations.

Nesmachnow et al. in [22] introduced a broker that resells reserved VMs in IaaS providers as on-demand VMs for the customers. The authors presented a specific model to deal with the Virtual Machine Planning Problem, which was defined as an optimisation problem that maximises the profit of the broker. This problem is mathematically well formed as well as the model that supports the broker representation and the static components. We consider the experiments presented in the paper as simulations that were performed using real data gathered from public reports. However, we considered the simulation feature only as partially covered since the work does not enable runtime simulations.

Decision models for service admission are presented in [23], all with mathematical background and covering fuzzy uncertainty. The proposed models are specific for admission control and explicitly used to perform simulations. On the other hand, the *resource types* used to model different elements in the cloud (e.g., CPU, storage) do not cover the concept of "component". In fact, the model considers the existence of resources, from which services depend, but it just models classes of resources and their economical behaviour related to service admission. Thus, we consider the concept feature "component" only partially covered. Also, the models presented can be compared with respect to revenue and service request acceptance rate, but the general structure of the models lacks comparison parameters.

In [24] an energy-saving task scheduling algorithm is presented, based on the vacation queueing model. The modelling is specific for task scheduling and energy consumption optimisation. The work has a strong mathematical background which enables the comparison of results, but does not have ability to compare the model structure, resulting in a partial coverage for "comparison" criterion. The evaluation of energy consumption in nodes motivated us to define the feature "components" as covered. Finally, the criterion "simulation" was reviewed from the previous analysis in [1] and we consider the model's characterisation as *covered* since the authors used discrete event simulation tool in Matlab, that is equivalent to runtime-like simulators as the CloudSim.

The comparison between the related works is presented schematically in Table I, where: the column "Class" specifies if a work is general or specific; "Formalism" evaluates the mathematical background that supports the models; the column "Components" presents the capacity of a model to express cloud components; the ability to compare structures is depicted in the column "Comparison"; and, "Simulation" expresses the capacity to perform simulations using the models.

Considering the gap in the existing cloud modelling techniques, our proposal intents to model the load propagation and evaluation functions over a graph to obtain expressiveness, whilst keeping the mathematical background and components' details. We opt to model the "load flow" because it is one of the most important information for managerial decisions, such as: load balance, resource allocation, scale up/down and migrations.

TABLE I: COMPARISON BETWEEN RELATED MODELS. ■ REPRESENTS A FEATURE COVERED, □ A PARTIALLY COVERED ONE AND - WHEN THE FEATURE IS NOT SUPPORTED.

Model	Class	Formalism	Components	Comparison	Simulation
CloudSim [10]	General	-	■	-	■
GreenCloud [12]	General	-	■	-	■
iCanCloud [14]	General	-	■	-	■
EMUSIM [15]	General	-	■	-	■
MDCSim [17]	General	-	■	-	■
Chang[24]	Specific	■	□	■	■
Püschel [23]	Specific	■	□	□	■
Nesmachnow [22]	Specific	■	□	■	■
Silva [20]	Specific	■	□	□	-
Vilaplana [18]	Specific	■	□	■	□
C_2LP	General	■	■	■	□

III. MODELLING LOAD FLOW IN CLOUDS

In this section we discuss the main components of cloud structures and propose a formal model based on a directed acyclic multigraph to represent the load flow in clouds. In the Subsection III-A we present the concept of load and its importance for cloud management, as well as, its representation in different abstraction levels. Subsection III-B presents the structural model and its main components. In Subsection III-C, we formally define the data structures to represent *loads*, *configurations*, *states* and *functions*. Finally, Subsection III-D discusses the computational details of the propagation of the loads and the evaluation of the states for each cloud component.

A. Loads and Abstraction Levels

The concept of *load* is central in CC management literature and it is related to the *qualitative* and *quantitative* effort that an element requires to perform a task. However, in CC, it is necessary to manage components related to processing, networking, storage and complex systems, in several abstraction levels. Materially, the loads and the consumers' data that must be transformed, transported and persisted are the same thing. Nevertheless, the system analysts are focused on the *behaviour of data* through the cloud structures, whereas the cloud manager must pay attention to the behaviour of *cloud structures* when the data is passing through them.

In a view based on data centre elements, the loads are traditionally mapped to metrics of processing, networking and storing. This *concrete* view is not complete for CC since the providers can work with elements in other levels of abstraction. Providers in a xAAS fashion can have any type of elements in their structures which must be modelled – from physical resources, till only third-party services as resources of an orchestration system. This heterogeneity in the abstraction levels of managed cloud elements, and their compositional nature (or fractal nature), produces the need to model the load propagation through the abstraction levels.

This load propagation through the technology stack is fundamental to understand how the abstract loads on services' interfaces become concrete loads in the resources. For example, supposing a photography storage service with mobile and web interfaces, the upload of an array of photos can represent a load in the server-side interface (expressed in number of photos), whereas, the same load must be expressed in several loads on (virtual) links, (virtual) processors, and (virtual) storages, not necessarily related to time. In fact, the upload of an array of photos is an abstract load and can be an useful to perform billing metrics, but it can be not useful to measure performance, requiring the detailing to concrete loads, according to the cloud's service implementation. An autonomic manager agent, responsible for planning and decision making in runtime, must understand the quantitative relations into the managed cloud structure to work in real time.

Thus, using a graph to express the dependences between elements in different levels, the abstracter elements (services' interface) must appear in the roots of the graph, the concreter elements (resources) must appear in the leaves, whereas the intermediary elements (systems) orchestrate resources in order to implement the services. These concepts of services interfaces, systems and resources become relative terms which can adapted for any cloud implementation, independent of absolute level of operation regards to the IaaS, PaaS and SaaS taxonomy.

B. Modelling Clouds with C_2LP

In C_2LP, the structural arrangement of cloud elements is based in a *directed acyclic multigraph* (DAM) where the nodes of the graph represent components. To start a horizontal decomposition must be considered the four main types for CC elements:

- *Resources* are the base of any cloud, and can be classified in three *elementary computational function*: as *Computing*, *Storage* and *Networking*; Therefore, these components are always leaf nodes, even when virtualized or based on service orchestration (e.g., a storage block device built on email accounts). The elements with these *computational functions* constitute the sources of computing power into a cloud. The term "computing power" is used here not only for processing, but also for networking and storage, since the CC paradigm effectively offer these last as services, exposing their economical value.
- *Systems* are abstractions of orchestrated resources that implement services. They can be, e.g., applications and platforms. In the model, systems must be directly linked to at least one of each type of resource: computing, storage and networking. Nevertheless, these resources might be replaced by other systems or third-party services. In such cases, the relationship between the system and the element that represents the resource (e.g., another system or the third-party service) must be explicitly defined using stereotypes (virtual computing, virtual networking or virtual storage).
- *Third-Party Services* represent: (i) resources to system components, when the relation is explicitly annotated with the appropriated stereotype, and (ii) entire systems which provide services and abstract the underlying layers (e.g., email services). The latter models, for example, hybrid clouds or composed services.
- *Services* are interfaces between the cloud and the consumers. They must be connected with a respective system that implement them and never are directly linked to resource or third-party services. Services interfaces are the points on which the specification of the consumer's needs (SLAs) are attached. In your model the services interfaces can receive loads from a hypothetical common source (*), that symbolizes the consumer.

Directed edges define to which elements each cloud component can transmit load. Nodes have two main processes: *propagation* of the load; and *evaluation* of the impact of the load in the node itself. Remarkably, the resources components do not propagate load and are the only nodes that actually run the assigned load, while other elements are abstract (e.g., applications, middlewares, platforms and operations systems). Moreover, we consider in the model also the configurations settings of nodes, which impact the propagation and evaluation processes.

Providers offers services and receive requests from consumers. These request represent an economical demand by work, which in providers' assets represent workloads, or just: *loads*. The loads vary according to each cloud component and are changing in quality and quantity along the computing chain that compose the providers' assets. Therefore, each node in the DAM represents a function that convert the input load to output load, from the services (sources) to the resources (sinks). In the resources occurs the work, realizing the load and consuming computing power.

In fact, just low abstraction loads would need to be represented in the model, e.g., supposing an IaaS provider: link, processor and storage. However, the patterns of behaviour in low level loads become chaotic and unmanageable without information about the abstract component that guide the resources usage. Therefore, distributing load propagation functions over a graph is a simple way to represent complex function compositions on a conceptual network. Assuming that the loads flow from the sources (services) to the sinks (resources), and a node must have all incoming loads available to compute the outgoing loads, the propagation must be made in a breadth-first fashion.

Since loads might have different forms, we model these relations enabling multiple edges between nodes, which simplifies the understanding of the model. For example, a service transmits 10 giga FLoating-point Operations Per Second (FLOPS) and 100 giga bytes of data to third-party service. This case is modelled using two edges, one for each type of load to the third-party. In case of change in the structure (e.g., the executor of the loads finds a cheaper storage provider) the model can be adjusted simply by removing the storage edge between these nodes and adding it to this new third-party provider.

When the loads are realized in the resources, they produce several effects which can be measured by the monitoring. For example: resource usage, energy consumption, fails, costs, etc. The modelling of qualitative and quantitative relations between loads and their effects over the resource is a mandatory task to enable managerial planning and decision making. Nevertheless, measurable effects in resources can also signify metrics in system and services. For example, the sum of energy consumed in the processors, network and storage, in order to download a photo of 10GB, means the amount of energy consume do resolve a load of type "download photo" of size "10GB", in service level.

However, is not only the loads which determine the behaviours of the resources, but also the configuration parametrized by the cloud manager, and the accumulated effects from previous loads. On the other hand, non-leaf elements – which the evaluations depend of lower level elements – must consider: incoming loads, the accumulated state (*a priori*) and the state of lower elements (target nodes). This is represented in the model as distinct evaluation functions. In the C_2LP were modelled a set of evaluated functions for leaf nodes, with two inputs, and a set for non-leaf nodes, with three inputs. The both type of functions output a new node state which can contain several sub-evaluations (measures).

The propagation of evaluations is done after the propagation of loads, from bottom to top. This procedure will provide the amount of loads in each element of the model. With the loads and the configurations and accumulated state (*a priori* state) in the resources elements, it is possible to compute the new configurations and accumulated state (the *a posteriori* state). So, in the non-leaf nodes it is possible to compute the *a posteriori* state with its the *a priori* state and the *a posteriori* states of its dependencies (lower level elements). To perform the evaluation of whole graph, from the root nodes, it is necessary to perform a depth-first computing though the graph.

Figure 1 presents the modelling of a scenario, in which a cloud provides two services: an email and Infrastructure-as-a-Service (IaaS). The IaaS is provided by a third-party cloud. The email service instead, employs a system component to represent a software email server (in this case a Postfix). This component uses local computing and networking and storage from a third-party cloud. The relation (edge) between these components is annotated accordingly.

In the proposed scenario, we exemplify the load propagation with a request from consumers to send 2 new emails using the email service. These 2 emails are converted by the service component into 2 loads of type "transaction" and sent for the email server where they are converted into another types of load and propagated to the resources linked to the server.

The evaluation process of this scenario uses different metrics in each node and is marked as "eval:". For example, in the service level, the load of 2 emails was measured in terms financial cost and energy necessary to complete the request.

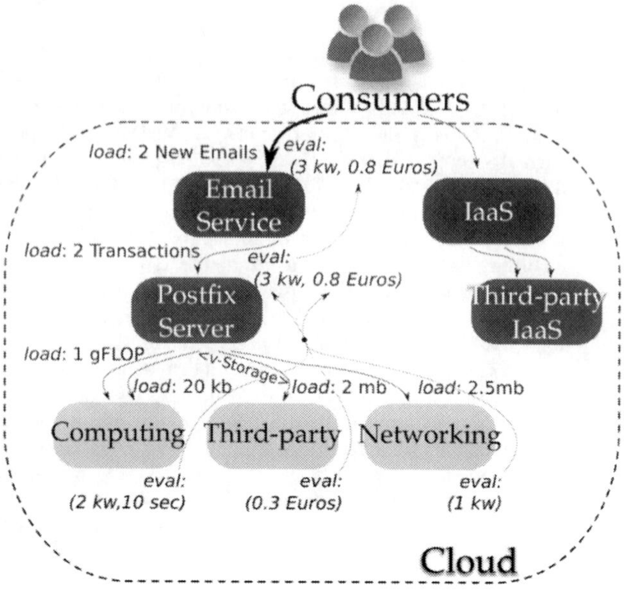

Figure 1: Example of the propagation of loads and the evaluation processes using the C_2LP model.

C. Formalisation of the Model

Formally, in C_2LP model, a cloud C can be expressed as $C = (V, E, \tau^V, \sigma, \Phi, \phi, \Gamma, \gamma, \Gamma', \gamma')$, where:

- V is the set of nodes $V = \{v_1, v_2, \ldots, v_n\}$ of the multigraph, such that every item in V represents one element of the cloud and has one respective node-weight w_v, that usually is a vector of values;
- E is the set of directed edges where $E = \{e_1, e_2, \ldots, e_m\} | e = (v, v')$, that describes the ability of a source node v to transmit a load to node v', such that each e_m also has a respective edge-weight $w_{v,v'}$;
- $\tau^V : V \to T^V$ is a bijective function which maps the nodes with the respective type, where the set T^V is the set of types of nodes, such that $T^V = \{'computing', 'storage', 'networking', 'system', 'service', 'third\_party'\}$;
- $\sigma : E_{\{\to system, \to third-party\}} \to \{none, vComputing, vStorage, vNetworking\}$ is a function which maps the edges that have systems and third-party services as target with the respective stereotype, characterising the relation between the source element with the target;
- Φ represents the set of propagation functions, where $\Phi = \{f_1, f_2, \ldots, f_v\}$ and ϕ is a bijective function $\phi : V \to \Phi$ that maps each node for the respective propagation function. Each function in the set Φ is defined as $f_v : \mathbb{N}^n, \mathbb{R}^i \to \mathbb{R}^o$, where: the set $\mathbb{N}^n$ represents the space where the n-tuple for the configuration is contained; the set $\mathbb{R}^i$ represents the space where the n-tuple of incoming edge-weights is contained; and, $\mathbb{R}^o$ is the space where the n-tuple of the outgoing edge-weights is contained. To simplify the model and the algorithms, we consider that configurations are stored in the node-weight, such that w_v^{conf} represents the configuration part of the node-weight vector.
- Γ is the set of sets that contains the evaluation functions for the leaf nodes, such that there exists one function for each distinct evaluation metric (e.g., energy use, CO2 emission, ...). Then, $\Gamma = \{\Gamma_1, \Gamma_2, \ldots \Gamma_k\}$, such that $\Gamma_k = \{g_{n+1}, g_{n+2}, \ldots, g_m\}$. Each set Γ_k is related to a leaf node $v \in V_{[leaf]}$ through the bijective function $\gamma : V_{[leaf]} \to \Gamma$. Every g_{n+m} is stored in a distinct position of the node-weight vector of the respective node – representing *a partial state* of v – such that the full new state can be computed through the expression: $w'_v = (c_1, \ldots, c_n, g_{n+1}(c_1, \ldots, c_n, w_v^i), g_{n+2}(c_1, \ldots, c_n, w_v^i), \ldots, g_{n+m}(c_1, \ldots, c_n, w_v^i))$, where: $c_1, \ldots, c_n$ is the n-tuple with the configuration part of the node-weight w_v; w_v^i is the n-tuple with all incoming edge-weights $w_{*,v}$ of v; and w'_v is the new node-weight (full state) for v. The complete evaluation procedure is detailed in Figure 6;
- Γ' is the set of sets that holds the evaluation functions for non-leaf nodes. Therefore, $\Gamma' = \{\Gamma'_1, \Gamma'_2, \ldots, \Gamma'_l\}$, such that each set $\Gamma'_l = \{g'_{n+1}, g'_{n+2}, \ldots, g'_m\}$ contains the evaluation functions g'_{n+m}. Every Γ'_l is associated with a non-leaf node v through the bijective

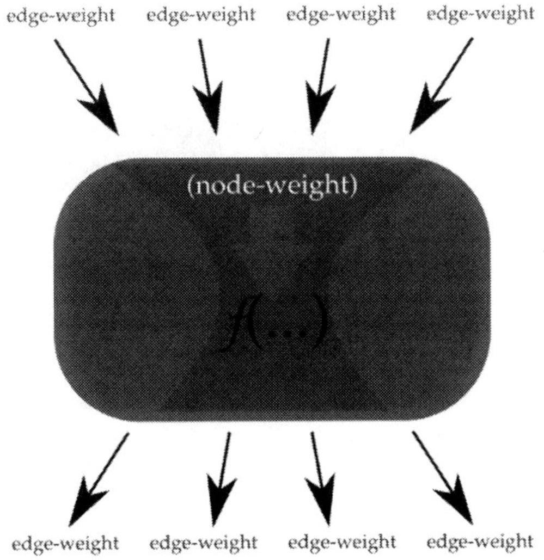

Figure 2: Illustration of load propagation in root or non-leaf nodes.

function $\gamma' : V_{non-leaf} \rightarrow \Gamma'$. Since the result of each function g'_{n+m} is stored in a distinct position of w'_v, it represents a partial state of the respective node v. A new full state of non-leaf nodes can be computed through the expression: $w'_v = (c_1, \ldots, c_n, g'_{n+1}(c_1, \ldots, c_n, w^i_v, w'_{u_v}), g'_{n+2}(c_1, \ldots, c_n, w^i_v, w'_{u_v}), \ldots, g'_{n+m}(c_1, \ldots, c_n, w^i_v, w'_{u_v}))$; where w'_v is the new node-weight of v, $c_1, \ldots, c_n$ is the n-tuple with the configuration part w^{conf}_v of the node-weight, w^i_v is the n-tuple with the incoming edge-weights $e_{*,v}$ of v, and w'_{u_v} is a tuple which puts together all node-weights of the successors of v (see Figure 6 for details).

The main objective of these formalisms is to specify the data structures that support a model validation, the load propagation, and elements evaluations. The details of each procedure concerned with propagation and evaluations are described in Subsection III-D.

D. Details on the Propagation and Evaluation

The load propagation consists in a top-down process that uses the *breadth-first* approach. In a breadth-first algorithm, all the incoming loads are available for a node before the inference of its outgoing loads. In the specific case on C_2LP the algorithm starts from the loads on the services, corresponding to the requests received from consumers. The Figure 2 illustrates the load propagation. The blue oblong represents a non-leaf element that has incoming edges, which the weights represent incoming loads. Alto, there is the node-weight that represents the *a priori* state, that contains the configurations and accumulated states. Both, the incoming loads and node-weight, are used as inputs for the node attached propagation function $f(\ldots)$, that produces a tuple with the output edge-weights.

The propagation process uses a queue with the service nodes (the roots of the graph). Then, a node v is picked from this queue and all its children are placed into the queue. Afterwards, a function $f_v = \phi(v)$ is executed to distribute the load, that is, to define all edge-weights for the outgoing edges of v. This procedure is repeated while the queue is not empty.

procedure BREADHTFIRSTPROPAGATION(C,W^V,W^E) ▷ Requires a cloud model $C = (V, E, \tau^V, \sigma, \Phi, \phi)$, the set of node-weights $W^V | \forall v \in V \wedge \exists! w_v \in W^V$ and the set of edge-weights $W^E | \forall e_{v,v'} \in E \wedge \exists! w_{v,v'} \in W^E$.
  $queue \leftarrow \varnothing$
  $enqueue(*)$
  repeat
    $v \leftarrow dequeue()$
    for each $u \in successorSet(v)$ **do**
      $enqueue(u)$
    end for ▷ enqueues the sucessor of each node
    $f_v \leftarrow \phi(v)$
    $w^{conf}_v \leftarrow configurationPart(w_v)$ ▷ gets the config. part of the node-weight (state).
    $w^i_v \leftarrow (w_{1,v}, w_{2,v}, \ldots, w_{u,v})$ ▷ builds the incoming edge-weights in a tuple w^i_v.
    $w^o_v \leftarrow f_v(w^{conf}_v, w^i_v)$ ▷ w^o_v contains the result of the propagation function.
    for each $w_{v,u} \in w^o_v$ **do**
      $W^E \leftarrow W^E \oplus w_{v,u}$ ▷ replaces the old value of $w_{v,u}$.
    end for▷ assign the values for the outgoing edges of v.
  until $queue \neq \varnothing$
  return W^E
end procedure

Figure 3: Breadth-first algorithm used for the load propagation.

The well defined method is detailed in Figure 3.

When the load is propagated to resources components (leaf nodes), they execute the load. This execution requires power and resources and can be evaluated in several forms. For example, *energy (kw)*, *performance*, *availability*, *accounting*, *security*, *CO_2 emissions* and other cloud specific feature units. This evaluation process takes every function $g_{n+m} \in \Gamma_k$ in order and computes each partial states, storing them into a position of the new node-weight w'_v. A finer description can be defined as: $w'_v = (w^{conf}_v, g_{n+1}(w^{conf}_v, w^i_v), \ldots, g_{n+m}(w^{conf}_v, w^i_v)$, such that w'_v represents the *a posteriori* state for the node v, w^{conf}_v are the configurations (*a priori* state) of v, w^i_v are the incoming edge-weights of v, and $g_{n+m} \in \gamma(v)$ are the evaluation functions associated with the node.

The process of evaluation in leaf nodes is depicted in the Figure 4, where the pink oblong represents a leaf node. In these nodes the edge-weights and the *a priori* node-weight serve as inputs for each function in the vector of evaluation functions, which produce a single value each one. These single values are grouped in a tuple that results in the *a posteriori* node weight.

The evaluations also include the non-leaf nodes since the load also passes through them and it is useful, e.g., to understand the load distribution and to identify bottlenecks. In the case of non-leaf nodes, the evaluation requires also the evaluation results of the bottom nodes. Therefore, this process is performed from the leaves to the roots using a *depth-first* approach.

A non-leaf node receives the tuples $(config, loads, children\_states)$, and evaluates by the processing of all $g'_{n+m} \in \gamma'(v)$ functions. A representation

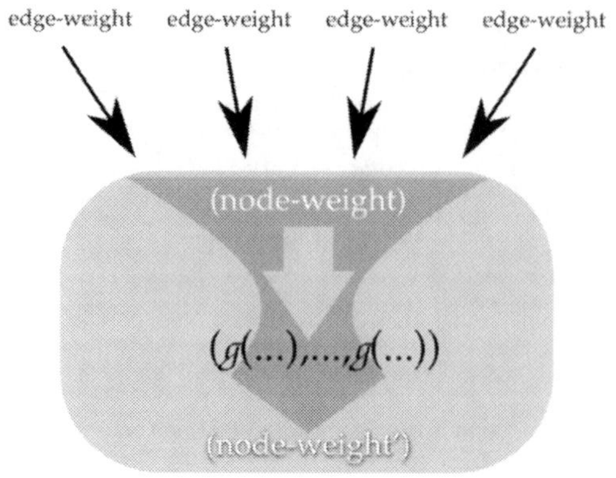

Figure 4: Illustration of evaluations in leaf nodes.

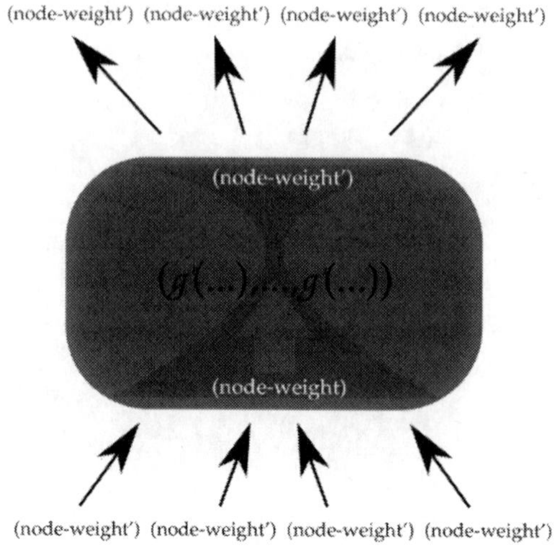

Figure 5: Illustration of evaluations in non-leaf nodes.

of this process can be described as: $w'_v = (w_v^{conf}, g'_{n+1}(w_v^{conf}, w_v^i, w'_{u_v}), \ldots, g'_{n+m}(w_v^{conf}, w_v^i, w'_{u_v}),$ such that w'_v represents the new node-weight (*a posteriori* state) for the node v, w_v^{conf} are the configuration part (*a priori* state) of node-weight into v, w_v^i represent the incoming edge-weights of v, w'_{u_v} are the computed node-weights of the successors of v, and $g'_{n+m} \in \gamma'(v)$ are the evaluation functions associated with the node.

The evaluation in a non-leaf node is depicted in the Figure 5, where the blue oblong represents a non-leaf. In this figure it is possible to observe the *a posteriori* node-weights from the lower level elements being "transmitted" through the edges. The proximity of node-weights with edges do not represent the association between them, but the transmission of one through the other. Into the node is depicted the vector of evaluation functions, which will receive: the *a priori* node-weight of the node itself and the *a posteriori* node-weights from the lower elements; and produce single values which are grouped, in order to compose *a posteriori* node-weight tuple for the node itself. This *a posteriori* node-weight is propagated for the upper elements through the edges. The node-weight in the superior edges have the same value, the computed *a posteriori* node-weight, for all edges. Also, the arrows do not represent the direction of the edges, but the information flow.

The complete evaluation process is detailed in Figure 6, where a stack is used to perform a depth-first computation. The first non-visited child of a current node is placed into the stack and will be used as current node. When all children of a node are evaluated, then the node is evaluated. If the node is a leaf node the g functions are used to compute the evaluations, otherwise, the g' functions are used instead.

These mathematical structures and algorithms provide a general framework for modelling and evaluation of clouds' elements behaviour in different abstraction levels. They can express and compute how service level loads are decomposed and converted, through the systems, till become resource level loads. In resource level, on concrete elements, the loads can be evaluated according to performance, availability and other objective metrics. At end, the same structures and algorithms can be used to compute objective metrics for abstract elements. The whole model serves to simulate and compare the impact of configuration's changes in any point of the cloud, supporting the managerial decision making.

IV. Experiments and Results

This section presents numerical experiments with the C_2LP model, based on a *service* modelling. These experiments serve to: (i) *test* the applicability of the model; (ii) illustrate the modelling with our formalism with an example; and (iii) *demonstrate* the model capacity to *generate quantitative behaviours* to manage loads, combining variations of propagation and evaluation functions.

To perform these experiments, we have implemented a use case using our model. This use case exemplifies the model's usage and serves to test its feasibility. The example of model's usage was made using hypothetical functions, since its objective is to prove the generation of simulations, the propagation and the evaluation. Nevertheless, our model can be used for modelling real-world clouds, provided that the propagation and evaluation functions are adjusted to the cloud instance.

As use case, we defined an *IaaS service* where consumers perform five operation: *deploy VM*, *undeploy VM*, *start VM*, *stop VM*, and *execute* tasks. To meet the demand for these services, we designed a hypothetical cloud infrastructure with which is possible to generate quantitative scenarios of propagation and evaluation – in a combinatorial fashion. Using this hypothetical infrastructure, we have tested some managerial configurations related to load distribution over the cloud elements, in order to evaluate the average utility for all quantitative scenarios. At the end, the configurations which achieve the best average utility for all quantitative scenarios were highlighted, depicting the ability of the model to simulate configuration consequences for the purpose of selecting configurations.

A. Use Case Modelling

To deal with the consumers' loads (deploy, undeploy, start, stop and execute) at service abstraction level, the infrastructure manages: the *service interface*; systems, such as *load balancers*, *cloud managers* and *cloud platforms*; and resources, such as *servers*, *storages* and *physical networks*. All operations invoked by consumers represent an incoming

```
procedure DEPTHFIRSTEVALUATION(C, W^V, W^E)    ▷ The same input described in Figure 3.
    β ← ∅                        ▷ initializes the set of visited nodes.
    stack ← ∅                    ▷ initializes the stack.
    push(*)                      ▷ starts from the hypothetical node.
    while stack ≠ ∅ do
        v ← peek()               ▷ gets a node without to remove it.
        for each u ∈ successorSet(v) do
            if u ∉ β then
                push(u)
                continue while
            end if
        end for  ▷ if the for loop ends, all successors have been evaluated.
        w^{conf} ← configurationPart(w_v)    ▷ gets the config. part for v.
        w^i_v ← (w_1, w_2, ..., w_{u,v})     ▷ builds the n-tuple with the incomings of v.
        if isLeaf(v) then
            w'_v ← (w^{conf}_v, g_{n+1}(w^{conf}_v, w^i_v), ..., g_{n+m}(w^{conf}_v, w^i_v)), ∀g_{n+m} ∈ γ(v)
                ▷ computes the partial states and builds the new node-weight.
        else
            w'_{u_v} ← (w'_{u_1}, w'_{u_2}, ..., w'_{u_o})
                ▷ builds the computed node-weights for all u|∃e_{v,u} ∈ E.
            w'_v ← (w^{conf}_v, g'_{n+1}(w^{conf}_v, w^i_v, w'_{u_v}), ..., g'_{n+m}(w^{conf}_v, w^i_v, w'_{u_v})), ∀g'_{n+m} ∈ γ'(v)
                ▷ computes the partial states and builds the new node-weight.
        end if
        W^V ← W^V ⊕ w'_v          ▷ replaces the old state of v into the node-weights.
        if v ∉ β then
            β ← β ∪ v
        end if  ▷ puts v in the visited set if it is not there.
        v ← pop()                ▷ gets and removes v from the stack.
    end while
    return W^V
end procedure
```

Figure 6: Depth-first algorithm to evaluate in specific metrics the impact of the load in each node.

load on the service interface, which is propagated to resources. In the resources the loads are evaluated to provide measures about *performance*, *availability*, *accounting*, *security* and *CO_2 emissions*. Once computed these measures for resource level elements it is possible to compute they also for systems and, at the end, for the service interfaces, getting service level measures.

The modelling of the use case was devised considering 21 components: 1 service, 9 systems, and 11 resources. The services represent the interface with customers. In this use case, the systems are: a *load balancer*; two *cloud manager* systems; and six *cloud platforms*. Also, between the resources there are: 8 physical computing servers (6 work servers and 2 managerial), 2 storages (1 work storage and 1 managerial), and 1 physical network. A detailed list of components is presented in Appendix I.

Regarding the edges and loads, each consumer's operation is modelled as an incoming edge in a *service interface node* – with the respective loads in the edge-weights. The service node forwards the loads for a *load balancer* system, where the propagation function decides to which *cloud manager* the load will be sent, whereas the *manager servers*, the *manager storage* and the *physical network* receive the loads by its operation. In the cloud mangers, the propagation function must decide to which *cloud platform* the loads will be sent and, at the same time, generate loads for the managerial resources. The cloud platform system effectively converts its loads into simple resource loads when uses the *work server*, *work storage* and *physical network*. The complete relation of load propagation paths is presented in Appendix I, where an element at the left side of an arrow can propagate loads for an element at the right. Furthermore, a graphical representation of these tables, which depicts the graph as a whole, is also presented in Appendix I.

Besides the node and the edges, the use case model required the definition of: • 4 types of propagation functions – one for the service and tree for each type of system; • 6 types of leaf evaluation functions – two specific performance evaluations, one for computing resources and another for storage and networking; plus, four common evaluation functions (availability, accounting, security and CO_2 emissions) for each type of resource; • 5 types of non-leaf evaluations functions.

We have modelled the possible combinations to distribute the loads {1-deployVM, 2-undeployVM, 3-startVM, 4-stopVM, 5-compute} as a partition set problem [25], resulting in 52 distinct possibilities of load propagation. Also, we introduced 2 possible configurations into each evaluation function for leaf nodes. These configurations are related to the choice of constants into the function. For example, the performance of a computing resource depends on its capacity, that can be: $a = 50GFLOPs$ or $b = 70GFLOPs$. Considering 5 distinct evaluation functions over 11 leaf nodes, we have got $(2^5)^{11} = 2^{55}$ possible distinct configurations to test.

B. Evaluations

The numerical experiments were performed running the propagation procedure, followed by the evaluation of every simulation. For each possible propagation, we tested and summarised the 2^{55} configurations for evaluation functions. Then, we analysed the average time (p, in seconds), average availability (av, in %), average accounting (ac, in currency units), average security (s, in % of risk of data exposition), and average of CO_2 emissions (c, in grammes). Each value was normalised according to the average for all propagations, tested and summarised in a global utility function, described in (1) – where the overlined variables represent the normalised values.

Such results can be used by cloud managers to choose the best scenario according to the priorities of the policy or to provide as input for a decision-making process, such as Markov Chains.

$$u = -(\overline{av} + \overline{s} - (\overline{p} + \overline{ac} + \overline{c})) \qquad (1)$$

The four best results of the fifty two numerical experiments are presented in Table II in ascending order. The configuration that achieves the best *average utility* is highlighted in bold. The *code* line in the table represents the propagation configuration, whereas the other lines contain the values obtained for each distinct evaluation type. The last row present the average utility

TABLE II: SUMMARY OF AVERAGE EVALUATIONS FOR EACH CONFIGURATION.

Criteria	Configuration			
Code	11221	11231	11232	**11212**
Time	180.59976	180.5999	180.60004	**180.59991**
Availability	0.9979606	0.99795955	0.9979587	**0.99795926**
Accounting	78.69924	78.69926	78.699234	**78.699265**
Security	0.9979606	0.99795955	0.9979587	**0.99795926**
Emissions	82848.31	82848.14	82848.51	**82848.74**
Utility	1.0526400204	1.0526410547	1.0526477776	**1.0526491889**

defined in Equation 1. To represent configuration we have adopted a set partition notation to express the propagation paths, such that each position in the code represents a type of load: 1-*deploy*, 2-*undeploy*, 3-*start*, 4-*stop*, and 5-*compute*. Considering that at leaves of the propagation graph there are 6 cloud platforms, a code 11212 indicates that the loads of type 1,2 and 4 were allocated on cloud platform 1, whereas the loads 3 and 5 ware allocated in the cloud platform 2.

These experiments present evidences that our model works as an engine to simulate and measure the impact of the propagation of loads through the several elements in the cloud. With the distribution of simple functions on a graph, we have demonstrated the capacity to compute a model that is rather complex,when treated purely with function composition and arithmetic. These experiments also shows that the metrics of behaviour can be simulated with the combinatorial representation of the parameters settings which generated the behaviour.

The breadth-first algorithm ensures that the nodes compute all loads before estimating their outputs. On the other hand, the model and the depth-first algorithm ensure that the computed measures generated by the actual resource consumption, which occurs in the leaves of the modelled cloud, can be composed. The loads are converted into different types (and units), according to the elements and specified functions. Also, the adjusts in the parameters in the node-weight allow the testing of several computed loads and measures, in different configuration scenarios. These parameters can be treated with combinatorics instead of programmatic simulators, since the total set of possible configurations becomes a well defined combinatorial problem.

V. CONCLUSION AND FUTURE WORKS

Several solutions have been proposed to model clouds. However, to the best of our knowledge, none is general and has mathematical formalism at the same time, which are essential characteristics for evaluation of decision making and autonomic management.

In this study, we have presented an approach with these characteristics to model clouds based in *Directed Acyclic Multigraph*, which has the flexibility of general models and the formalism of the specifics. Therefore, C_2LP is a flexible well-formed modelling tool to express flows of loads through the cloud components. This model supports the specification of elements in distinct abstraction levels, the generation of combinatorial variations in a use case modelling and the evaluation of the consequences of different configuration in the load propagation.

We developed a simulation software tool for the modelling of IaaS services and demonstrated the applicability of our approach through a use case. In this use case, we simulated several graph network theoretic analysis, evaluated and compared different configurations and, as a result, supplied the cloud managers with a numeric comparison of cost and benefits of each configuration. These experiments, demonstrated that this tools provides an essential support for the management of cloud.

In the future works we intent to develop a description language to specify the rules of association between cloud elements in order to compose de graph. Yet, we intent to study the fractal phenomena in cloud structures, in order to improve the managerial view about the relation between abstract and concrete elements, and the model's granularity. Also, is our desire to investigate how the different models – among the possible aggregations of metrics and parameters – impact the planning and decision making in management of cloud at runtime. At last, we intent to improve the C2LP adding order relations between the states, attached to nodes, in order to enable the model to encompass policies and SLAs.

ACKNOWLEDGEMENT

The present work was done with the support of CNPq agency, through the program Ciência sem Fronteiras (CsF), and the company Eletrosul Centrais Elétricas S.A. – in Brazil. The authors also would like to thank professor Rocco De Nicola and the group of SysMA research unit in Institute for advanced studies Lucca (IMT).

REFERENCES

[1] Rafael de S. Mendes, Rafael B. Uriarte, and Carlos B. Westphall, "C2LP: Modelling Load Propagation and Evaluation through the Cloud Components," In ICN 2016, The Fifteenth International Conference on Network, IARIA XPS Press, 2016, pages 28–36.

[2] Sekharipuram S. Ravi and Sandeep K. Shukla, "Fundamental Problems in Computing: Essays in Honor of Professor Daniel J. Rosenkrantz," Springer Netherlands, 2009.

[3] Rajkumar Buyya, Rodrigo N. Calheiros, and Xiaorong Li, "Autonomic cloud computing: Open challenges and architectural elements," In *Emerging Applications of Information Technology (EAIT), 2012 Third International Conference on.* IEEE, 2012, pp. 3–10.

[4] Rafael de S. Mendes et al., "Decision-theoretic planning for cloud computing," In ICN 2014, The Thirteenth International Conference on Networks, Iaria, vol. 7, no. 3 & 4, 2014, pages 191–197.

[5] Itzhak Gilboa, "Theory of Decision under Uncertainty," Cambridge University Press, 2009.

[6] Cliff Ragsdale, "Modeling & Decision Analysis," Thomson, 2008.

[7] Alexandre A. Flores, Rafael de S. Mendes, Gabriel B. Bräscher, Carlos B. Westphall, and Maria E. Villareal, "Decision-theoretic model to support autonomic cloud computing," In ICN 2015, The Fourteenth International Conference on Networks, Iaria, vol. 8, no. 1 & 2, 2015, pages 218–223.

[8] Rafael B. Uriarte, "Supporting Autonomic Management of Clouds: Service-Level-Agreement, Cloud Monitoring and Similarity Learning," PhD thesis, IMT Lucca, 2015.

[9] Rafael B. Uriarte, Francesco Tiezzi, and Rocco De Nicola, "SLAC: A formal service-level-agreement language for cloud computing," In Proceedings of the 2014 IEEE/ACM 7th International Conference on Utility and Cloud Computing, IEEE Computer Society, 2014, pages 419–426.

[10] Rodrigo N. Calheiros, Rajiv Ranjan, Anton Beloglazov, Csar A. F. De Rose, and Rajkumar Buyya, "Cloudsim: a toolkit for modeling and simulation of cloud computing environments and evaluation of resource provisioning algorithms," Software: Practice and Experience, Wiley Online Library, vol. 41, no. 1, 2011, pages 23–50.

[11] Rajkumar Buyya and Manzur Murshed, "Gridsim: A toolkit for the modeling and simulation of distributed resource management and scheduling for grid computing," Concurrency and computation: practice and experience, Wiley Online Library, vol. 14.no. 1315, 2002, pages 1175–1220.

[12] Dzmitry Kliazovich, Pascal Bouvry, and Samee Ullah Khan, "GreenCloud: a packet-level simulator of energy-aware cloud computing data centers," The Journal of Supercomputing, Springer, 2012, page 1263–1283.

[13] Teerawat Issariyakul and Ekram Hossain, "Introduction to network simulator NS2," Springer Science & Business Media, 2011.

[14] Alberto Núñez et al., "iCanCloud: A flexible and scalable cloud infrastructure simulator," Journal of Grid Computing, Springer, vol. 10, no. 1, 2012, pages 185–209.

[15] Rodrigo N. Calheiros, Marco A.S. Netto, César A.F. De Rose, and Rajkumar Buyya, "EMUSIM: an integrated emulation and simulation environment for modeling, evaluation, and validation of performance of cloud computing applications," Software: Practice and Experience, Wiley Online Library, vol. 43, no. 5, 2013, pages 595–612.

[16] Rodrigo N. Calheiros, Rajkumar Buyya, and Csar A. F. De Rose, "Building an automated and self-configurable emulation testbed for grid applications," Software: Practice and Experience, Wiley Online Library, vol. 40, no. 5, 2010, pages 405–429.

[17] Seung-Hwan Lim, Bikash Sharma, Gunwoo Nam, Eun Kyoung Kim, and Chita R. Das, "MDCSim: A multi-tier data center simulation, platform," In Cluster Computing and Workshops, 2009. CLUSTER'09. IEEE International Conference on, IEEE, 2009, pages 1–9.

[18] Jordi Vilaplana, Francesc Solsona, and Ivan Teixidó, "A performance model for scalable cloud computing," In 13th Australasian Symposium on Parallel and Distributed Computing (AusPDC 2015), ACS, vol. 163, 2015, pages 51–60.

[19] James R. Jackson "Networks of Waiting Lines," Operations Research, vol 5, no. 4, 1957, pages 518–521.

[20] Paulo F. Silva, Carlos B. Westphall, and Carla M. Westphall, "Model for cloud computing risk analysis," ICN 2015, Iaria, vol. 8, no. 1 & 2, 2015, page 152.

[21] Nada Ahmed and Ajith Abraham, "Modeling cloud computing risk assessment using machine learning," In Afro-European Conference for Industrial Advancement, Springer, 2015, pages 315–325.

[22] Sergio Nesmachnow, Santiago Iturriaga, and Bernabe Dorronsoro, "Efficient heuristics for profit optimization of virtual cloud brokers," Computational Intelligence Magazine, IEEE, vol. 10, no. 1, 2015, pages 33–43.

[23] Tim Püschel, Guido Schryen, Diana Hristova, and Dirk Neumann, "Revenue management for cloud computing providers: Decision models for service admission control under non-probabilistic uncertainty," European Journal of Operational Research, Elsevier, vol. 244, no. 2, 2015, pages 637–647.

[24] Chunling Cheng, Jun Li, and Ying Wang, "An energy-saving task scheduling strategy based on vacation queuing theory in cloud computing," Tsinghua Science and Technology, IEEE, vol. 20, no. 1, 2015, pages 28–39.

[25] Toufik Mansour, "Combinatorics of Set Partitions," CRC Press, 2012.

APPENDIX I: IMPLEMENTATION DETAILS

TABLE III: THE CLOUD ELEMENTS – NODES OF THE GRAPH.

CS - computing service	**CP21** - platform 21	**WS12** - work server 12
LB - load balancer	**CP22** - platform 22	**WS13** - work server 13
CM1 - cloud manager 1	**CP23** - platform 23	**WS21** - work server 21
CM2 - cloud manager 2	**MS1** - manager server 1	**WS22** - work server 22
CP11 - platform 11	**MS2** - manager server 2	**WS23** - work server 23
CP12 - platform 12	**MSTO** - manager storage	**WSTO** - work storage
CP13 - platform 13	**WS11** - work server 11	**PN** - physical network

TABLE IV: THE LOAD PROPAGATION RELATIONS – EDGES OF THE GRAPH.

$\xrightarrow{5}$CS	CM1$\xrightarrow{5}$CP11	CP11 → WS11	CP21 → PN
CS$\xrightarrow{5}$LB	CM1$\xrightarrow{5}$CP12	CP11→PN	CP21→WSTO
LB$\xrightarrow{5}$CM1	CM1$\xrightarrow{5}$CP13	CP11→WSTO	CP22→W22
LB$\xrightarrow{5}$CM2	CM1 → PN	CP12→WS12	CP22 → PN
LB → MS1	CM2 → MS2	CP12 → PN	CP22 → WSTO
LB → MS2	CM2 → MSTO	CP12 → WSTO	CP23 → W23
LB → WSTO	CM2 $\xrightarrow{5}$ CP21	CP13→ W13	CP23 → PN
LB → PN	CM2 $\xrightarrow{5}$ CP22	CP13→ PN	CP23 → WSTO
CM1 → MS1	CM2 $\xrightarrow{5}$ CP23	CP13 → WSTO	
CM1 → MSTO	CM2 → PN	CP21 → W21	

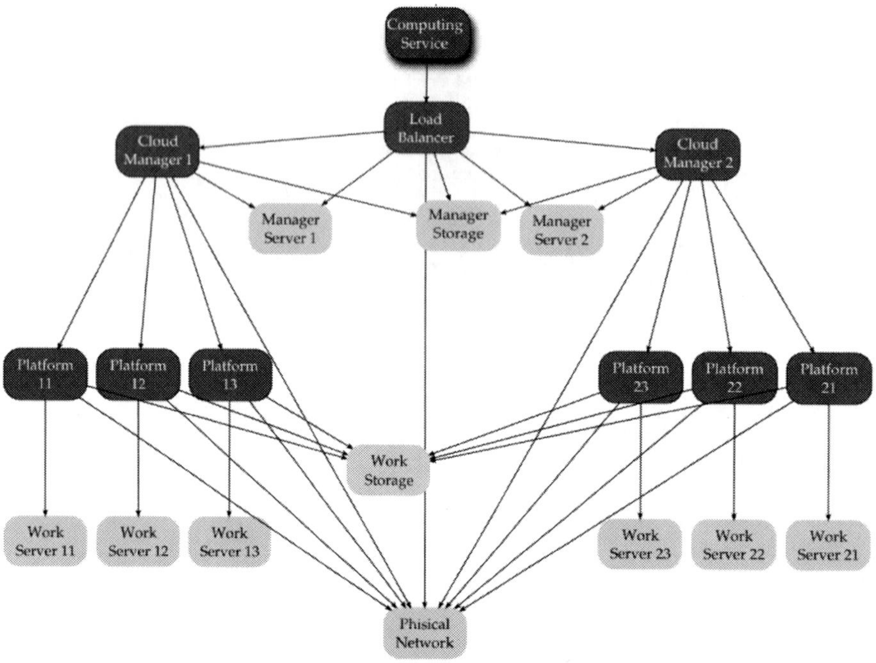

Figure 7: Graphical representation of structural arrangement for the modelling use case.

TABLE V: PROPAGATION FUNCTIONS.

Types	Declarations	Definitions
service	$(w_1,\cdots,w_5) \xmapsto{f^{CS}} (w'_1,\cdots,w'_5)$.	w_n is the weight for $\xrightarrow{n} CS)$. w'_n is the weight for $(CS \xrightarrow{n} LB)$. $w'_n = w_n \mid \forall w'_n \in f^{CS}$.
balancer	$(c_1,\ldots,c_5,w_1,\cdots,w_5) \xmapsto{f^{LB}}$. $(w'_1,\ldots,w'_{14})$	$c_n \in \{CM1, CM2\}$, are the configurations which represent the targets of each load $w_n \mid 1 \leqslant n \leqslant 5$. $w'_n = \left\{ \begin{array}{ll} w_n & \text{if } c_n = CM1 \\ 0 & \text{otherwise} \end{array} \right| 1 \leqslant n \leqslant 5$. $w'_{n+5} = \left\{ \begin{array}{ll} w_n & \text{if } c_n = CM2 \\ 0 & \text{otherwise} \end{array} \right| 1 \leqslant n \leqslant 5$. $w'_{1 \geqslant n \geqslant 5}$, are the weights in the edges LB$\xrightarrow{5}$CM1. $w'_{6 \geqslant n \geqslant 10}$, are the weights in the edges LB$\xrightarrow{5}$CM2. $w'_{11} = 1Gflop$, is the a constant computing load in LB→MS1. $w'_{12} = 1Gflop$, is the a constant computing load in LB→MS2. $w'_{13} = 50GB$, is the a constant storage load in LB→MSTO. $w'_{14} = w_1 + 40$, is the load over LB→PN, such that w_1 is the VM image size in *GB*, comes from *deploy VM* operation, and 40 is a constant value in *GB* for the another operations.
cloud manager	$(c_1,\ldots,c_5,w_1,\cdots,w_5) \xmapsto{f^{CMn}}$ $(w'_1,\ldots,w'_{18})$	$c_n \in \{CPm1, CPm2, CPm3\}$, are the configurations which represent the targets of each load $w_n \mid 1 \leqslant n \leqslant 5$. $w'_n = \left\{ \begin{array}{ll} w_n & \text{if } c_n = CPm1 \\ 0 & \text{otherwise} \end{array} \right| 1 \leqslant n \leqslant 5$. $w'_{n+5} = \left\{ \begin{array}{ll} w_n & \text{if } c_n = CPm2 \\ 0 & \text{otherwise} \end{array} \right| 1 \leqslant n \leqslant 5$. $w'_{n+10} = \left\{ \begin{array}{ll} w_n & \text{if } c_n = CPm3 \\ 0 & \text{otherwise} \end{array} \right| 1 \leqslant n \leqslant 5$. $w'_{16} = 1Gflop$, is the a constant computing load in CMn→MSn. $w'_{17} = 50GB$, is the a constant storage load in CMn→MSTO. $w'_{18} = w_1 + 40$, is the load over CMn→PN, such that w_1 is the VM image size in *GB*, comes from *deploy VM* operation, and 40 is a constant value in *GB* for the another operations.
cloud platform	$(w_1,\cdots,w_5) \xmapsto{f^{CPnn}}$ (w'_1, w'_2, w'_3).	$w_1,\cdots,w_5$, are the main loads come from the service, associatively, w_1 – deploy VM, w_2 – undeploy VM, w_3 – start VM, w_4 – stop VM, and w_5 – compute tasks. w'_1, w'_2 and w'_3 are, respectively, the edge-weight for the arcs CPnn→WSnn, CPnn→WSTO and CPnn→PN, where: $w'_1 = w_1 - w_2 + w_3 - w_4 + w_5$; $w'_2 = w_1 - w_2 + 1MB$; $w'_3 = w_1 + w_3 - w_4 + 1MB$.

TABLE VI: EVALUATION FUNCTIONS FOR LEAF NODES.

Types	Functions
computing specific functions	*performance (duration)*: $d(load) = \frac{load}{capacity}$, where $load$ is expressed in GFlop, $capacity$ is a constant of 70GFLOPs and d is the total time to resolve the load.
	energy increment (kWh): $energy_{increment}(load)$ here is considered a linear function which returns the amount of energy necessary to process the load above the average consumption of standby state. For computing have been considered $0.001kW$ per GFLOP.
storage and network specific functions	*performance (duration)*: $d(load) = \frac{load}{capacity}$, where $load$ is expressed in GByte, $capacity$ is a constant of 1GBps and d is the total time to resolve the load. For the networking resources this concept is intuitively associated with the network throughput, however, for storage is necessary to explain that the performance refers to throughput of the data bus.
	energy increment (kW): $energy_{increment}(load)$ for data transmission is assumed as linear, and was here considered $0.001kW$ per GB transferred.
common functions	*availability*: $av(load) = 1 - p_{fault}(d(load))$, where p_{fault} is the probability which a fault occurs during the load processing. Here will be considered a linear naive probability, such that $p_{fault}(d) = d \times 0.01$.
	accounting: $ac(load) = price_{energy} \times energy_{total}$, where $price_{energy}$ is a constant of $0.38US\$/kW$ or $0.58US\$/kW$, depending on node configuration; and $energy_{total} = energy_{increment}(load) + energy_{average}(d(load))$, such that $energy_{average}(d(load)) = d(load) \times 0.1kW$ is the shared energy spent by the cloud by time slot, and $energy_{increment}(load)$ is the increment of energy result of resource usage.
	security (risk of data exposition): $s(load) = 1 - p_{exposure}(load)$, where $p_{exposure}(load)$ is the probability that the load processing results in data exposure and $s(load)$ is the trustability of the operation. The $p_{exposure}(load)$ is calculated as 0.001 for each second of operation.
	CO_2 emission: $c = energy_{total} \times 400$, where $energy_{total}$ was defined in the accounting evaluation function and 400 is a constant which represents the grammes of CO_2 per kW.

TABLE VII: EVALUATION FUNCTIONS FOR NON-LEAF NODES.

Types	Declarations	Definitions
performance	maximum duration of loads sent for successor nodes.	$p_v(w_1, \ldots, w_5, w'_1, \ldots, w'_n) = max(w'_1[p], \ldots, w'_n[p])$, where p_v represents the total time to process the incoming loads, and $w'_n[p]$ represents the specific part of in the node-weight of n successor nodes, regards to the duration to process the loads sent by the node v.
availability	the product of the availability of successor nodes according to the sent loads.	$av_v(w_1, \ldots, w_5, w'_1, \ldots, w'_n) = \prod w'_n[av]$, where av_v represents the total availability of a node v according its dependencies, and $w'_n[av]$ represents the availability part in node-weights of the successors of v, related to the loads sent.
accounting	the sum of costs relative to the sent loads for successor nodes.	$ac_v(w_1, \ldots, w_5, w'_1, \ldots, w'_n) = \sum w'_n[ac]$, where ac_v is the total cost related to v and regards to the loads processed in the successors, and $w'_n[ac]$ is the accounting part of the successors' node-weight.
security	the product of security (regards to data exposition) of successor nodes according to the sent loads.	$s_v(w_1, \ldots, w_5, w'_1, \ldots, w'_n) = \prod w'_n[s]$, where s_v represents the total security measure of a node v, and $w'_n[s]$ represents the security measure part in node-weights of the successors of v, related to the loads sent.
CO_2 emission	the sum of total emissions relative to the loads sent to the successor nodes.	$c_v(w_1, \ldots, w_5, w'_1, \ldots, w'_n) = \sum w'_n[ac]$, where c_v is the total CO_2 emission associated with a node v, and $w'_n[ac]$ is the node-weight part associated with the emissions caused by the loads sent from v.

Multiradio, Multiboot Capable Sensing Systems for Home Area Networking

Brendan O'Flynn, Marco De Donno, Wassim Magnin
Tyndall National Institute
University College Cork
Cork, Ireland

email: brendan.oflynn@tyndall.ie. marco.dedonno@tyndall.ie, wassim.magnin@tyndall.ie

***Abstract*—The development of Wireless Sensor Networking technology to deploy in smart home environments for a variety of applications such as Home Area Networking has been the focus of commercial and academic interest for the last decade. Developers of such systems have not adopted a common standard for communications in such schemes. Many Wireless Sensor Network systems use proprietary systems so interoperability between different devices and systems can be at best difficult with various protocols (standards based and non-standards based) used (ZigBee, EnOcean, MODBUS, KNX, DALI, Powerline, etc.). This work describes the development of a novel low power consumption multiradio system incorporating 32-bit ARM-Cortex microcontroller and multiple radio interfaces - ZigBee/6LoWPAN/Bluetooth LE/868MHz platform. The multiradio sensing system lends itself to interoperability and standardization between the different technologies, which typically make up a heterogeneous network of sensors for both standards based and non-standards based systems. The configurability of the system enables energy savings, and increases the range between single points enabling the implementation of adaptive networking architectures of different configurations. The system described provides a future-proof wireless platform for Home Automation Networks with regards to the network heterogeneity in terms of hardware and protocols defined as being critical for use in the built environment. This system is the first to provide the capability to communicate in the 2.4GHz band as well as the 868MHz band as well as the feature of multiboot capability. A description of the system operation and potential for power savings through the use of such a system is provided. Using such a multiradio, multiboot capable, system can not only allow interoperability across multiple radio platforms in a Home Area Network, but can also increase battery lifetime by 20 – 25% in standard sensing applications.**

Keywords - Smart Sensing; Low Power Consumption Protocols, Home Area Networks (HAN); Energy Management; Multiradio Systems.

I. INTRODUCTION

Wireless Sensor Network (WSN) systems have the potential to be ubiquitous in today's Society in a myriad of applications such as Smart Homes, Building Energy Management (BEM), Home Area Networking (HAN), micro grid management, environmental monitoring and smart cities. New architectures, such as those described in the conference paper [1] and from which this paper evolved, are required to offer improved inter-operability, to improve reliability of data communications and to address the spread spectrum requirements associated with next generation sensor systems through the development of smart radio systems. Currently available platforms exist that have multiple radios but these tend to operate in a single Industrial, Scientific and Medical (ISM) band (typically 2.4GHz) – and not in combination with the 868MHz ISM Band, which is ideal for the built environment due to its long range, low data rate properties.

This type of architecture has some interesting commercial applications for interoperable networks, Home Area Networks, commercial buildings and smart cities. Compared to single-end radio devices, it has the potential to provide increased connectivity in deployment, and can potentially reduce the interference impact on the network because the system can hop from ISM band to ISM band in an autonomous and opportunistic manner. The development of multiradio sensing architectures lends itself to interoperability between the different technologies that typically make up a heterogeneous network of sensors.

The value of WSNs as a sensing system is clear when you compare them to traditional wired sensing systems. Typically wired sensor systems are expensive to install with 70-90% of the cost of a sensor system installation relating to labor and wiring, which ranges from $40 to $2000 per linear foot of wiring [2]. As such, the wireless nature of WSN technologies makes them easier and cheaper to deploy than wired technologies.

However, a number of challenges still need to be addressed to ensure WSN technology achieves its' full potential across all application areas. An abundance of communications technologies persist within the HAN domain, with no single technology identifying itself as the "one size fits all" solution.

The *AUT*onomic *H*om*E* area *N*e*T*work *I*nfrastru*C*ture (AUTHENTIC) project [3][4] funded by the International Energy Research Centre (IERC) [5], sought to develop and deploy a HAN infrastructure capable of supporting opportunistic decision making pertaining to effective energy management within the home. This required the integration of key enabling heterogeneous technologies including a variety of physical sensors within the home (temperature, contact sensors, passive infra-red), cyber sensor sources (services) outside of the home (e.g., meteorological data, energy providers dynamic pricing sites) together with effective interfacing with the smart grid beyond the home. As part of the AUTHENTIC project (final demonstrators were presented in 2015) the WSN group at Tyndall were developing the embedded systems and communications platforms to sense and transfer data in the built environment. The platform developed enables communications between the heterogeneous sensing systems that typically make up a HAN scenario in a power efficient implementation.

Section I of this paper introduces the subject matter and application space associated with wireless sensing solutions for the built environment. Section II reviews some of the state of the art in current wireless sensing system technologies, with emphasis on multiradio systems. Section III describes the "AUTHENTIC Board" developed within the project [1]. Section IV describes the multiradio functionality and Section V examines the results of initial range testing trials and tests carried out using the system to investigate power consumption characteristics of the platform. Section VI investigates the power savings enabled by this multiradio, multiboot platform, through the implementation of different communications protocols based on the system level tests carried out in Section V. Section VII concludes the work and outlines some directions for future research in this area.

II. PREVIOUS WORKS

There are a variety of standards available (proprietary and non-proprietary), which are widely used within the many deployments of HAN that exist. ZigBee, Bluetooth LE (Low Energy), IEEE 802.11x (Wi-Fi) are globally recognized as references in wireless communications and go far beyond the scope of WSN. Those technologies have been developed using the license-free ISM band of 2.4-2.5GHz, although ZigBee has an implementation for the 868MHz and the latest 802.11.n standard used by Wi-Fi offers support for both 2.4 and 5GHz. Indoor range above the GHz frequency is quite limited especially for indoor applications with dense obstacles. The Wi-Fi technology surpasses those issues with higher transmission power (up to 100 times higher than ZigBee/802.15.4), which is of course not suitable for battery powered systems in low power WSN deployments.

Although some manufacturers provide WSN systems using 868MHz or even 433MHz, it is more common to see them designed around proprietary technologies such as ZigBee. An interesting trade off investigated in this paper is the development of a system with the ability to adapt its communications channel to use the best radio link depending on the throughput and range requirements in any configuration.

Multiradio platforms are a subject of research for WSN as they offer some attractive characteristics and improvements over single radio WSN platforms. Multiradio systems with radios covering Wi-Fi, Bluetooth and 6LoWPAN (IPv6 over Low power Wireless Personal Area Networks) operating at the 2.45 GHz ISM band have reported to achieve enhanced robustness, latency and energy characteristics [6]. In a variety of implementations, multiradio systems operating at the 433MHz and 2.45 GHz ISM bands have been reported which use a preamble sampling technique in a wakeup radio implementation [7]. These multiradio platforms have been used to evaluate the performance of communications protocols in terms of power consumption and latency over different duty cycle values and under various amounts of traffic loads. Kusy [8] reports on the development of a new dual radio network architecture to improve communication reliability in a wireless sensor network, but the approach was limited to a single channel implementation, where the 900MHz and 2.4GHz radios were used in parallel rather than in conjunction with power saving protocols. A multiradio platform for on the body WSN applications operating in 433MHz and 868Mz is reported in [9] with focus on the platform architecture. More consideration on the issues of antenna design for such devices is found in [10] [11]. A comprehensive survey of MAC protocols is given by Jurdak et Al in [12]. They survey, classify, and analyze 34 MAC layer protocols for wireless ad hoc networks, ranging from industry standards to research activites.

The BtNode V3 [13] platform features two radios. It incorporates a Chipcon CC1000 low power radio (433-915 MHz) and also has an additional ZV4002 Bluetooth radio (2.4 GHz) as shown in Figure 1.a. Similarly the Shimmer mote [14] and the Wasp Mote [15] feature a CC2420 IEEE 802.15.4 radio and can also be configured with an optional Bluetooth radio shown in Figure 1.b and Figure 1.c respectively. The Wasp Mote also has separate 868MHz and 900MHz radio modular plug-in boards however, in this instance only a single radio module can be operated at a time and true multiradio operation is not feasible. Similarly, the Tyndall Mote (Figure 1.d), has the capability for adding multiple radios. With the Tyndall mote, because of the planar implementation, several different radios could be stacked on top of each other and operate simultaneously.

The AUTHENTIC board described in this publication is not only a radio sensing platform but it can also be a repeater increasing the range of the network. Moreover, at the same time, the user can connect to each single platform in the network using a tablet or a smartphone via Bluetooth (for maintenance or data visualization).

The AUTHENTIC board has been designed with interoperability in mind, it can be used in existing deployments that use ZigBee or 868MHz protocols, to improving the network range without increasing the interference. From a protocol perspective, each board can work as an end node or base station/coordinator as well. In fact, if there are some changes in the network one node can reboot and operate as in base station mode using its multiboot functionality.

Similarly, the OPAL platform is an example of a multiradio platform where increased performance in terms of the network realization, latency, data throughput and power consumption were achieved compared to single radio platforms [16]. The OPAL platform is a high throughput sensing module that includes two onboard 802.15.4 radios operating in the 900MHz and 2.4GHz bands to provide communication diversity and an aggregate transfer rate of 3 Mbps. It embeds a 96 MHz Cortex SAM3U processor with dynamic core frequency scaling, a feature that can be used to fine-tune processing speed with the higher communication rates while minimizing energy consumption.

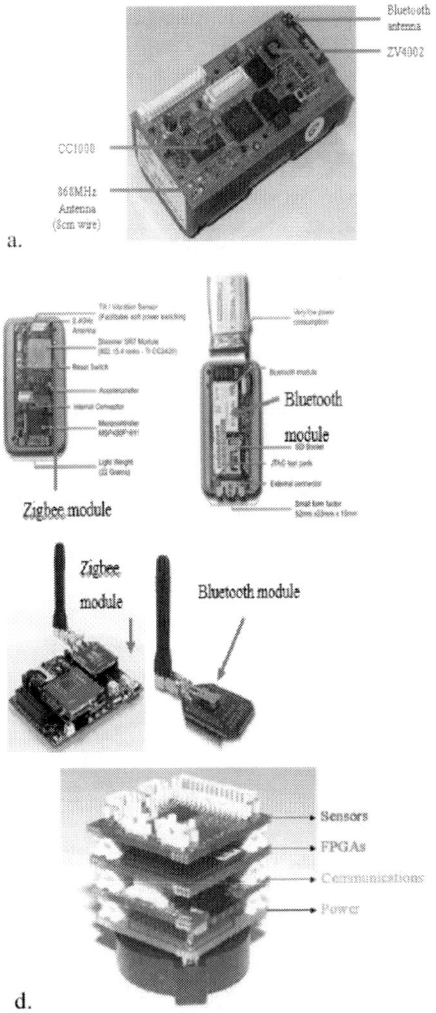

Figure 1. Multiradio systems. a) Dual Radio BTnodeRev3 b) Dual Radio Shimmer c) Wasp Mote ZigBee & Bluetooth Modules d) The Tyndall 25mm modular system

III. System Implementation

The aim of this system development is to provide a future-proof wireless platform for HAN with regards to the network heterogeneity in terms of hardware and protocols currently in use and under development.

A specification process was undertaken with industry partners and service providers in the area of building management – to identify the core requirements associated with a wireless system for deployment in homes and offices.

The platform described in the following sections of this paper is a novel low power consumption multiradio system incorporating a 32-bit ARM-Cortex microcontroller and multiple radio interfaces - ZigBee/6LoWPAN/Bluetooth LE/868MHz platform, which features autonomous behavior to enable interoperability between systems utilizing different radio front ends. It provides a solution for network congestion in environments such as HAN and Commercial Buildings in a credit card sized form factor shown in Figure 2. It also provides better interoperability than the usual wireless sensor devices approach, enhancing the communicability between different network entities (sensor nodes, smart meters, media, smartphones), and driving the wireless sensor networks to the smart cities application space.

Figure 2. AUTHENTIC Credit Card Form Factor Platform.

The four main issues that need to be considered prior to selecting any unit or design approaches are: over all power consumption, cost, complete module size and user friendliness. Technical features assessed and considered included: functionality requirements as regards actuation and control, quality of service, latency, number and types of sensors/meters and interfaces, programming methods (wireless/non wireless), power supplies/energy harvesting compatibility, radio frequency band, standards/non standards communications and data transmission range.

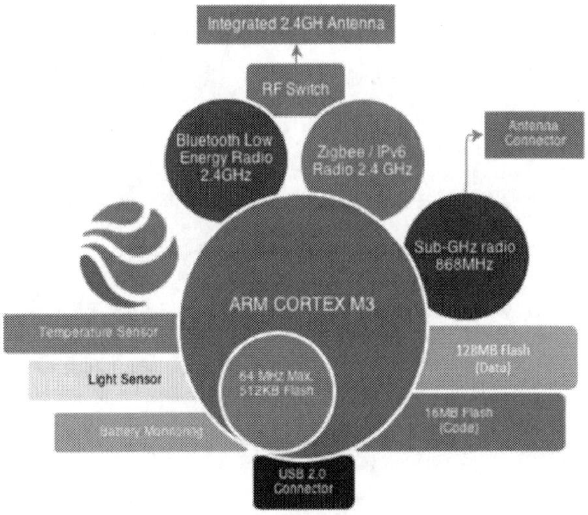

Figure 3. Block diagram of AUTHENTIC Platform functionality.

In conjunction with these end users, as part of our system specification, three communication standards were identified as being needed within the HAN environment: ZigBee – 2.4GHz, 6LoWPan – 2.4GHz, Bluetooth Low Energy – 2.4GHz, as well as a non-standards based ISM band 868MHz transceiver as a response to the 2.4GHz limitations identified - bandwidth congestion and data loss associated with non line of sight (NLOS) effects of the building structure limited RF range. The board has been designed around the standard ARM CORTEX-M3 based microcontroller, which offers a good trade-off between power consumption and performance. See Figure 3 for an overview of features and functionalities.

The final embedded system was designed around a credit card form factor (shown in Figure 4) and deployed in offices and homes for preliminary tests and characterization

Microcontroller: The heart of the system is the ATMEL SAM3S8C microcontroller, a 32-bit ARM Cortex M3 Core. 64MHz Maximum, 512KB flash, 64KB RAM, USB 2.0.

External Flash Memories: Two external flash memories: 128MB NAND flash for data logging, 16MB NOR-flash for code execution. The two memories are connected to the microcontroller External Bus Interface (EBI).

Radio Communication: The platform integrates three radio chips: Bluetooth Low Energy radio chip, (manufacturer: NORDIC, model: NRF8001), ZigBee/6LoWPAN radio chip, (manufacturer: ATMEL, model: AT86RF231), Sub-GHz radio chip (868MHz), (manufacturer: ST Microelectronics, model: SPIRIT1).

Sensors: Two sensors were interfaced via an I^2C interface: temperature sensor, accuracy: ±0.5°C, (manufacturer: MAXIM, model: MAX31725MTA+), light sensor, range: 0.045 Lux to 188,000 Lux, (manufacturer: MAXIM, model: MAX44009EDT+T). These are used for detecting in-home activity monitoring occupancy through lighting usage.

Battery: The battery used is a lithium prismatic battery with a capacity of 1300mAh, which is recharged through the USB port or through the use of energy harvesting systems compatible with the built environment [17].

1- Bluetooth Low Energy Radio Chip
2- Zigbee/6LowPAN Radio Chip
3- Sub-GHz Radio Chip
4- Cortex M3 Microcontroller Unit
5- Temperature Sensor
6- Light Sensor
7- Battery connector
8- USB micro B connector
9- On/Off Switch
10- Interrupt Switch
11- 868MHz Antenna connector
12- RF Switch
13- 2.4GHz PCB Antenna
14- RF connector for prototype evaluation

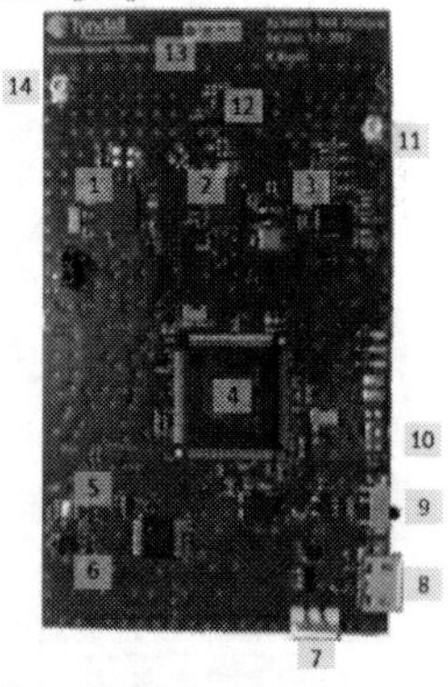

Figure 4. AUTHENTIC multiradio embedded system.

IV. MULTIRADIO FUNCTIONALITY

In this section the functionality of the AUTHENTIC platform is presented in terms of its communication architectures, the multiradio and multiboot capabilities embedded in the system.

A. *Communication Architectures using Multiradio Systems*

In the context of "crowded radio frequency spectrum", a wireless sensor network composed with a number of the proposed devices' architectures can automatically adapt to the most reliable frequency communication channel based on the local interferences. This type of architecture has some interesting commercial applications for interoperable networks, HAN's, commercial buildings and smart cities. Compared to single-end radio devices, it has the potential to provide increased connectivity in deployment, and can potentially reduce the interference impact on the network as the system can hop from ISM band to ISM band in an autonomous and opportunistic manner.

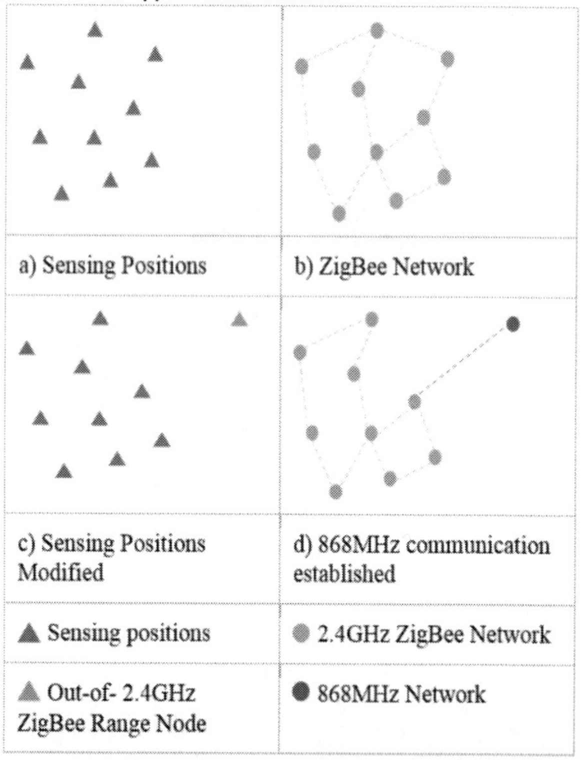

Figure 5. AUTHENTIC multiradio system in operation

By developing smart mechanisms for multi-protocol routing between the different radios, this architecture can potentially reduce the number of repeaters (and thus the infrastructure cost) compared to a standard single ended radio platform. In addition, multiradio systems provide better interoperability with Off-The-Shelf wireless devices, many of which operate on a variety of different standards and which may constitute a typical smart home deployment.

From a research point of view, such a platform can be used to develop and evaluate firmware/wireless protocols using different frequency bands.

The multiradio concept is illustrated in Figure 5 which shows how, by jumping between the 2.4GHz and 868MHz frequency bands, a connection can be made between remote clusters of ZigBee nodes, which are in different locations or separated by a congested spectrum making communication at 2.4GHz difficult.

Thus the network automatically switches to the 868MHz frequency in order to maintain communication with the out of range node. In that case, one node from the first cluster will act as a virtual "dual sensing" node, providing two inputs to the ZigBee Network.

B. Multiradio Aspect

The Bluetooth and 868MHz multiradio functionality has been tested as a proof of concept in a HAN as part of the AUTHENTIC deployment in office environments and in homes (for open field testing, the system was deployed temporarily outside).

To evaluate the capabilities of the multiradio functionality, the remote node sends data (light, temperature or other peripheral sensor) to the base station using the 868MHz radio or the 2.4GHz ZigBee network. The base station then sends the received data to a Smart Phone/HAN gateway using the Bluetooth interface that displays the data stream (in this case, temperature and light level from the remote sensor) as shown in Figure 6.

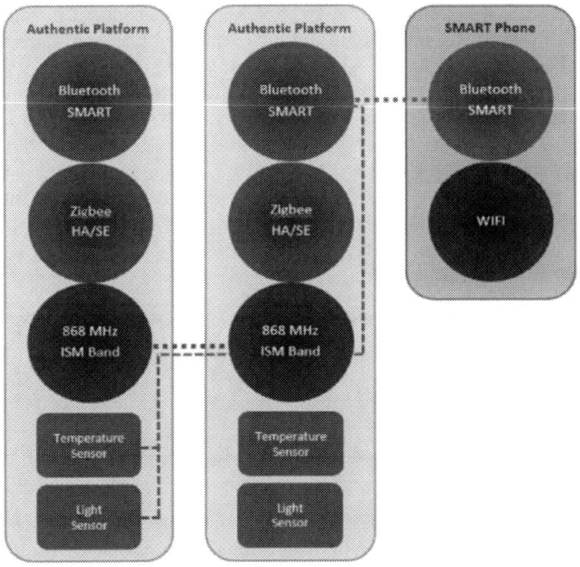

Figure 6. AUTHENTIC multiradio system

C. Multiboot - Autonomous System Implementation

Multiboot capability enables the system to boot up and run according to various boot images [18] [19], which are stored in various sectors (region) of memory – see Figure 7.

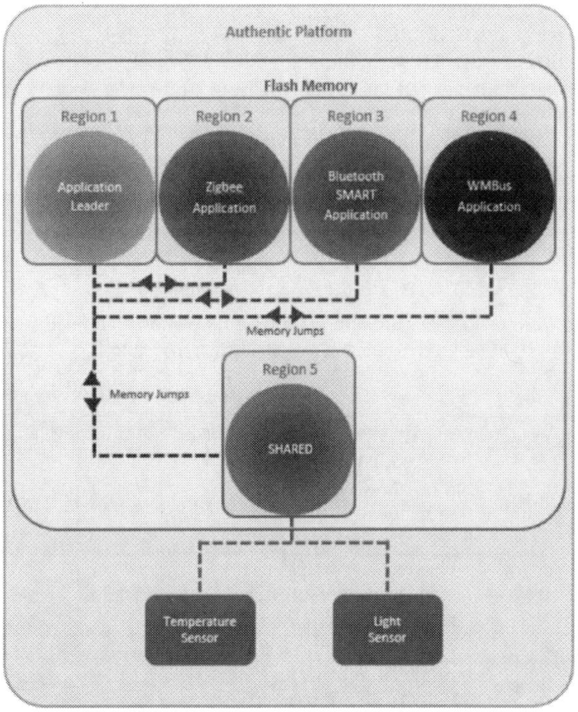

Figure 7. AUTHENTIC Multiboot reconfigurability

To facilitate energy savings at an embedded system level, the multiboot configuration of the system will allow the platform to host two different applications and jump between them (via a boot loader). The applications can and will use different radios in future deployments, which will be useful for overcoming transmission issues in a congested/noisy environment. The targeted example is the mote running a ZigBee 2.4GHz application and an 868MHz application. Failing to transmit data at 2.4GHz due to electromagnetic effects or long range requirements, the node would switch to the 868MHz application to operate in a less congested ISM band. This behavior would be coordinated among the network nodes in protocols under development. In this case, the idea is to allocate memory regions to specific applications.

The **Multi-Application Software Management** tool acts as a main application that we will call "**Leader**". The **Leader** is programmed in a specific area of the memory and will act as what is commonly known as a Bootstrap Loader. The particular boot state functionality can be associated with a range of communications modalities say ZigBee, Bluetooth or Wireless Modbus according to application requirements associated with energy consumption, latency or Quality of Service.

The **Leader** can access any location of the memory. The applications that will contain the required functionalities of the system (e.g., sensing, communication) will be described as "**Users**". The **Leader** can then grant the leadership to the different **Users** that will need to return the leadership to the **Leader** (different solutions are possible for the latter).

The **Leader** will provide an API (Application Programming Interface) in order to modify intrinsic parameters of the system (e.g., system clock frequency, timers etc.). Thus, this functionality will considerably reduce the complexity of the development from the user developer's point of view.

From a smart home/building management system deployment perspective, it will provide an essential software management tool for multiradio platforms.

V. RESULTS

A. AUTHENTIC Board Power Characterization

To carry out the energy consumption tests, the following modalities were implemented as shown in Table I.

TABLE I. SYSTEM POWER CONSUMPTION IN DIFFERENT MODES

Symbol	Operational Mode Measured	Value	Unit
I_{TX868}	Current consumption in TX mode 868MHz module, POUT = +12 dBm, all components on	43.98	mA
I_{sb868}	Current consumption in standby mode 868MHz module, all components on	28.24	mA
I_{TXBLE} 0dBm	Current consumption in TX mode BLE module, POUT = 0 dBm, all components on	24.80	mA
I_{sbBLE}	Current consumption in standby mode (between 2 transmissions) BLE module, all components on	17.29	mA
ITX, ZigBee 1	Current consumption in TX mode ZigBee module, POUT = +3 dBm, all components on, 1 led on	64.07	mA
ITX, ZigBee 2	Current consumption in TX mode ZigBee module, POUT = +3 dBm, all components on, 1 led off	71.12	mA
Isleep1	Current consumption in sleep mode (microcontroller) and all the other components on	15.73	mA
Isleep2	Current consumption in sleep mode (microcontroller) and all the other components off	3.18	mA
Isleep3	Current consumption in deepest sleep mode (microcontroller) and all the other components on	3.1	mA
Isleep4	Current consumption in deepest sleep mode and components off / removed	3.5	µA

The MCU is programmed to turn on all the devices, setting the output power of the module to (+12 dBm for 868 MHz module, 0 dBm for BLE, +3 dBm for ZigBee), start the transmission of a single packet (1 byte length) and then put it in standby mode. Sleep mode tests include the MCU turning on all the devices before going into sleep mode, turning off all the devices and entering sleep mode, turning on all the devices and entering deepest sleep mode and turning off all the devices and going into deepest sleep mode.

For the 868 MHz tests, GFSK (Gaussian frequency-shift keying) modulation with the Gaussian filter "BT Product" set to 1 was used. For the Bluetooth LE modules the default Gaussian filter used is 0.5. For the ZigBee module quadrature phase-shift keying (QPSK) modulation was used. Table I shows the results of all tests in different modes. These provide the building blocks for developing low-power networking algorithims for optimising the lifetime of the WSN systems and QoS parameters.

B. Multiradio Range Test Comparison

1) Indoor Non Line of Sight (NLOS) range testing

This section focuses on the NLOS testing of the 868 MHz, Bluetooth and ZigBee radio modules on the AUTHENTIC Board. Two boards are used: one acts as a sensing node and one as a Base Station.

The node reads data from the temperature sensor as well as received signal strength indication (RSSI) values. This is then sent to the Base Station where it is converted into a value expressed in °C (minimizing energy consumption associated with processing on the node), which is in turn sent to our visual interface (a smartphone connected via Bluetooth).

The test took place in an office environment consisting of open plan cubicles, closed offices, coffee dock facilities and meeting rooms in a simulated "home environment". The node (represented by the star) was kept stationary while the base station and the smartphone moved around the entire area for data gathering at the different frequencies under test. In Figures 8, 9, 10, the areas where the data is received perfectly are reported in green, in orange the areas where the signal is poor and the data is received intermittently, in red the areas where there is no signal and data is not received.

Theory would suggest that the range associated with lower frequency (868MHz) ISM bands would significantly outperform higher frequency ISM bands (2.4GHz). In this experiment, the difference is little more than a 10% improvement (see Table II).

TABLE II. COMPARISON OF RANGE FOR INDOOR NLOS TESTS

Radio	Appoximate Area Covered	Max. distance (Line of sight)
868 MHz	130.4 m^2	11.4 m
Bluetooth LE	60.04 m^2	7 m
ZigBee	108.6 m^2	10.6 m

We expected 868MHz to be much better than ZigBee, a possible reason (under investigation) is that the 868MHz data rate (500 kbps) is higher than the ZigBee one (250 kbps) and there is a tradeoff between the range and the data rate. Moreover, the modulation used by the modules are different: the value of Eb/N0 (noise power per unit bandwidth) of the offset-QPSK is less than that of the GFSK; this means that the bit error rate is better for the ZigBee module operating at

2.4GHz. To improve the 868MHz range, it is possible to increase the power of the module (it can reach +16 dB) and reduce the data rate. Further experiments were carried out to validate this (as shown in Table III).

Figure 8. 868MHz range test

Figure 9. Bluetooth LE range test

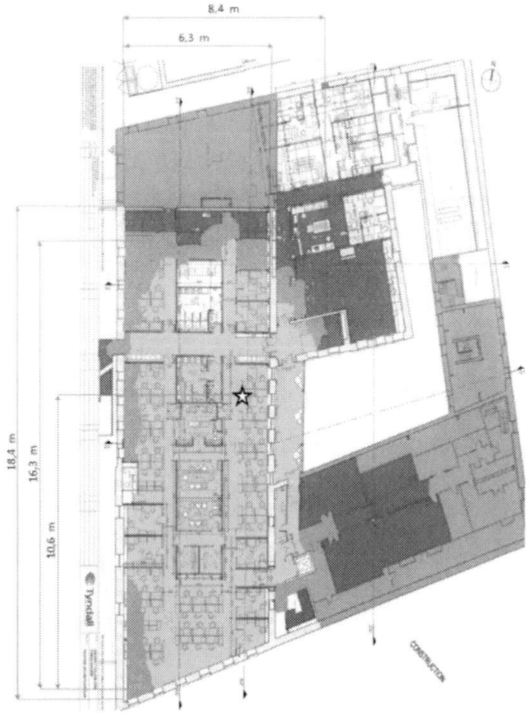

Figure 10. ZigBee 2.4GHz range test

2) Sub-GHz range improvement.

To improve the 868MHz range, 3 solutions have been adopted: the output power of the sensing node was increased up to +12 dBm (initially +11dBm). In addition, the data rate was reduced to 100 kbps (from 250 kbps). Finally, the GFSK modulation with BT product was set to 0.5 (from 1). BT is the Bandwidth Time. It is the product of adjacent signal frequency separation and symbol duration. A BT product of 0.5 corresponds to the minimum carrier separation to ensure orthogonality between signals in adjacent channels. The beneficial result of this is the signal on one frequency channel does not interfere with the signal on the adjacent frequency channel.

The sub-GHz radio chip uses an external crystal oscillator that provides a clock signal for the frequency synthesizer. The channel center frequency has been programmed to be 868MHz. So as to ensure that this is the actual frequency used, it was measured using a Spectrum Analyser.

We measured that the two boards in the deployment (remote multi radio node and multi radio base station) send and receive data at 868.027 MHz (+10.70 dBm) and 868.0181 MHz (+11.02 dBm) respectively. This is found to be due to the crystal inaccuracy. To compensate the inaccuracy, a correction term (f_{offset}) has been implemented in the firmware to ensure that the frequency for send and receive is exactly set to 868MHz.

$$f_{offset} = \frac{f_{XO}}{2^{18}} \cdot FC\_OFFSET$$

Where fxo is the frequency of the crystal oscillator (52MHz) and FC_OFFSET is a 12-bit integer set by the FC_OFFSET registers of the radio chip.

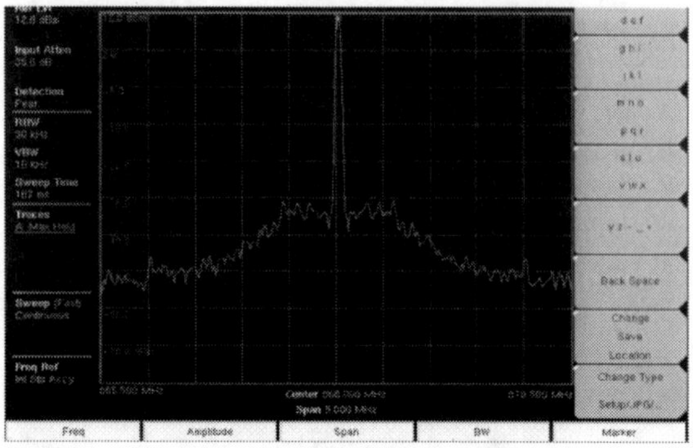

Figure 11. Output power.

After this compensation, the 2 boards had the center frequency at 868.00MHz (Figure 11) and another range test has been made in the same environment of the previous tests with 2 AUTHENTIC boards (one as node remote and one as base station) and the result has been reported in Figure 12 and Table III below showing the maximum range obtained using the 868MHz radio.

Figure 12. 868MHz range test after compensation

As can be seen from a comparison with the initial set of results reported in [1] and shown here in Table II, we achieved an improvement of 60% in performance (area covered) with the new configuration settings for the AUTHENTIC boards operating in the 868 MHz band.

TABLE III. RANGE TESTING 868 MHZ BAND USING OPTIMISED CONFIGURATION SETTINGS

Radio	Approximate Area Covered
868MHz (Test 1)	130,4 m^2
868MHz (Test 2)	211,5 m^2

3) Outdoor Line of Sight (LOS) range testing

An open field is one of the simplest and most commonly used environments for RF range tests. In this section, tests for the three modules on the AUTHENTIC Board (868MHz, Bluetooth, and ZigBee) are reported. The tests took place in a sports field in University College Cork, which offered a long range LOS measurement.

868MHz: To test the Sub-GHz module, two AUTHENTIC boards were used, one as Node Remote and one as Base Station. The first reads data every four seconds from the temperature sensor and sends it to the Base Station. The maximum range measured was 193m.

Bluetooth: For this test, two devices were used: one AUTHENTIC Board and a smartphone. The board was left stationary and the smartphone was moved around the area checking if the connection was still available or not. The maximum LOS distance measured was 18.4m.

ZigBee: To test the ZigBee module, two AUTHENTIC boards (one as Trust Center and one as Occupancy Sensor) were used along with a RF231USB-RD USB Stick (as Remote Control). The Trust Center creates the network and the other two devices join it. After this, the Occupancy Sensor reads the value of the LED (on/off) and sends it every four seconds to the Remote Control that moves around the area. The maximum range measured was 193m.

The maximum distance measured in Line of Sight for both the ZigBee and 868MHz system was 193m, but this value could be greater and additional tests need to be carried out to establish the maximum range for each. The maximum range achieved was due to the presence of physical obstacles (walls/buildings, which would have interfered with the LOS measurements at the maximum extremity of the test location. The results are tabulated in Table IV.

TABLE IV. COMPARISON OF RANGE FOR OUTDOOR LOS TESTS

Radio	Max. distance (Line of Sight)
868MHz	193m *
Bluetooth LE	18.4m
ZigBee	193m *

* Limit of the field measurement, not the technology

VI. AUTHENTIC MULTI HOP PROTOCOL IMPLEMENTATION

The AUTHENTIC network has been designed to be an auto configurable network, this means that the network is autonomous in operation and has the capability to reconfigure itself. It is composed of one base station (that acts as both a router and gateway) and sensor nodes (sensing nodes that read data from the sensors on board and send the sensor data values to the base station/gateway) as shown in Figure 13.

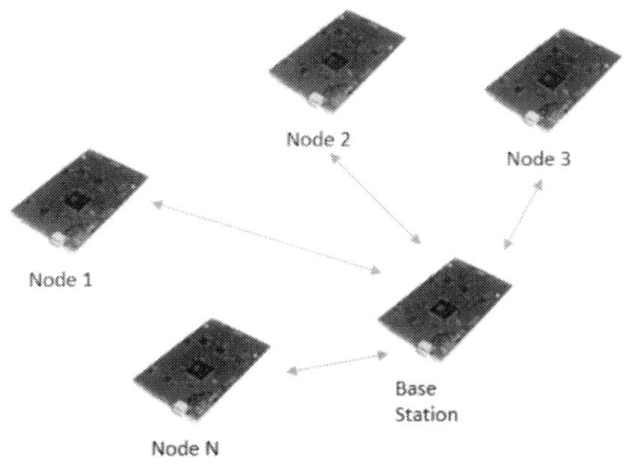

Figure 13. The AUTHENTIC network topology

At system start up, the base station creates a sub-1GHz network with the sensor nodes by transmitting a broadcast message to the nodes and waiting for their reply.

When the node receives the broadcast packet, it saves the base station's address in its memory and replies with an ACK to confirm that it has received the message.

When the base station receives the ACK, it checks the Received Signal Strength Indication (RSSI) to be sure that the link with the node is a robust one. If the RSSI value is higher than the threshold (it is taken to be -75 dBm), then the base station saves the node's address in its list of the sub-1GHz addresses, so as to be able to build an appropriate routing table. If the RSSI value is lower than the threshold, the base station sends another message to the node in order to change the radio communication to ZigBee. The default start up mode is in the 868MHz band operation mode. Two possible factors can affect the RSSI value: interference and the distance between the node and the base station. In these cases it is better to switch to another frequency.

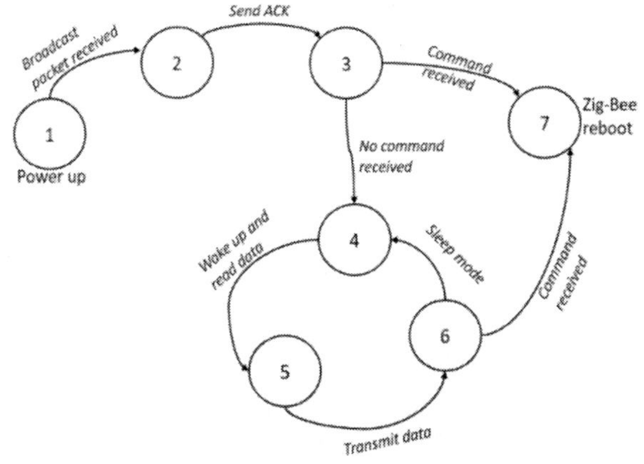

Figure 14. Node's state machine

The node goes into RX mode every time it sends a packet to the base station in order to receive the command to switch to ZigBee. The protocol state machine for the node is shown in Figure 14. The node, after sending the ACK message regarding the broadcast packet, goes into RX mode for a certain period (it is taken for the purposes of these experiments to be 1 second). During this period the only message that it can receive is the command to change its communication to ZigBee due to the RSSI level measurements taken. If so, it will reboot (using the multi boot functionality described in [1]) with the ZigBee application and waits for the creation of the ZigBee network.

If the node doesn't receive any command from the base station it assumes that it is part of the sub-1GHz (868MHz) network, and goes into sleep mode (to reduce power consumption) for a random period between 4 and 5 minutes (T_{sleep}). The node then wakes up, reads the data from the sensors on board (temperature and light level) and sends them to the base station. Once the data packet is sent, the node again enters in RX mode for 2 seconds so as to receive an appropriate command from the base station, after that it goes into sleep mode for T_{sleep}, then it wakes up, sends the sensors readings and so on.

T_{sleep} is a randomly assigned value to avoid the case that all the nodes send their sensor readings at the same time. This will reduce the probability of packet collision between the transmissions with the resultant requirement for retransmissions and increase in associated energy consumption.

The base station, after the broadcast message, communicates with each node that has replied to the broadcast, and saves all their addresses in 2 lists, one for the sub GHz network (that contains the nodes' addresses with RSSI higher than the threshold) and one for the ZigBee network (that contains the nodes' addresses with RSSI lower than the threshold). Based on these tables, the coordinator is in a position to develop an appropriate network structure. The sub GHz network is created first, after which the base station starts the creation of the ZigBee network. Once the two networks have been defined, the basestation enters sleep mode to save power. The system can be woken up by receiving sensor data messages from the nodes associated with the 2 networks created. This wake up is instigated by an interrupt based on a received data packet used to wake the microcontroller up out of standby mode.

For each message received, the base station sends the sensor data to a GUI enabled device connected via the Bluetooth interface on the AUTHENTIC Board (to any standard smartphone, tablet, PC etc.). The GUI displays data in real time from the different nodes and stores these in an associated database for analysis. The base station checks if the RSSI value of that node is higher or lower than the threshold (in this case -75 dBm). Only if it is lower than -75 dBm will the base station send a message to the node in order to switch to ZigBee network. When the node receives this command it sends an ACK to the base station to confirm that the message has been received and it reboots with the ZigBee application mode operational.

When the base station receives the ACK, it removes the node's address from the sub GHz addresses list and adds it to the ZigBee addresses list. The packet structure is shown in Figure 15.

Preamble	Sync	Length	Dest. Address	Source Address	Control	Seq. No.	ACK	Payload	CRC

Figure 15. The AUTHENTIC Board Zigbee packet structure

Where:

- Preamble is a signal to synchronize transmission timing and it is a programmable field from 1 to 32 bytes;
- Sync is the synchronization word;
- Length is the packet length;
- Dest. Address is the destination address and can be set to a single, broadcast or multicast address;
- Source Address is the address of the transmitting board;
- Control is the control field of the packet;
- Seq. No. contains the sequence number of the transmitted packet. It is incremented automatically every time a new packet is transmitted;
- ACK is the acknowledgement field. If set to 1 means that it is the acknowledgement packet;
- Payload is information data;
- CRC is the error detecting code to detect errors in the data.

The base station sends periodically (every 15 minutes) the general broadcast message in order to contact new nodes that did not reply at the first message or to contact any of the nodes that need to reboot so they can join the network. Nodes that are already in the network will ignore the message.

The use of this protocol shows the interoperability between the different wireless technologies (Bluetooth, ZigBee, and 868MHz). It is proposed that this system is a solution for network congestion because it reduces interference in one particular frequency band. If interference is encountered in one band then the system simply changes the operational ISM band to avoid it.

It is also a good solution to reduce power consumption associated with an individual nodes' operation. In the first instance, power savings are enabled due to the fact that the nodes and the base station are in low-power sleep mode if they don't need to transmit data. Moreover, since the base station is monitoring the RSSI signal levels, redundant and energy wasteful transmissions are eliminated (in the case that the node continues to transmit data but the base station can't receive them - because it is out of range or there is too much interference in the network).

An evaluation of potential power savings associated with the new protocol has been carried out regarding a network composed of one Base Station and three nodes and based on the power consumption reported in Table I, assuming to power the boards with a 3V battery, to transmit data every 5 minutes and then go in sleep mode.

In a scenario where three nodes join the sub-1GHz network and when the RSSI level referring to one node is lower than the threshold it joins the ZigBee network, the estimated power consumption of the Base Station is 52.13mW and 14.43mW for a single node.

As previously outlined, the Base Station is in standby mode when it is not transmitting or receiving and the nodes go into sleep mode after sending the data read from the temperature and light sensors.

In a single radio scenario, where only the ZigBee network is available, it can happen that the nodes send the sensors data to the Base Station but it cannot receive them because of the interferences or long range issues, so the nodes transmit uselessly wasting power. In this case the estimated power consumption of the Base Station is 55.87mW and 16.83mW for a single node.

System energy consumption for the multiradio platform was calculated based on a model which was developed using empirically derived power measurements. These measurements are reported in Table I, and are based on the board being powered by a 3V battery. The operational duty cycle for the sensor nodes was selected to be 5%. The system is considered to be in sleep mode for the rest of the cycle.

From this energy model, we can see that the power consumption of the node that uses an appropriate communication protocol associated with a multiradio system (14.43mW) is reduced by approximately 15% compared to a node that works in a single radio system (16.83mW). This will translate to an increase in battery lifetime of 10-15% in a typical application (based on a standard AA battery).

VII. Conclusions & Future Work

Interoperability between communications protocols operating using different radio technologies is a major issue within the realm of wireless sensor technology where numerous wireless sensor technologies could be operating in the same vicinity. Middleware is one software solution that aims to overcome this problem. Middleware runs at either the gateway or cloud level and incorporates drivers for numerous protocols (ZigBee, Z-Wave and EnOcean for example).

This paper has shown how multi radio architectures and networks offer the possibility of increased interoperability and energy savings at a network and node level and thus are ideal for use in such HAN architectures. In addition, the multiradio architectures described address some of the issues associated with the fact that in the resource-constrained systems typically used in sensing systems for the built environment, energy is often the primary constraint and impacts on all aspects of the sensor system.

This work describes the development and preliminary characterization of a novel low power consumption multiradio system incorporating multiple radio interfaces - ZigBee/6LoWPAN/Bluetooth LE/868MHz platform. It provides a solution for network congestion in environment such as Home Area Network and Commercial Buildings in a credit card sized form factor. The multiradio sensing system shows the potential for such systems to improve interoperability between the different wireless technologies enhancing the communications between heterogeneous network entities (Sensor Nodes, Smart Meters, Media, Smart Phones), and driving the Wireless Sensor Networks use case in the built environment. The configurability of the system can increase the range between single sensor points and can enable the implementation of adaptive networking architectures of different configurations.

Additional characterization and optimization of the system in a variety of environments is underway and development of frequency hopping protocols to maximize the potential of the multiradio system and its possibilities to maximize system lifetime of a WSN in a Smart Home or office environment through the development of networking protocols leveraging off the platforms capabilities.

ACKNOWLEDGMENT

The authors would like to acknowledge the support of Enterprise Ireland and the International Energy Research Centre (IERC) for funding the AUTHENTIC project (TC20121002A/B). This publication has emanated from research supported in part by Science Foundation Ireland (SFI) and is co-funded under the European Regional Development Fund, Grant Number 13/RC/2077-CONNECT. Aspects of this work have been funded by the European Union Horizon 2020 project MOEEBIUS under grant agreement 680517.

REFERENCES

[1] B. O'Flynn, M. De Donno, and W. Magnin, "Multiradio Sensing Systems for Home Area Networking and Building Management," The Fifth International Conference on Smart Cities, Systems, Devices and Technologies (SMART 2016), IARIA, May 2016, pp. 25-30, ISSN: 2308-3727, ISBN: 978-1-61208-4763.

[2] F. Zhao and L. Guibas, Wireless Sensor Networks: An Information Processing Approach, ISBN-9781558609143, Elsevier, Chapter 8, pp. 294, 2004.

[3] AUTHENTIC Webpage, http://www.creativedesign.ie/ierc_test/?homeareanetworks=AUTHENTIC-for-home-area-networks-han 2016.11.25

[4] K.Curran, Recent Advances in Ambient Intelligence and Context-Aware Computing, IGI global book series Advances in Computational Intelligence and Robotics (ACIR)(ISSN: 2327-0411), Chapter 10, pp. 155-169.

[5] IERC Website, http://www.ierc.ie/ 2016.11.25

[6] M. T. Delgado, H. Khaleel, C. Pastrone, and M. A. Spirito, "Underlying connectivity mechanisms for multi-radio wireless sensor and actuator networks," The 9th International Conference on Wireless and Mobile Computing, Networking and Communications (WiMob 2013), IEEE, Oct 2013, pp. 408-413.

[7] J. Ansari, X. Zhang, and P. Mahonen, "Multi-radio medium access control protocol for wireless sensor networks," Int. J. Sen. Networks, 8(1):47-61, 2010.

[8] B. Kusy et al., "Radio diversity for reliable communication in wsns," in Proc. Int. Symp. Inform. Process. Sensor Networks.,Chicago, IL, 2011, pp. 270–281.

[9] J. Buckley et al.,"A novel and miniaturized 433/868mhz multi-band wireless sensor platform for body sensor network applications," Ninth International Conference on Wearable and Implantable Body Sensor Networks (BSN 2012), May 2012,, pp. 63-66, ISBN: 978-0-7695-4698-8.

[10] L. Loizou, J. Buckley, and B. O'Flynn," Design and analysis of a dual-band inverted-f antenna with orthogonal frequency-controlled radiation planes," Antennas and Propagation, IEEE Transactions on, 61(8):3946-3951, 2013.

[11] L. Loizou, J. Buckley, B. O'Flynn, J. Barton, C. O'Mathuna, and E. Popovici," Design and measurement of a planar dual-band antenna for the Tyndall multiradio wireless sensing platform," In Sensors Applications Symposium (SAS 2013) IEEE, Feb 2013 pp. 11-14, ISBN: 978-1-4673-4636-8.

[12] R. Jurdak, C. V. Lopes, and P. Baldi, "A survey classification and comparative analysis of medium access control protocols for ad hoc networks." IEEE Commun. Survey. Tutorials, vol. 6, pp. 2–16, Jan. 2004.

[13] BTNode http://www.btnode.ethz.ch/ 2016.11.25

[14] Shimmer Mote link www.shimmer.com 2016.11.25

[15] http://www.libelium.com/products/waspmote/hardware 2016.11.25

[16] R. Jurdak, K. Klues, B. Kusy, C. Richter, K. Langendoen, and M. Brunig, "Opal. A multiradio platform for high throughput wireless sensor networks," Embedded Systems Letters, IEEE, 3(4):121-124, 2011.

[17] C. O'Mathuna, T. O'Donnell, R. Martinez-Catala, J. Rohan, and B. O'Flynn, "Energy Scavenging For Long-Term Deployable Wireless Sensor Networks," Talanta, 75 (3):613-623.

[18] D. Fuji, T. Yamakami, and K. Ishiguro, "A fast-boot method for embedded mobile Linux: Toward a single-digit user sensed boot time for full-featured commercial phones," Proc. - 25th IEEE Int. Conf. Adv. Inf. Netw. Appl. Work., (WAINA 2011), March 2011, pp. 81–85, ISBN 978-0-7695-4338-3.

[19] C. W. Chang, C. Y. Yang, Y. H. Chang, and T. W. Kuo, "Booting time minimization for real-time embedded systems with non-volatile memory," IEEE Trans. Comput., vol. 63, no. 4, pp. 847–859, 2014.

Analyzing the Performance of Software Defined Networks vs Real Networks

Jose M. Jimenez, Oscar Romero, Albert Rego, Jaime Lloret
Universidad Politécnica de Valencia
Camino Vera s/n 46022, Valencia (Spain)
email: jojiher@dcom.upv.es, oromero@dcom.upv.es, alrema91@gmail.com, jlloret@dcom.upv.es

***Abstract*—Emulators and simulators provide an easy way to reduce hardware needs in experiments. Because of that, network researchers use applications that allow them to emulate or simulate networks, like Mininet in Software Defined Networks. It is desired to obtain very close results between the ones given in a virtual network and the ones obtained when the real network hardware is implemented in order to avoid using too much hardware in complex experiments without gathering unreal results. In this paper, we compare the experimental results obtained when a virtual network is generated by using Mininet versus a real implemented network. We have compared them varying the Maximum Transmission Unit (MTU) on Internet Protocol version 4 (IPv4) packets. Ethernet, Fiber Distributed Data Interface (FDDI), and Wireless Local Area Network 802.11 (WLAN 802.11) MTUs have been used in our experimental tests. We have worked with different link capabilities and generated traffic with different bandwidth.**

Keywords- SDN; OpenFlow; Mininet; MTU; virtualization; bandwidth; jitter.

I. INTRODUCTION

In the field of computer networks, the researches usually use programs that allow us to emulate or simulate networks. This is because, in most cases, we do not have the necessary devices needed to create complex networks, but we need to know if these programs are reliable [1]. There are emulators and simulators as Omnet++ [2], OPNET [3], NS-2 [4], NS-3 [5] Netsim [6], GNS3 [7], etc. that are frequently used to create computer networks.

Deployment of network is very quick in virtual environment, even if it is needed a large number of resources, which is always practically almost impossible to implement with real hardware. Problem solving or troubleshooting capability is still easier than real implementations. Note that a network researcher has to keep in mind that the results obtained from a virtual network should be similar from those obtained by the real hardware network. If there is a significant difference between results of virtual network and real network, then the research work should not be taken into consideration. As a network test bed gives almost the same results as the real implemented network, then it saves a large amount of time, complexity and a lot of resources.

In general, network devices perform the transport and the control function. But, configuring a great amount of devices and changing the configuration efficiently to work properly, it means a big challenge for networking professionals.

Today's, computer network world is able to offer a large amount of functionalities suited to the requirements of users. A new technology, named Software Defined Networking (SDN) [8] appears to increase the efficiency and reduce the cost of network configuration.

Figure 1 shows the components of SDN in a layered structure. The first layer consists of some frequently used tools of monitoring and depuration. The tool "Oftrace" is used for analyzing and parsing Openflow message from network dump. "Oftrace" provides a library which analyzes and parses the message from TCP dump or Wireshark [9]. Loops or cyclic path can cause critical problems in SDN. "Oflops" is a tool to catch the loop mechanism in the software defined networks. It mentions the data packets in the loop which are not able to leave the network [10]. "Openseer" is a CGI script which helps to plot that data effectively in SDN [11]. In Controllers Layer there are few controllers which are used in SDN. More often, controllers are called the Brain of Network which controls and manages the software defined network. Floodlight, Open Daylight, Beacon, Nox are among the frequently used controllers in SDN [12]. Flow Visor ensures that multiple isolated logical networks can share the same topology and hardware resources of a network. It places as a transparent proxy between OpenFlow switches and OpenFlow controllers. The isolated logical network is named slice of the network and flow visor is named slicing software in SDN [13]. In SDN environment, OpenFlow switches are used to forward the packets. OpenFlow switches are either a software program or a hardware device which is compatible with OpenFlow protocols. Some of the commercial switches are available in market like HP, Nec, Juniper, etc. [14]. Mininet is used to create realistic virtual network within seconds on a single machine that could be able to run real kernel, switch and application code [15].

There are few emulators and simulators which are frequently used to run and control the technology SDN from a single screen. Some of them are NS-3, Estinet 9.0 [16], OmNet ++, Mininet, etc.

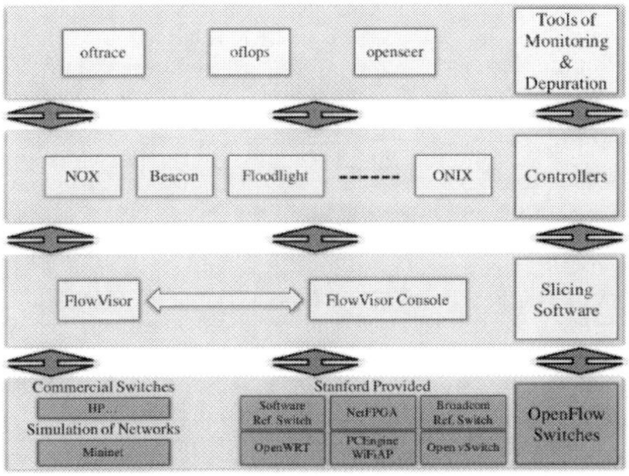

Figure 1.Key component of SDN in layered structure.

In this paper, we show the comparison among the obtained results from the virtual networks and from the real implemented networks. With the assessment of these results we are able to find the significant differences, which may be very useful for the researchers who all are performing their research work in Networking Industry. We have performed different experiments over Mininet and real implementation to have a good understanding of the network behavior in both scenarios. To do a detailed study, we must send data packets of different properties and compare the results. We used the data packets with different Maximum Transmission Unit (MTU) on IPv4. These sizes of packets are usual for Ethernet version 2, Ethernet with Logical Link Control (LLC), Point-to-Point Protocol over Ethernet (PPPoE), WLAN, Token Ring and FDDI.

This paper is an extended version of a conference paper published in [1].

The rest of the paper is structured as follows. In Section II, we discuss existing related works. In Section III, we introduced all resources that we used in our test bench. Measurement results and our discussion and analysis are shown in Section IV. Section V shows the conclusion and future works.

II. RELATED WORKS

In the past, a few researchers have accomplished their work in the area of SDN and investigated the performance of multimedia delivery over SDN. Furthermore, in the last years, emulators have been developed in order to provide an easy way to manage virtual networks and perform the research experiments. These emulators reduce the costs associated to the hardware needed to build the network. Inside the SDN research, the emulators have a great importance because of the great number of tests and the specific hardware that are necessary.

In the following section, we are going to discuss about some previous research work that helps us to get a deep understanding of SDN. Then, we will describe the previous researches in which emulators provide a useful way to test the experiments.

Recently, in our previous research article [17], we tried to evaluate the performance of multimedia streaming delivery over Mininet compared to real network implementation. We considered different properties of multimedia delivery, i.e., bandwidth, delay, jitter, and we found some significant differences over mininet and real test network. Kreutzet et al. [18] discussed the SDN, and analyzed the significance of SDN over traditional networking. Authors explained about the key components of SDN by using a bottom-up layered approach and focused on challenges, troubleshooting and debugging in SDN. Noghaniet et al. [19] introduced a framework based on SDN that could enable the network controller to deploy IP multicast between source and subscribers. The network controller was also able to control the distributed set of sources where multiple description coded (MDC) video content is available by using a simple northbound interface. Due to this SDN-based streaming multicast framework for medium and heavy workload, the Peak Signal-to-Noise Ratio (PSNR) of the received video is increasing considerably. Authors noticed that the received video, which had a very poor quality before, was having a significant increase in the quality of video now. Nam et al. [20] proposed a mechanism to solve the congestion problem and improve the video quality of experience (QoE). Authors tried to develop an SDN based application to improve the quality of video that can monitor conditions of network in real time streaming, and change routing paths dynamically by multi-protocol label switching (MPLS).

Egilmezet et al. [21] give a unique design of an Openflow controller for multimedia delivery over SDN with end to end Quality of Service (QoS) support. The authors tried to optimize routes of multimedia flows dynamically. After experiments over real test network, the authors found better results than HTTP based multi-bitrate adaptive streaming. They ensured that OpenQoS can guarantee the video delivery with little or no video artifacts experienced by the end-users. In another publication, Egilmezet et al. [22] gave new distributed control plane architectures for multimedia delivery over large-scale, multi-operator SDN. The extensions included in the design of architecture were: (a) to acquire network topology and the state information by topology aggregation and link summarization, (b) to propose an optimized framework for flowing based end to end over multi-domain networks, and (c) two distributed control plane designs by addressing the messaging between controllers for scalable and secure routing between two domains. By applying these extensions on layered video streaming, authors obtained a better quality of received video, reduced cost and memory overhead. This architecture was effectively scalable for large networks. Kassleret et al. [23] tried to negotiate the service and parameter for network communication between end users, and assign multimedia delivery paths in network according to prefixed service configuration. The idea behind this system was to centralize multi-user optimization of path assignments, which provides the better quality of experience by considering network topology, link capacities, delay and account service utility. Due to optimization, the system was able to use Openflow to set up forwarding paths in network.

In [24] Yang et al. have proposed a novel time-aware software defined networking (TaSDN) architecture for OpenFlow-based datacenter optical networks, by introducing a time-aware service scheduling (TaSS) strategy. The strategy can arrange and accommodate the applications with required QoS considering the time factor, and enhance the responsiveness to quickly provide for datacenter demand.

Dramitinoset et al. [25] have discussed about different aspects of video delivery over next generation cellular networks, which includes the software defined networks and cloud computing. The authors have been focused on next generation cellular networks which employ SDN in core due to increased demands of video streaming commercially. In our paper we are trying to explore the performance of multimedia delivery over Software Defined Networks as compared to real test networks in terms of some important parameters.

Some of these researches test their experiments with emulators. As told before, in [17] we evaluated the performance of Mininet. Mininet is the most used emulator in SDN researches. In the paper "Using Mininet for Emulation and Prototyping Software-Defined Networks" [26], Oliveira et al. concluded that despite some limitations related with the fidelity of performance between the real network and the emulated one, Mininet has several positive aspects like the capacity of fast and simplified prototyping, the possibility of showing and sharing results, its applicability and low cost.

In addition, Wette et al. tried in [27] to create a large network emulation using Mininet. Their goal was to do an emulated network almost as large as e.g. data center networks, which are composed by thousands of nodes. They presented a framework called Maxinet, based on Mininet, able to emulate 3200 hosts in a cluster of only 12 physical machines, although they concluded that, even a larger network could be emulated with Maxinet using better hardware available than they used in the research.

This last research proves the power of emulators like Mininet, and the performance that can be obtained from Mininet shows why it has become the most used emulator, especially in the SDN field.

However, there are other emulators that are used in the literature in order to obtain the results of the research. In this section we are going to enumerate some cases where emulators are used to set up a virtual SDN. There are some other emulators, for instance, OpenvSwitch. It is an emulator widely used to test experiments about networking, emulating an OpenFlow software-based switch. In [28] Akella and Xiong made a study about QoS in SDN networks. They presented a bandwidth allocation approach by using Open vSwitch. Their study is useful for most of cloud applications like gaming, voice IP and teleconference. They achieved the guarantee bandwidth allocation to all cloud users by introducing queuing techniques and considering the performance metrics of response time and the number of hops.

On the other hand, other tools like GNS3 are used to emulate the SDN designed in the experiments. For example, in [29] Jingjing et al. researched the deployment of routing protocols over SDN emulated by GNS3. They used and optimized an architecture called Kandoo, a distributed control plane architecture, to enhance routing in SDN. They also analyze BGP and OSPF routing protocols and concluded their routing strategies are superior to the traditional ones based on BGP and OSPF. They used for the simulation GNS3 emulator, which is essential to evaluate their results and finalizing the research.

Other test bed used in several researches is the OFELIA project, based in OpenFlow. It is an experimental SDN designed to research about networking in SDN. In [30] Salsano et al. discussed and proposed a general and long term solution to support ICN (Information Center Networking) over a large scale SDN based on Openflow using OFELIA to experimenting their proposal.

Furthermore, networks designed in order to simulate the experiments, like OFELIA, provide new opportunities to develop other tools like VeRTIGO, expanding the SDN possibilities over any topology.

Gerola et al. tested VeRTIGO [31] to demonstrate this new tool has the power of allowing investigators work with OpenFlow-based SDN in a large scale in terms of topology. VeRTIGO has been developed within the framework OFELIA project.

Beside the emulators, which can virtualize networks in order to test the proposals, there are simulators, which try to simulate components and network behavior. Usually, emulators achieve a better performance than simulators. In [32] Wang et al. introduced EstiNet, a new tool to make experiments which consists on a mix of emulator and simulator. They presented it for testing performance of SDN OpenFlow controller's application programs. Without any modification, they could run OpenFlow controllers into an EstiNet virtual network. They concluded that EstiNet, by combining simulation and emulation, take the advantages of both approaches and it is able to avoid their disadvantages. Finally, they made a comparison between EstiNet, Mininet and ns-3 simulator, concluding EstiNet is even better than Mininet because it is more scalable, although it takes more time simulating more OpenFlow switches, and generates correct performance, while Mininet performance and results are untrustworthy. This comparison is detailed in [33], written by Wang.

III. TEST BENCH

In this section, we are going to introduce the SDN emulator and the real network topology used in our test bench.

A. *Devices and equipement*

In this subsection, we explain the devices and equipment used to perform our study.

The real topology is composed by the following equipment:

- 1 Layer 3 Switch, Cisco Catalyst WS-C3560-24PS-E [34] that runs an IOS C3560-IPSERVICESK9-M,Versión 12.2 (53) SE2, release software (fc3). It has 24 Fast Ethernet and 2 Gigabit Ethernet interfaces and 16 Mbytes of flash memory;

- 1 Desktop PC that has an Intel Core Quad Q9400 CPU @2.66 Ghz processor, 6 Gb of RAM memory, 1 Network Interface Card (NIC) Intel 82579V Gigabit Ethernet and Windows 7 Professional - 64 bits operative system;
- • 1 Desktop PC that has an Intel Core i5-2400 CPU @3.10 Ghz, 4 Gb RAM memory, 1 NIC Intel 82579V Gigabit Ethernet and Windows 7 Enterprise - 64 bits as operating system.

To design and develop the virtualized topology we have used a laptop composed by an Intel i7-4500UCPU @ 2.70 Ghz processor, 16 Gb RAM memory, 1 10/100/1000 Mbit/s NIC, and Ubuntu 14.04 - 64 bits as operating system.

B. Software used

With Mininet, we can create a realistic virtual network, running real kernel, switch and application code, on a single machine. The machine can be a virtual machine running on a local PC, or a machine virtualized through the cloud, or a native machine. For our study, we have used Mininet version 2.2.1, with a native installation on Ubuntu 14 as shown in Figure 2.

We used a software application named gt, programmed with a C Linux compiler and developed by us, which allow us to send traffic with different MTU and bandwidths set by the user. Varying the frame interdelay and frame size, it is easy to get any desired speed, as far as it not higher than the physical interface speed. The components of the transport line are not significant four these tests

In both, real and virtualized topologies, to capture and analyze the received traffic, we have used Wireshark [35], version 1.10.

C. Characteristics of traffic transmited

In our work, we send traffic with different MTUs that represents the packet sizes in different standards. Table I shows different sizes of MTU that was sent in our network topologies.

As can be observed in Table I, sizes of MTU that was sent in our topology do not have standard values. This is because of the need to establish a GRE tunnel in the real topology, to connect the two hosts that have been created in Mininet, thus changing the frame size. Traffic was transmitted through UDP protocol. To calculate the jitter (J), we use the expression presented in RFC 4689 (Terminology for Benchmarking Network-layer Traffic Control Mechanisms) [36]. Therefore, we use the formula (1), where S_i is the transmission timestamp from packet i, and R_i is the reception timestamp of arrival packet i. For two consecutive packets i and j.

$$J = |(R_j - S_j) - (R_i - S_i)| \quad (1)$$

D. Physical topology

The real topology consists of two computers connected by straight-through cable, using one real switch (Cisco Catalyst WS-C3560-24PS-E), as shown in Figure 3. The data transfer rates used is 10 Mbps.

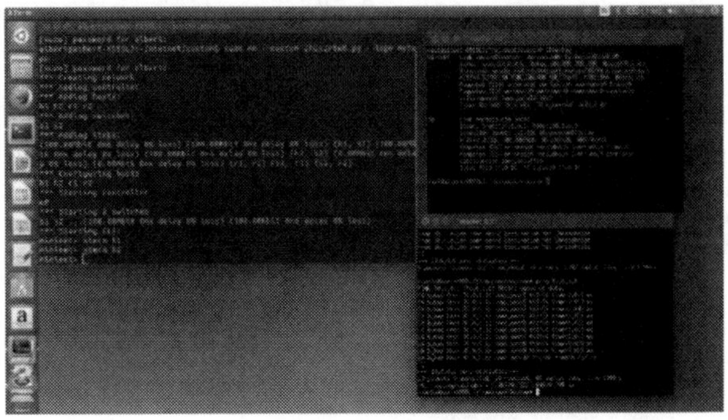

Figure 2. Host running in Mininet.

TABLE I. MTU PACKETS IN TOPOLOGIES

Frame Differentiation	
Media	**MTU (bytes)**
Ethernet wit LLC and SNP, PPPoE	1518
FDDI	4370
WLAN 802.11, Ethernet Jumbo Frame	7999

Figure 3. Real topology.

In the software defined network, we used a computer with Mininet, where we set up the same topology as the real one.

IV. MEASURAMENT AND DISCUSSION

This section shows the results obtained in both cases, when traffic is being delivered over the real network and in the virtual topology using Mininet. Here we present measures of traffic, when link bandwidth was configured at 10 and 100 Mbps, and the traffic generator was transmitting at 10 and 100 Mbps. Our intention is to test the ability of the devices to process packets of several sizes. For that, MTU of every interface is configured to allow those different packet sizes. The parameters observed are bandwidth and jitter of packets with three different MTUs: 1518, 4370 and 7999, corresponding at size of packets for traffic Ethernet, FDDI and WLAN 802.11.

The two Mininet networks running at different PCs were interconnected through a GRE tunnel established between both PCs. The GRE encapsulation is showed in Figure 4.

The experiments are described as follows. First, we group the experiments according to the maximum bandwidth available in the links of our topology. Then, we present the results obtained in words of bandwidth and jitter from both topologies, the real and the virtual one, for every MTU value we test.

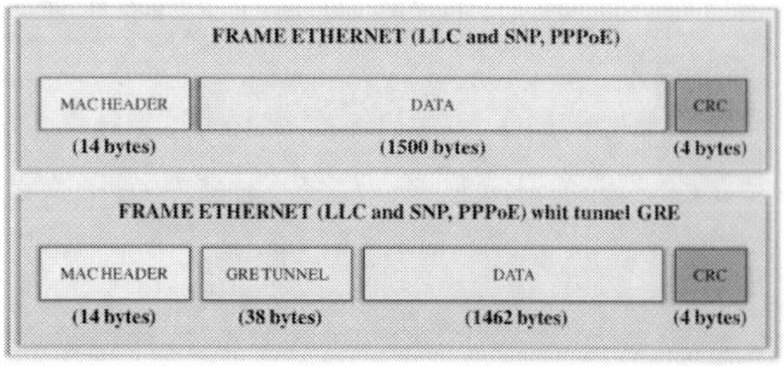

Figure 4. GRE tunnel.

1) Traffic links bandwidth 10 Mbps - Traffic generated 10 Mbps.

a) MTU - 1518

In Figure 5, we can see the bandwidth consumption values of the real topology and the values obtained in the virtual topology. The data have similar values for both topologies when the transmission is stabilized. Although, in real topology is less than in virtual topology. The mean value of bandwidth in real topology is 9.5 Mbps while for virtual topology is 10 Mbps. The maximum and minimum values for real and virtual topologies are different, 9.9 Mbps and 20.8 Mbps for maximum and 6.7 Mbps and 9.9 Mbps for minimum. Observe that in the virtual topology, at the beginning of the transmission we obtain bandwidth values higher than 10 Mbps, meaning that in this situation the emulator is not accurate since the maximum bandwidth for a emulated 10 Mbps physical link should be 10 Mbps. After a few transmitted packets, the measured bandwidth is already providing more accurate values.

In Figure 6, we can see the jitter values of the real topology and the values obtained in the virtual topology. The values of the real topology are higher than those from the virtual topology. The mean value of jitter in real topology is 0.690 ms while for virtual topology is 0.001 ms. The maximum values real and virtual topologies are different, 3.169 ms and 0.607 ms. The minimum values for both topologies are the same, 0 ms.

b) MTU - 4370

In Figure 7, we can see the bandwidth consumption values of the real topology and the values obtained in the virtual topology. The data have similar values for both topologies, when the transmission is stabilized, although in real topology is less than in virtual topology. The mean value of bandwidth in real topology is 9.5 Mbps while for virtual topology is 10 Mbps. The maximum and minimum values for real and virtual topologies are different, 9.8 Mbps and 31.5 Mbps for maximum, and 4.2 Mbps and 9.9 Mbps for minimum. As in the previous case, MTU 1518 bytes, in the virtual topology, we can observe that the bandwidth values are not realistic at the beginning of the transmission. After several transmitted packets, the values obtained are already close to the real network values.

In Figure 8, we can see the jitter values of the real topology and the values obtained in the virtual topology. The values of the real topology are higher than those from the virtual topology. The mean value of jitter in real topology is 0.228ms while for virtual topology is 0.002 ms. The maximum values for real topology are different, 9.189 ms and 1.277 ms. The minimum values for real topology and virtual topology are the same, 0 ms.

c) MTU - 7999

In Figure 9, we can see the bandwidth consumption values of the real topology and the values obtained in the virtual topology. The data have similar values for both topologies, when the transmission is stabilized, although in real topology is less than in virtual topology. The mean value of bandwidth in real topology is 9.5 Mbps while for virtual topology is 10 Mbps. The maximum and minimum values for real topology and virtual topology are different, 9.9 Mbps and 23 Mbps for maximum and 3.9 Mbps and 10 Mbps for minimum. Once again, the virtual topology is not providing realistic bandwidth values at the beginning of the transmission and, after transmitting a few packets, the bandwidth values are quite similar to those from the real network.

In Figure 10, we can see the jitter values of the real topology and the values obtained in the virtual topology. The values of the real topology are higher than those from the virtual topology. The mean value of jitter in real topology is 0.345 ms while for virtual topology is 0.001 ms. The maximum and minimum values for real topology and virtual topology are different, 25.091 ms and 0.844 ms for maximum and 0.037 ms and 0 ms for minimum.

As a conclusion, the packet size does not seem to have much impact on the observed bandwidth, but more on the jitter.

2) Traffic links bandwidth 100 Mbps - Traffic generated 10 Mbps.

a) MTU - 1518

In Figure 11, we can see the bandwidth consumption values of the real topology and the values obtained in the virtual topology. The data have similar values for both topologies, when the transmission was stabilized, although in real topology is less than in virtual topology. The mean value of bandwidth in real topology is 9,9 Mbps while for virtual topology is 10 Mbps. The maximum and minimum values for real topology and virtual topology are different, 10,0 Mbps and 10,3 Mbps for maximum and 9,9 Mbps and 9,8 Mbps for minimum.

In Figure 12, we can see the jitter values of the real topology and the values obtained in the virtual topology. The values of the real topology are higher than the ones of the virtual topology. The mean value of jitter in real topology is 0,015 ms while for virtual topology is 0,001 ms. The maximum values for real and virtual topology are different, 1,26 ms and 2,691 ms. The minimum values for real topology and virtual topology are the same, 0 ms.

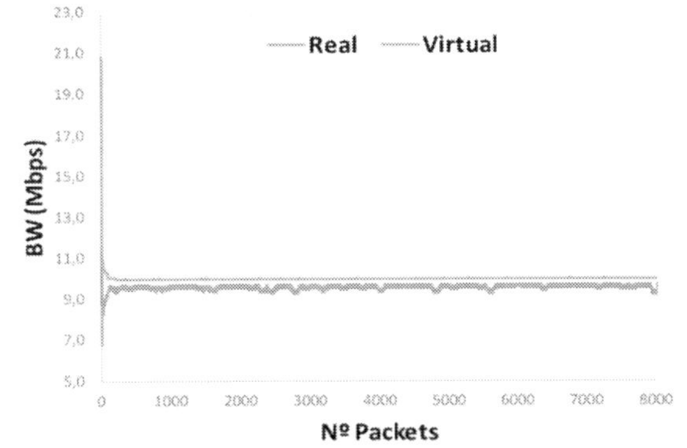

Figure 5. BW at 1518.

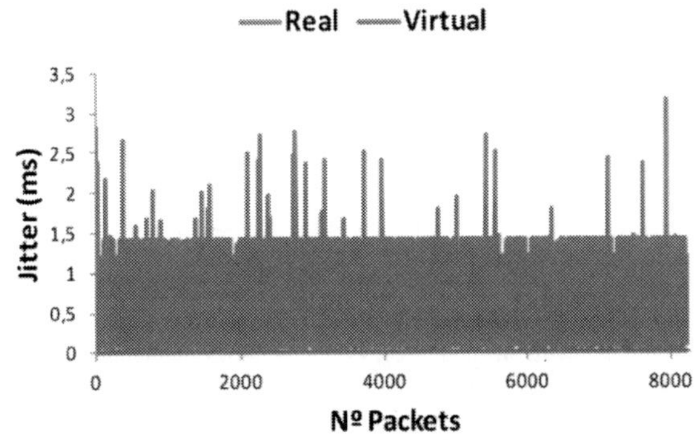

Figure 6. Jitter at 1518.

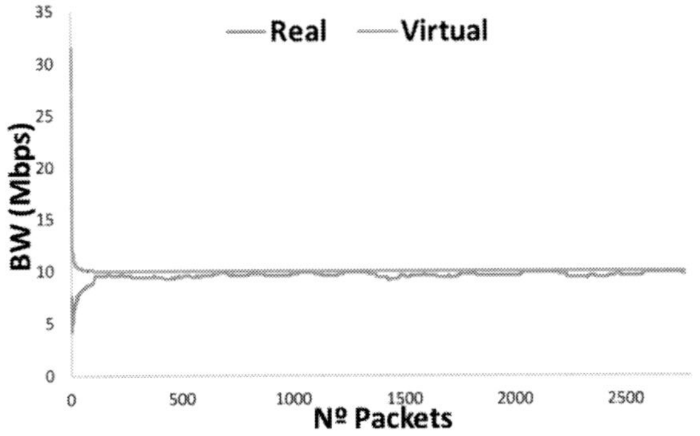

Figure 7. BW at 4370.

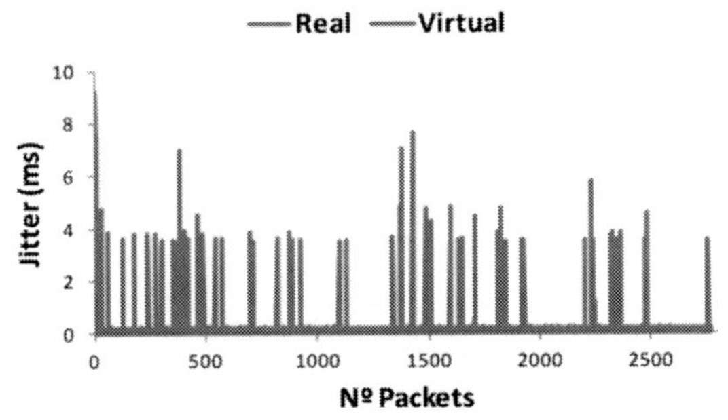

Figure 8. Jitter at 4370.

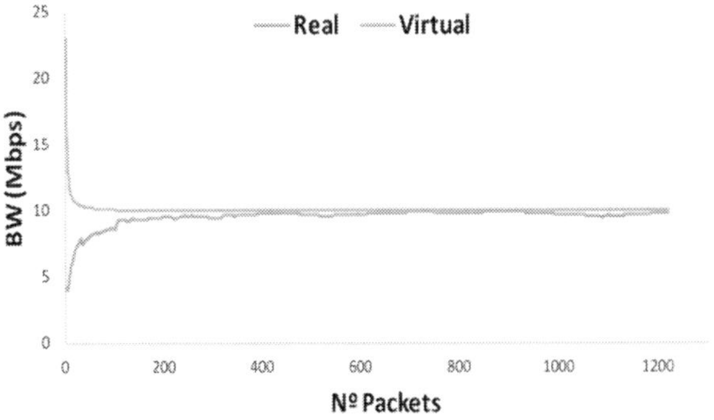

Figure 9. BW at 7999.

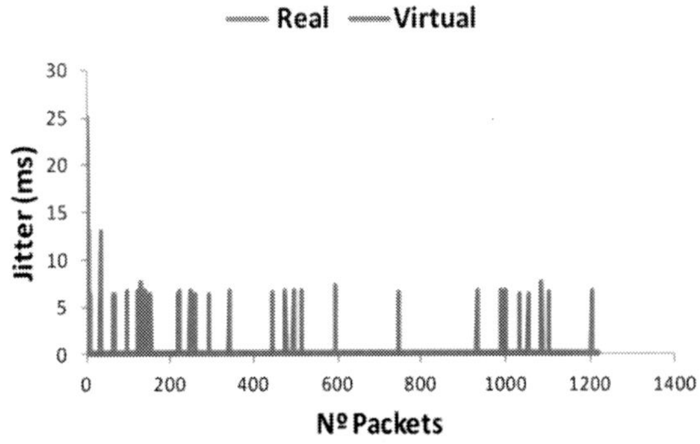

Figure 10. Jitter at 7999.

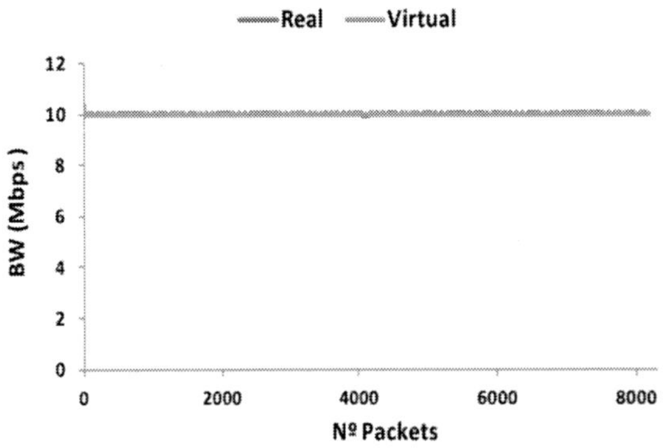

Figure 11. BW at 1518.

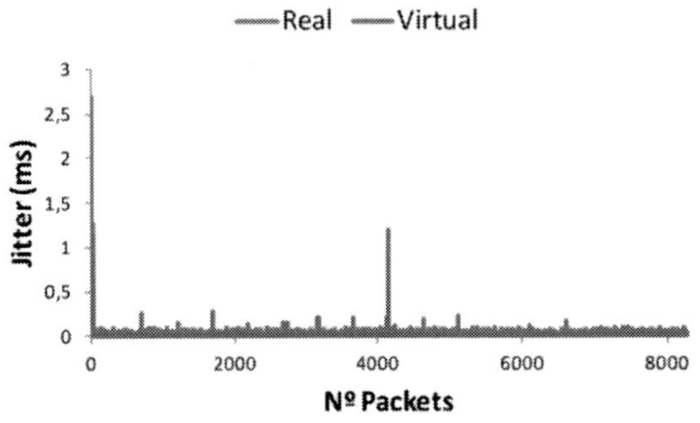

Figure 12. Jitter at 1518.

b) MTU - 4370

In Figure 13, we can see the bandwidth consumption values of the real topology and the values obtained in the virtual topology. The data have similar values for both topologies, when the transmission was stabilized. Although in real topology is less than in virtual topology. The mean value of bandwidth in real topology is 9.9 Mbps while for virtual topology is 10 Mbps. The maximum values for real and virtual topology are the same 10 Mbps. The minimum values for real topology and virtual topology are different 9.8 Mbps and 9.9 Mbps.

In Figure 14, we can see the jitter values of the real topology and the values obtained in the virtual topology. The values of the real topology are higher than the ones of the virtual topology. The mean value of jitter in real topology is 0.019 ms while for virtual topology is 0.004 ms. The maximum values for real topology and virtual topology are different, 3.433 ms and 0.898 ms. The minimum values for real topology and virtual topology are the same, 0 ms.

This section shows the results obtained in both cases, when traffic is being delivered over the network and in the virtual topology using Mininet.

c) MTU - 7999

In Figure 15, we can see the bandwidth consumption values of the real topology and the values obtained in the virtual topology. The data have similar values for both topologies, when the transmission was stabilized.. The mean value of bandwidth in real and virtual topology is 10 Mbps. The maximum and minimum values for real topology and virtual topology are the same, 10 Mbps for maximum and 9.9 Mbps for minimum.

In Figure 16, we can see the jitter values of the real topology and the values obtained in the virtual topology. The values of the real topology are higher than the ones of the virtual topology. The mean value of jitter in real topology is 0.021 ms while for virtual topology is 0.005 ms. The maximum values for real topology and virtual topology are different, 1.177 ms and 1.756 ms. These values occurred at the very beginning and the virtual peak hide the one related with the real topology. The minimum values for real topology and virtual topology are the same, 0 ms.

Sending less traffic than the maximum bandwidth available seems that introduces less discrepancy between the virtual topology and the real one.

3) Traffic links bandwidth 100 Mbps - Traffic generated 100 Mbps.

a) MTU - 1518

In Figure 17, we can see the bandwidth consumption values of the real topology and the values obtained in the virtual topology. The data have similar values for both topologies, when the transmission was stabilized, although in real topology is less than in virtual topology. The mean value of bandwidth in real topology is 96 Mbps while for virtual topology is 100 Mbps. The maximum and minimum values for real topology and virtual topology are different, 100 Mbps and 101 Mbps for maximum and 94.3 Mbps and 7.3 Mbps for minimum.

In Figure 18, we can see the jitter values of the real topology and the values obtained in the virtual topology. The values of the real topology are higher than then ones of the virtual topology. The mean value of jitter in real topology is 0.011 ms while for virtual topology is 0.001 ms. The maximum values for real topology and virtual topology are different, 0.25 ms and 3.26 ms. The minimum values for real topology and virtual topology are the same, 0 ms.

b) MTU - 4370

In Figure 19, we can see the bandwidth consumption values of the real topology and the values obtained in the virtual topology. The data have similar values for both topologies, when the transmission was stabilized, although in real topology is less than in virtual topology. The mean value of bandwidth in real topology is 98.559 Mbps while for virtual topology is 100 Mbps. The maximum and minimum values for real topology and virtual topology are different, 100 Mbps and 120.344 Mbps for maximum and 95.474 Mbps and 99.931 Mbps for minimum. Once again, the virtual topology is not providing realistic bandwidth values at the beginning of the transmission. But also, after transmitting a few packets the bandwidth values are similar to those from the real network.

In Figure 20, we can see the jitter values of the real topology and the values obtained in the virtual topology. The values of the real topology are higher than the ones of the virtual topology. The mean value of jitter in real topology is 0.017 ms while for virtual topology is 0 ms. The maximum values for real topology and virtual topology are different, 0,908 ms and 0.028 ms. The minimum values for real topology and virtual topology are the same, 0 ms.

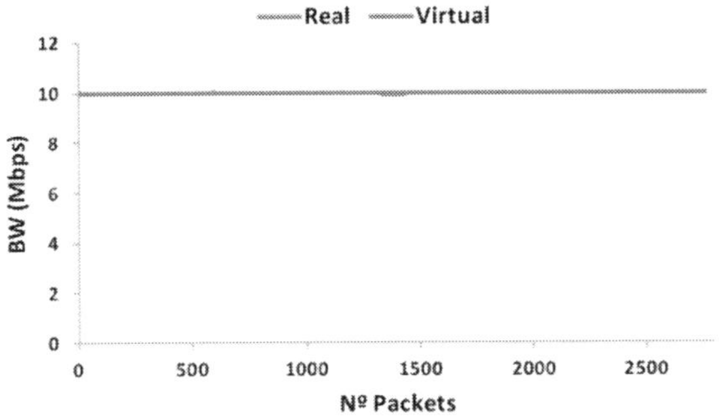

Figure 13. BW at 4370.

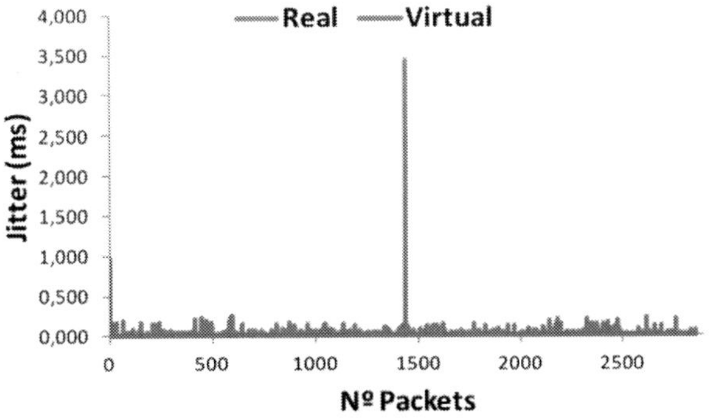

Figure 14. Jitter at 4370.

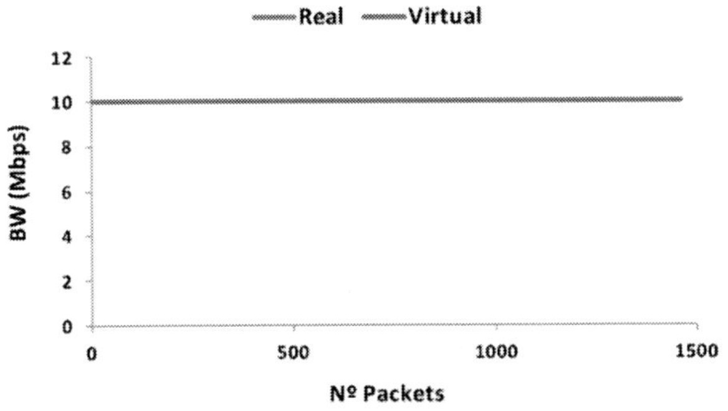

Figure 15. BW at 7999.

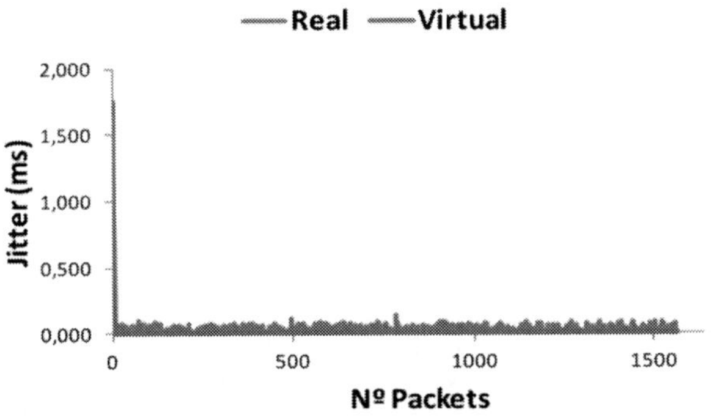

Figure 16. Jitter at 7999.

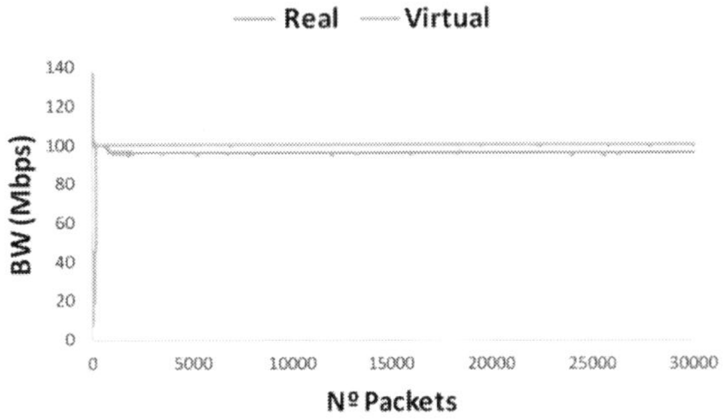

Figure 17. BW at 1518.

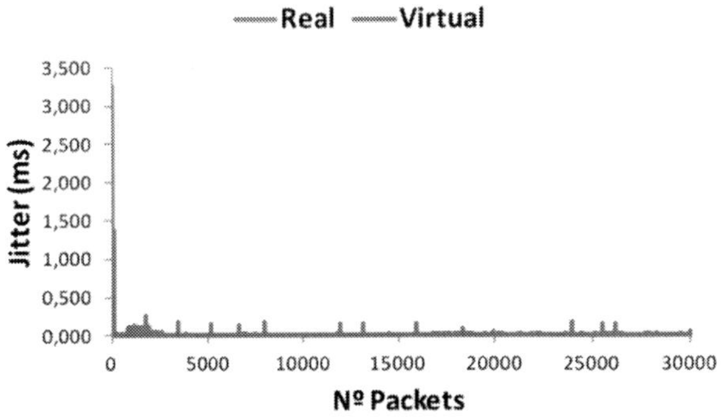

Figure 18. Jitter at 1518.

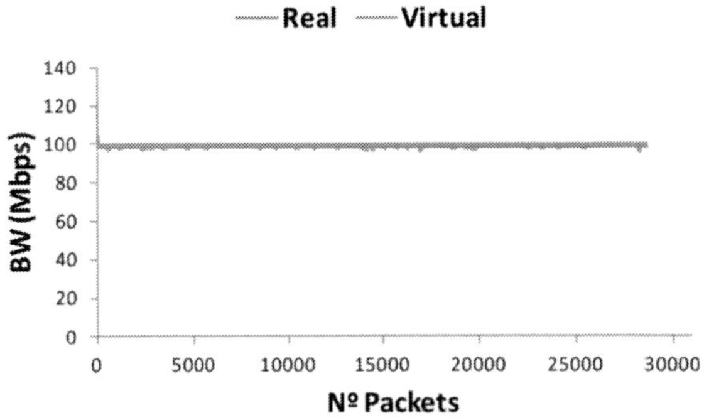

Figure 19. BW at 4370.

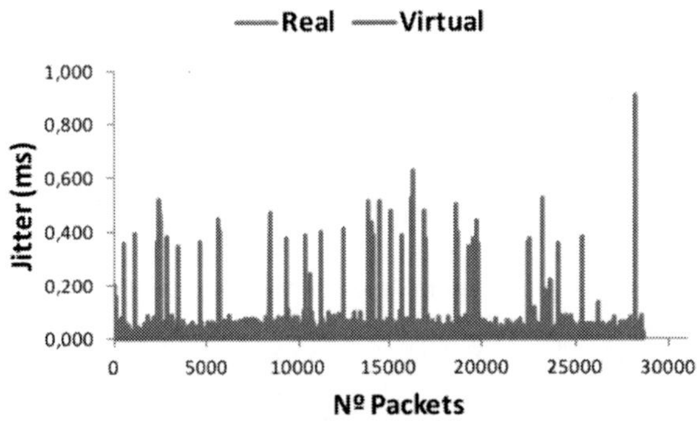

Figure 20. Jitter at 4370.

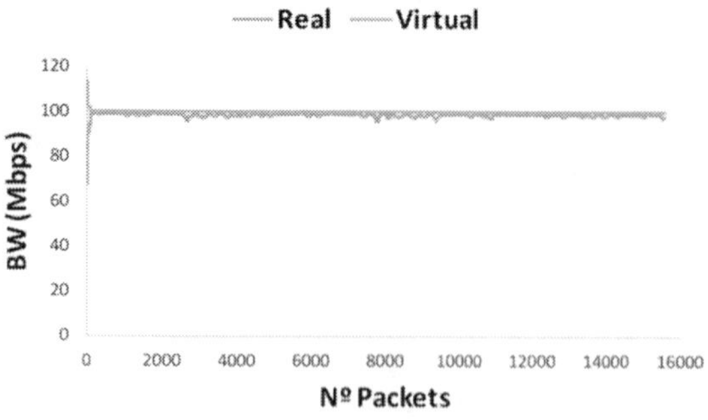

Figure 21. BW at 7999.

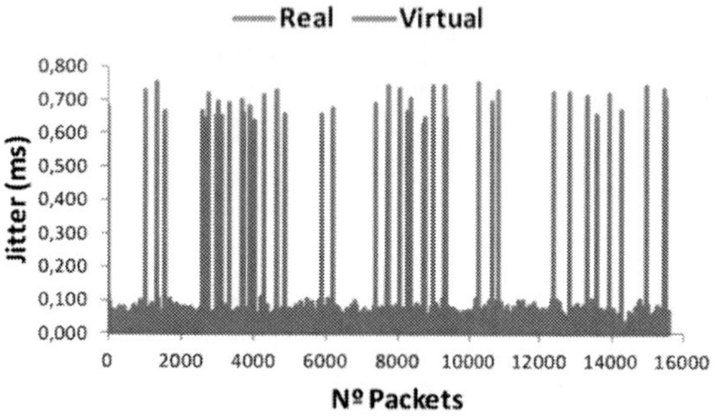

Figure 22. Jitter at 7999.MTU - 7999

This section shows the results obtained in both cases, when traffic is being delivered over the network and in the virtual topology using Mininet.

In Figure 21, we can see the bandwidth consumption values of the real topology and the values obtained in the virtual topology. The data have similar values for both topologies, when the transmission was stabilized. The mean value of bandwidth in real topology is 98.911 Mbps while for virtual topology is 100 Mbps. The maximum and minimum values for real topology and virtual topology are different, 99.502 Mbps and 113.581 Mbps for maximum and 67.687 Mbps and 100 Kbps for minimum (due to the initial interval that some devices need to start sending messages). As previously, virtual topology is not providing realistic bandwidth values at the beginning of the transmission.

In Figure 22, we can see the jitter values of the real topology and the values obtained in the virtual topology. The values of the real topology are higher than the ones of the virtual topology. The mean value of jitter in real topology is 0.016 ms while for virtual topology is 0 ms. The maximum values for real topology and virtual topology are different, 0.749 ms and 0.123 ms. The minimum values for real topology and virtual topology are the same, 0 ms.

These lasts measurements indicate that the virtual topology can consume more bandwidth than the available in the real network.

V. Conclusion

In this paper, we have studied the performance of virtual networks and compared with real networks. For this study, we have transmitted packets with different MTU sizes, which correspond to Ethernet, FDDI, and WLAN 802.11 (also Jumbo Ethernet frames) packets and we have used different link capabilities and traffic through the network. It can be seen that the variation of the bandwidth between the real and virtual topologies are very low. However, in virtual networks, the first packets are usually sent with an unreal bandwidth. The results obtained for the jitter show that there are major deviations, although, we are working with a very low time scale, as we are dealing with milliseconds. In our future work, we will compare real and virtual networks using more complex topologies, and with Openflow compatible equipment.

Acknowledgment

This work has been supported by the "Ministerio de Economía y Competitividad", through the "Convocatoria 2014. Proyectos I+D - Programa Estatal de Investigación Científica y Técnica de Excelencia" in the "Subprograma Estatal de Generación de Conocimiento", Project TIN2014-57991-C3-1-P and the "Programa para la Formación de Personal Investigador – (FPI-2015-S2-884)" by the "Universitat Politècnica de València".

References

[1] J. M. Jimenez, O. Romero, A. Rego, A. Dilendra, J. Lloret, Performance Study of a Software Defined Network Emulator, The Eleventh International Conference on Internet Monitoring and Protection (ICIMP 2016), May 22 - 26, 2016 - Valencia, Spain

[2] Omnet++. Available at https://omnetpp.org/ [Last access November 8, 2016]

[3] OPNET is now part of Riberved. Available at http://es.riverbed.com/products/performance-management-control/opnet.html / [Last access November 8, 2016]

[4] The Network Simulator - ns-2. Available at http://www.isi.edu/nsnam/ns/ [Last access November 8, 2016]

[5] NS-3. Available at NS-3 website: https://www.nsnam.org/ [Last access November 8, 2016]

[6] NetSim NETWORK SIMULATOR. Available at http://www.boson.com/netsim-cisco-network-simulator [Last access November 8, 2016].

[7] GNS3 The software that empowers networks professionals. Available at https://www.gns3.com/ [Last access November 8, 2016].

[8] Software-Defined Networking: A Perspective from within a Service Provider Environment. Available at: https:// tools.ietf.org/pdf/rfc7149.pdf [Last access November 8, 2016]

[9] Liboftrace. Available at http://archive.openflow.org/wk/index .php/Liboftrace [Last access November 8, 2016]

[10] OFLOPS. Available at https://www.sdxcentral.com/projects/ oflops/ [Last access November 8, 2016]

[11] OpenSeer. Available at http://archive.openflow.org/wk/ index.php/OpenSeer [Last access November 8, 2016]

[12] What are SDN Controllers (or SDN Controllers Platforms)?. Available at https://www.sdxcentral.com/resources/sdn/sdn-controllers/[Last access November 8, 2016]

[13] OpenFlow network virtualization with FlowVisor. Available at https://www.os3.nl/_media/2012-2013/courses/rp2/p28_report.pdf [Last access November 8, 2016]

[14] OpenFlow switch. Available at http://searchsdn.techtarget.com/definition/OpenFlow-switch [Last access November 8, 2016]

[15] Mininet An Instant Virtual Network on your Laptop (or other PC). Available at http://mininet.org [Last access November 8, 2016]

[16] EstiNet Technologies Inc. Available at EstiNet Technologies website: http://www.estinet.com/index.php [Last access November 8, 2016].

[17] J. M. Jimenez, O. Romero, A. Rego, A. Dilendra and J. Lloret, "Study of Multimedia Delivery over Software Defined Networking", in Network Protocols and Algorithm, vol. 7, No. 4, 2015, pp. 37-62, 2015, doi:10.5296/npa.v7i48794

[18] D. Kreutz, F. M. V. Ramos, P. Esteves Verissimo, C. Esteve Rothenberg, S. Azodolmolky, and S. Uhlig, "Software-Defined Networking: A Comprehensive Survey", Proceedings of the IEEE, Volume103, Issue 1, Jan. 2015, pp. 14-76, 2015, http://dx.doi.org/10.1109/JPROC.2014.2371999

[19] K. A. Noghani and M. O. Sunay, "Streaming Multicast Video over Software-Defined Networks", Proceedings of the IEEE 11th International Conference on Mobile Ad Hoc and Sensor Systems (MASS) (2014), 28-30 Oct. 2014, pages 551-556, 2014, doi: 10.1109/MASS.2014.125

[20] H. Nam, K. Kim, J. Y. Kim and H. Schulzrinney, "Towards QoE-aware Video Streaming using SDN", Global Communications Conference (GLOBECOM), Dec. 2014, pp 1317-1322, 2014, doi: 10.1109/GLOCOM.2014.7036990

[21] H. E. Egilmez, S. T. Dane, K. Tolga Bagci and A. Murat Tekalp, "OpenQoS: An OpenFlow controller design for multimedia delivery with end-to-end Quality of Service over Software-Defined Networks", Signal & Information Processing Association Annual Summit and Conference (APSIPA ASC), 2012 Asia-Pacific, 3-6 Dec. 2012, Hollywood (USA), pp 1-8, 2012

[22] H. E. Egilmez, and A. M. Tekalp, "Distributed QoS Architectures for Multimedia Streaming Over Software Defined Networks", Multimedia, IEEE Transactions on , Volume:16 , Issue: 6 , Sept. 2014, pages: 1597 – 1609, 2014; doi:10.1109/TMM.2014.2325791

[23] A. Kassler, L. Skorin-Kapov, O. Dobrijevic, M. Matijasevic, and P. Dely, "Towards QoE-driven Multimedia Service Negotiation and Path Optimization with Software Defined Networking", Software, Telecommunications and Computer Networks (SoftCOM), IEEE, Sept. 2012, Split (Croatia), pages: 1-5, 2012, ISBN: 978-1-4673-2710-7

[24] H. Yang, J. Zhang, Y. Zhao, Y. Ji, J. Han, Y. Lin, S. Qiu, Y. Lee, Time-aware Software Defined Networking for OpenFlow-based Datacenter Optical Networks, Network Protocols and Algorithms, Vol 6, No 4 (2014). pp. 77-91.

[25] M. Dramitinos, N. Zhang, M.. Kantor, J. Costa-Requena, I. Papafili, "Video Delivery over Next Generation Cellular Networks", Network and Service Management (CNSM), 2013 9th International Conference, IEEE, 14-18 Oct. 2013, Zurich (Switzerland), pp. 386-393, doi> 10.1109/CNSM.2013.6727862t

[26] R. L. S. de Oliveira, A. A. Shinoda, C. M. Schweitzer, L. Rodrigues Prete, "Using Mininet for Emulation and Prototyping Software-Defined Networks", Communications and Computing (COLCOM), 2014 IEEE Colombian Conference, IEEE, 4-6 June 2014, Bogota (Colombia), pp. 1 - 6, DOI 10.1109/ColComCon.2014.6860404

[27] P. Wette, M. Dräxler, A. Schwabe, F. Wallaschek, M. H. Zahraee, H. Karl, "MaxiNet: Distributed Emulation of Software-Defined Networks", Networking Conference, 2014 IFIP, 2-4 June 2014, Throndheim (Norway), pp. 1-9, DOI 10.1109/IFIPNetworking.2014.6857078

[28] A. V. Akella, K. Xiong, "Quality of Service (QoS) Guaranteed Network Resource Allocation via Software Defined Networking (SDN)", Dependable, Autonomic and Secure Computing (DASC), 2014 IEEE 12th International Conference, 24-27 Aug. 2014, IEEE, Dalian (China), pp. 7-13, DOI 10.1109/DASC.2014.11.

[29] Z. Jingjing, C. Di, W. Weiming, J. Rong, W. Xiaochun, "The Deployment of Routing Protocols in Distributed Control Plane of SDN", in The Scientific World Journal, Volume 2014, Article ID 918536, 8 pages, http://dx.doi.org/10.1155/2014/918536

[30] S. Salsano, N. Blefari-Melazzi, A. Detti, G. Morabito, L. Veltri, "Information centric networking over SDN and OpenFlow: Architectural aspects and experiments on the OFELIA testbed", Computer Networks, Volume 57, Issue 16, 13 November 2013, pp. 3207-3221, DOI 10.1016/j.comnet.2013.07.031

[31] M. Gerola, R. Doriguzzi Corin, R. Riggio, F. De Pellegrini, E. Salvadori, H. Woesner, T. Rothe, M. Suñé, L. Bergesio, "Demonstrating in ter-testbed network virtualization in OFELIA SDN experimental facility", Computer Communications Workshops (INFOCOM WKSHPS), 2013 IEEE Conference, 14-19 April 2013, Turin (Italy), pp. 39-40, DOI 10.1109/INFCOMW.2013.6970724

[32] S.-Y. Wang, C.-L. Chou, C.-M. Yang, "EstiNet OpenFlow Network Simulator and Emulator", in Communications Magazine, IEEE (Volume:51 , Issue: 9), IEEE, September 2013, pp. 110-117, DOI 10.1109/MCOM.2013.6588659

[33] S.-Y. Wang, "Comparison of SDN OpenFlow Network Simulator and Emulators: EstiNet vs. Mininet", in Computers and Communication (ISCC), 2014 IEEE Symposium, 23-26 June 2014, Funchal (Portugal), pp 1-6, DOI 10.1109/ISCC.2014.6912609

[34] Cisco Catalyst 3560 Series Switches Data Sheet. Available at Cisco website: http://www.cisco.com/c/en/us/products/collateral/switches/catalyst-3560-series-switches/product_data_sheet09186a00801f3d7d.html [Last access January 14, 2016]

[35] Wireshark software. Available at Wireshark website: https://www.wireshark.org/ [Last access January 14, 2016]

[36] Terminology for Benchmarking Network-layer Traffic Control Mechanisms. Available at https://www.ietf.org/rfc/rfc4689.txt.txt [Last access January 14, 2016]

iaria journals

www.iariajournals.org

International Journal On Advances in Intelligent Systems
issn: 1942-2679

International Journal On Advances in Internet Technology
issn: 1942-2652

International Journal On Advances in Life Sciences
issn: 1942-2660

International Journal On Advances in Networks and Services
issn: 1942-2644

International Journal On Advances in Security
issn: 1942-2636

International Journal On Advances in Software
issn: 1942-2628

International Journal On Advances in Systems and Measurements
issn: 1942-261x

International Journal On Advances in Telecommunications
issn: 1942-2601